# Queenship and Power

Series Editors
Charles Beem
University of North Carolina
Pembroke, NC, USA

Carole Levin
University of Nebraska
Lincoln, NE, USA

This series focuses on works specializing in gender analysis, women's studies, literary interpretation, and cultural, political, constitutional, and diplomatic history. It aims to broaden our understanding of the strategies that queens—both consorts and regnants, as well as female regents—pursued in order to wield political power within the structures of male-dominant societies. The works describe queenship in Europe as well as many other parts of the world, including East Asia, Sub-Saharan Africa, and Islamic civilization.

More information about this series at
http://www.palgrave.com/gp/series/14523

Estelle Paranque

# Elizabeth I of England through Valois Eyes

## Power, Representation, and Diplomacy in the Reign of the Queen, 1558–1588

palgrave
macmillan

Estelle Paranque
New College of the Humanities
London, UK

Queenship and Power
ISBN 978-3-030-01528-2        ISBN 978-3-030-01529-9    (eBook)
https://doi.org/10.1007/978-3-030-01529-9

Library of Congress Control Number: 2018960042

This Palgrave Macmillan imprint is published by the registered company Springer Nature
Switzerland AG
The registered company address is: Gewerbestrasse 11, 6330 Cham, Switzerland

*For my parents, Bernard and Joëlle Paranque,*
*for their unconditional love and support.*
*With all my love and gratitude.*

# A Note on Translation

Translating is a very difficult task. I have done my best to translate sixteenth century French sources into modern English. Yet some passages remain problematic (as the source is also). I have sometimes opted for literal translations and sometimes I have taken some liberties to make it more comprehensible to an English language audience. This is why I have decided to keep all French in footnotes to be as transparent as possible. Any errors are mine.

# Acknowledgments

This book would have never existed without the incredible and ongoing support and encouragements of Carole Levin. In July 2009, I made one of the best decisions of my life: I emailed Carole in the hope of one day collaborating with her. She immediately replied that she would be thrilled to discuss research topics and help me pursue my dream in any way she could. I knew from that moment that I had found a true gem—not only a brilliant scholar but also a dear friend. Four years later, in March 2013, I met her in person in Omaha, USA, at the Queen Elizabeth I Conference. Thereafter, she became my mentor, wrote references, read and commented on my thesis, advised me in terms of careers and publication prospects, and, most importantly, became a shoulder on which I could lean when necessary. Without a doubt, I am forever indebted to her for her kindness, support, generosity, and benevolence. Carole, thank you from the bottom of my heart for believing in me and my project since the first day we exchanged emails.

I am also indebted to two fantastic scholars who became dear friends: Michael Questier and Elena (Ellie) Woodacre. I met Michael when I moved to London in January 2011. Despite his busy schedule, he always offered to read my work and helped me improve it. He supported me, believed in me, encouraged me, and helped me bear some gloomy days. Thank you, Michael, for your wit, generosity, and friendship. I met Ellie at my first conference: Kings and Queens 1 at Bath Spa University back in 2012. Ellie offered help and assistance whenever needed from the very start. She cheered me up, supported me, and encouraged me throughout my Ph.D. and beyond. She read the whole thesis and offered invaluable feedback. Thank you so much, Ellie.

I would also like to extend great thanks to Dr. John Cooper. He was not only an exceptional external examiner during my viva, but continued to support and encourage me thereafter—writing (far too) many references and offering advice and counsel regarding job applications and publications. Thank you, John. This book would not have been possible without your insightful feedback and ongoing support (especially at our meetings at Patisserie Valerie).

I am hugely indebted to many other scholars and friends whom I have met throughout this journey and who have helped to make it wonderful: my anonymous readers, Philip Parr, Anya Riehl Bertolet, Lucy Kostyanovsky, Emma Wells, Helen Hackett, Lucinda Dean, Tracy Borman, Joanne Paul, Linda Shenk, Suzannah Lipscomb, and Hallie Rubenhold.

I would like to thank my friends and family for putting up with my passion: my sister Sandrine Doré, my niece Charlotte Collomb, my nephew and godson Mathias Collomb, Justine Brun and my goddaughter Juliette Alvès-Brun and their family, my cousin Nicolas Paranque, my great-uncle Régis Paranque, my childhood friends Gina Ros and Thomas Cavalier, my university friends Fella Hannachi, Laetitia Calabrese, Marie Armilano, and Laurence Baudoin, my history-loving friends Adrian Blau, Marius Ostrowski, Katie Elphick, Paul Bradshaw, Cassandra Auble, Natalie Sproxton, Laura Gray, and Eilish Gregory, my former and current students Kyle Fenn, Gabrielle Bissett, Rebecca Bourne, Raluca Chereji, Rebekah Ingle, Megan Jones-Khan, Annie Néant, Daisy Gibbs, Tierney Cowap, and all my former and current students at NCH, and everyone who has always believed in me.

Thanks to my wonderful colleagues at the New College of the Humanities—Lars Kjaer, Oliver Ayers, and Edmund Neill—for their kind words and positive energy as well as my colleagues at the Centre for the Study of the Renaissance—Ingrid de Smet and Penny Roberts—who have supported and believed in my research.

I would also like to thank the amazing series editors—Charles Beem and Carole Levin (again)—for making this book possible as well as the editors at Palgrave Macmillan—Megan Laddusaw and Christine Pardue—who have replied to all my enquiries and requests with great kindness and patience.

Last but not least, I would like to thank the people to whom this book is dedicated: the loves of my life, my parents Bernard and Joëlle Paranque.

For my mother who has encouraged my love and passion for history since my childhood. For my mother who has converted me to color-coding and meticulous organization when writing. For my mother who has taught me never to give up: no matter how tired you feel, get up and do the job! For my father who is my warrior of light and, in many ways, has shaped my approach to life. For my father who would always kindle my curiosity with topics as diverse as politics and astronomy. For my father who has literally held my hand in difficult times when I felt that I could not carry on. For my parents for their tremendous generosity with their emotional and financial support throughout the years. For my parents who have always believed in me no matter what and who have done everything in their power to ensure that I would make my dream come true. For my parents because I could not have hoped for better ones, with all my love.

# Contents

# ABBREVIATIONS

BL                                British Library
BNF                               Bibliothèque Nationale de France
*Correspondence diplomatique*     *Correspondence diplomatique de Bertrand de*
                                  *Salignac de la Mothe Fénélon, ambassadeur de*
                                  *France en Angleterre, de 1568 à 1575*
*LCM*                             *Lettres de Catherine de Médicis* publiées par M. Le
                                  Cte Hector de la Ferrière
MS Fr                             Manuscript Français
ODNB                              Oxford Dictionary of National Biography
SP                                State Papers
TNA                               The National Archives

# CHAPTER 1

# Introduction: In Valois Eyes

On September 7, 1533, Elizabeth Tudor was born. Her parents had married just months before, generating shock and disapproval all around Europe. In his dispatch to Francis I of France, Jean de Dinteville, the French ambassador to the English court, reported the June 1 coronation of "Anne de Boulen" and Henry VIII's displeasure on learning that many courtiers were gossiping about it.[1] The relationship between Elizabeth's parents swiftly deteriorated, and in 1536 Anne Boleyn was accused of high treason for incestuous and promiscuous relationships with several men, including her brother George. On May 19, she was beheaded. Soon after, Elizabeth was declared bastard and illegitimate, precipitating more than a decade of tumult for the young princess. She was third in line to the throne, after her half-brother Edward and her half-sister Mary. During their respective reigns, Elizabeth survived countless false accusations and even imprisonment in the Tower of London.

Events in England, France, and Spain were usually locked together. The Italian wars that ravaged Europe from 1494 to 1559 had a profound impact on diplomatic relations between the three countries.[2] Francis I of

---

[1] Jean de Dinteville to Francis I, king of France, June 10, 1533, BNF MS. Fr. 15,971, fol. 5.

[2] See Albert Guérard, *France: A Modern History* (Ann Arbor: University of Michigan Press, 1959); Bert S. Hall, *Weapons and Warfaire in Renaissance Europe: Gunpowder, Technology, and Tactics* (Baltimore: Johns Hopkins University Press, 1997); Robert J. Knecht, *Renaissance Warrior and Patron: The Reign of Francis I* (Cambridge: Cambridge University Press, 1994); Angus Konstam, *Pavia 1525: The Climax of the Italian Wars* (Oxford: Osprey Publishing, 1996); John Julius Norwich, *A History of Venice* (New York: Vintage Books,

© The Author(s) 2019
E. Paranque, *Elizabeth I of England through Valois Eyes*, Queenship and Power, https://doi.org/10.1007/978-3-030-01529-9_1

France (and before him Charles VIII and Louis XII) and Charles V of Spain had been fighting over the duchy of Milan and the kingdom of Naples in an atmosphere of seemingly irreconcilable tension between the two royal houses.[3] In 1522, Henry VIII of England had chosen to join the league formed by the Pope Leo X and Charles V of Spain against France. Following a military catastrophe at Pavia in 1525, in January of the following year Francis was forced to sign the Treaty of Madrid, by which he renounced his claims to Italy, Flanders, and Burgundy.[4] However, Clement VII, who had succeeded to the papacy in 1523, did not wish to see Charles V's empire grow any further. Another alliance was formed, this time with France and England ranged against Spain, but it collapsed and Charles V surrounded the papal states.[5]

Francis I died on March 31, 1547. Four years later, his son, Henry II, declared war on Spain in a bid to regain some glory and the Italian territories. In 1556, Charles V abdicated, leaving his imperial title to his brother Ferdinand and his Spanish crown to his son Philip II. The latter was married to Mary I of England, which paved the way for a political and military alliance. Two years later, the French invaded and regained control of Calais, which had been under English jurisdiction since 1347. In 1559, the Peace of Cateau-Cambrésis brought the Italian wars to an end by forcing Henry II to renounce his Italian claims. But Calais remained French.

Mary I had died on November 17, 1558, whereupon, to many people's surprise, Elizabeth had become Queen of England. The loss of Calais during her sister's reign was a profound national disgrace, and Elizabeth was determined to reclaim it.[6] In 1562, ostensibly to help the Huguenots in their struggles against French Catholics, she sent 6000 troops to Newhaven (Le Havre), and expressed the hope that "the English occupation of Le

1989) and Michael Mallet and Christine Shaw, *The Italian Wars: 1494–1559* (Harlow: Pearson Education, 2012).

[3] Rhea Marsh Smith, *Spain: A Modern History* (Ann Arbor: University of Michigan Press, 1965), 145.

[4] Michael Mallet and Christine Shaw, *The Italian Wars: 1494–1559*, 155.

[5] Mallet and Shaw, *The Italian Wars: 1494–1559*, 160–4.

[6] Raphael Holinshed, *Holinshed's chronicles of England, Scotland and Ireland*, 1587, vol. 4 England, ed. Sir H. Ellis (London: J. Johnson, 1808), 952. Cyndia Susan Clegg examines how this work was seen as propaganda and ended up being censored by the English government; see the discussion in Cyndia Susan Clegg, "Censorship and Propaganda," in *The Elizabethan World*, eds. Susan Doran and Norman Jones (Oxford: Routledge, 2011), 167–71.

Havre could be treated for the return of Calais."[7] However, the English expedition ended in failure as the French forces united against Elizabeth's troops and Calais was lost forever.[8] Despite the 1572 Treaty of Blois, which stated that England and France would form an alliance against Spain, relations between the two courts continued to be characterized by mistrust.[9]

## REPRESENTATIONS OF ELIZABETH: POWER, PERSUASION, AND PERPETUAL YOUTH

This book focuses on how Elizabeth was perceived by the French royal family and their ambassadors from 1558 to 1588. It also examines the dynamics of Anglo-French relations at that time and argues that, contrary to assumptions based on the fact that France was a Catholic country while England was officially Protestant, the representations of Elizabeth in French diplomatic correspondence were not entirely negative. Indeed, the general traffic of diplomatic correspondence offers a wide range of perspectives on the English queen.

These representations of the English queen have fascinated scholars for centuries. Interestingly, her contemporaries in France—Charles IX and Henry III—have not attracted nearly as much attention, and the French historiography covering their reigns does not engage so intensively with their representations.[10] From the portrayals of Elizabeth as the Virgin Queen and Deborah the Israelite judge who freed her people from oppression, the image of a Protestant heroine who managed to rule effectively amid a horde of Catholic enemies has been extensively studied

[7] Paul E. J. Hammer, "The Catholic Threat and the Military Response," in *The Elizabethan World*, 629.

[8] Hammer, "The Catholic Threat and the Military Response," 630. See also Paul E. J. Hammer, *Elizabeth's Wars: War, Government and Society in Tudor England, 1544–1604* (New York: Palgrave Macmillan, 2003), 48–53 and 62–66.

[9] See Lynn A. Martin, "Papal Policy and the European Conflict, 1559–1572," in *Sixteenth Century Journal*, vol. 11, 2 (1980): 35–48.

[10] On Charles IX of France, see Pierre Champion, *Charles IX, la France et le contrôle de l'Espagne: Tome I, Avant la Saint-Barthélémy et Tome II: Après la Saint-Barthélémy* (Paris: Bernard Grasset, 1939); Denis Crouzet, "Charles IX ou le roi sanglant malgré lui?" in *Bulletin-Société de l'histoire de protestantisme français* vol. 141, (1995). On Henry III, see Jacqueline Boucher, *La cour de Henri III* (Rennes: Ouest-France, 1986); Nicolas Le Roux, *Un régicide au nom de Dieu* (Paris: Gallimard, 2006) and Robert J. Knecht, *Hero or Tyrant: Henry III, King of France, 1574–1589* (Farnham: Ashgate, 2014).

and developed, notably by Sir John Neale and Roy Strong.[11] But this image is a complex one,[12] not least because her depiction as Protestant heroine was as much imposed upon Elizabeth as it was generated by the actions and proclamations of the queen herself.[13] Indeed, in many ways, she was a reluctant heroine of the Reformation, because, while she could not ignore the struggles of continental Protestants, she had no desire to go to war against her neighbors in order to defend her coreligionists.[14]

Another image of Elizabeth that has been explored in depth is "mother of her country."[15] Her gender has been studied as a significant part of her queenship, and a number of scholars, such as Maria Petty and Ilona Bell, have attempted to problematize the gendered representations of the

[11] On the Protestant champion, see the works of John Neale, *Queen Elizabeth I* (London, 1934) and Roy Strong, *The Cult of Elizabeth: Elizabethan Portraiture and Pageantry* (London: Pimlico, 1999). On Deborah, see Carol Blessing, "Elizabeth I as Deborah the Judge: exceptional women of power," in *Goddesses and Queens: The Iconography of Elizabeth I*, eds. Annaliese Connolly & Lisa Hopkins (Manchester and New York: Manchester University Press, 2007), 19–30.

[12] Elizabeth's religious belief has influenced scholars and their representations of her as a Protestant champion or a defender of the Protestant faith, see the works of Sir John E. Neale, "The via media in politics," *Elizabethan Essays* (London: Jonathan Cape Thirty Bedford Square, 1958), 114–5; Shenk, *Learned Queen*, 23 and 44 and Susan Doran, *Elizabeth I and Religion, 1558–1603* (London and New York: Routledge, 1994), 6–7. On a more negative image of Elizabeth due to her politics, see Peter Lake, *Bad Queen Bess? Libels, Secret Histories, and the Politics of Publicity in the Reign of Queen Elizabeth I* (Oxford: Oxford University Press, 2016).

[13] Thomas S. Freeman and Susan Doran, "Introduction," in *The Myth of Elizabeth*, eds. Susan Doran and Thomas S. Freeman (New York: Palgrave Macmillan, 2003), 6.

[14] On Elizabeth's Protestant saviour image developed in John Foxe's *Acts and* Monuments and in the *Bishop's* Bible, see John N. King, *Tudor Royal Iconography: Literature and Art in an Age of Religious Crisis* (Princeton: Princeton University Press, 1989), 105–6, 153–4 and 234–5. And on Elizabeth as a Deborah, see the works of Anne McLaren, "Elizabeth I as Deborah: Biblical typology, prophecy and political power," *Gender, Power and Privilege in Early Modern Europe*, eds. Jessica Munns and Penny Richards (London: Longman, 2003), 90–107 and Alexandra Walsham, "'A Very Deborah?' The Myth of Elizabeth I as a Providential Monarch," in *The Myth of Elizabeth*, eds. Susan Doran and Thomas S. Freeman (New York: Palgrave Macmillan, 2003), 143–70.

[15] See Christine Coch, "'Mother of my Contreye': Elizabeth I and Tudor Constructions of Motherhood," *English Literary Renaissance*, 26.3 (1996): 423–50 and Helen Hackett, *Virgin Mother, Maiden Queen: Elizabeth I and the Cult of the Virgin Mary* (GB: Palgrave Macmillan, 1994). Other works have also paid attention to Elizabeth's gender and how it influenced her representations; see e.g. Christopher Haigh, *Elizabeth I* (London and New York: Longman, 1988).

queen.[16] In *The Heart and Stomach of a King: Elizabeth I and the Politics of Sex and Power*, Carole Levin evolves a more complex image of Elizabeth.[17] Though Levin does not dismiss the importance of Elizabeth's sex, she rightly explains that, as she remained single, she was both Queen and King of England, which played an important role in her self-representation.[18] This duality—a male and female representation of the Tudor queen—is also examined by Kevin Sharpe, for example in his analysis of the famous 1588 Tilbury speech.[19] Many other historians have similarly explored Elizabeth's image in the context of her warlike rhetoric.[20] This dual representation of Elizabeth as both King and Queen of England was echoed in French writings, too—demonstrating that her reign was perceived as unusual both inside and outside the borders of her realm.

Elizabeth's portraits have also drawn the attention of numerous scholars.[21] For instance, Anna Riehl Bertolet focuses on the English queen's

---

[16] On Elizabeth's writings, see Maria Perry, *The word of a prince* (Woodbridge: The Boydell Press, 1990). Also see Ilona Bell, *Elizabeth I: The Voice of a Monarch* (New York: Palgrave Macmillan, 2010). For the queen's speeches, as previously mentioned, see Allison Heisch, "Queen Elizabeth I and the Persistence of Patriarchy" and Frances Teagues, "Queen Elizabeth in her speeches," in *Gloriana's Face: Women, Public and Private, in the English Renaissance*, eds. S.P. Cerasano and Marion Wynne-Davies (Detroit: Wayne State University Press, 1992), 63–78. On Elizabeth's writing in general, see Donatella Montini and Iolanda Plescia (eds.), *Elizabeth I in Writing: Language, Power and Representation in Early Modern England* (New York: Palgrave Macmillan, 2018).

[17] Carole Levin, *The Heart and Stomach of a King: Elizabeth I and the Politics of Sex and Power* (Philadelphia: University of Pennsylvania Press, 1994, 2nd edition 2013).

[18] Levin, *The Heart and Stomach of a King*, 4 and 148.

[19] Kevin Sharpe, *Selling the Tudor Monarchy: Authority and Image in Sixteenth Century England* (New Haven: Yale University Press, 2009), 458.

[20] See Anna Whitelock, "'Woman, Warrior, Queen?': Rethinking Mary and Elizabeth," in *Tudor Queenship: the Reigns of Mary and Elizabeth*, eds. Alice Hunt and Anna Whitelock (New York: Palgrave Macmillan, 2010), 173–89; Ben Spiller, "Warlike Mates? Queen Elizabeth and Joan La Pucelle in 1 Henry VI," in *Goddesses and Queens: the Iconography of Elizabeth I*, eds. Annaliese Connolly and Lisa Hopkins (Manchester and New York: Manchester University Press, 2007), 34–44 and Estelle Paranque, "The representations and ambiguities of the warlike female kingship of Elizabeth I of England," in *Medieval and Early Modern Representations of Authority in Scotland and Great Britain*, eds. Katherine Buchanan and Lucinda Dean (London: Routledge, 2016), 163–76.

[21] The most famous works remain Roy Strong, *The Cult of Elizabeth: Elizabethan Portraiture and Pageantry* and Roy Strong, *Gloriana: Portraits of Queen Elizabeth I* (London: Thames and Hudson, 1987); also see Catherine Loomis, "'Bear your Body More Seeming': Open-Kneed Portraits of Elizabeth I," in *The Emblematic Queen: Extra-Literary Representations of Early Modern Queenship*, ed. Debra Barrett-Graves (New York: Palgrave

face and its importance in both written accounts and portraiture.[22] Meanwhile, Frances Yates explores Elizabeth's representation as Astraea, the Greek goddess of innocence, in literary works and links this depiction to the queen's faith.[23] More recently, Mary Villeponteaux and others have examined how the English viewed their queen and shaped some of her images.[24] These works have established that Elizabeth's reputation and representation were multi-layered in England, and I argue that this was also the case within the French court.

In this study, I suggest a series of fresh and complementary approaches on these issues by looking at the French royal family and their ambassadors' letters and official reports. Close examination of these royal and diplomatic sources has revealed that some familiar images, such as Elizabeth as Protestant champion, were not reported by the Valois, while other, often rather different, images and perceptions of Elizabeth did emerge in their correspondence.

Monarchs tended to use familial tropes when engaging with one another and to maintain alliances. While this is hardly surprising, the way in which they shaped fictional familial relationships is intriguing.[25] The following chapters investigate the important categorization of Elizabeth as

Macmillan, 2013), 53–68; Janet Arnold, *The Queen's Wardrobe Unlock'd* (Leeds: Maney Publishing, 1988); Susan Frye, *Elizabeth I: The Competition for Representation* (Oxford: University Press, 1996); Louis Montrose, *The Subject of Elizabeth: Authority, Gender, and Representation* (Chicago: University of Chicago Press, 2006) and Kevin Sharpe and his chapter on "The portrait and picture of the Queen's Majesty," in Kevin Sharpe, *Selling the Tudor Monarchy: Authority and Image in Sixteenth Century England*, 358–412.

[22] Anna Riehl Bertolet, *The Face of Queenship, Early modern Representations of Elizabeth I* (New York: Palgrave Macmillan, 2010).

[23] Frances A. Yates, *Astraea* (London and New York: Routledge, 1999, first published in 1975), 29–87.

[24] Mary Villeponteaux, *The Queen's Mercy: Gender and Judgment in Representations of Elizabeth I* (New York: Palgrave Macmillan, 2014). And see Sharpe, *Selling the Tudor Monarchy*, 451–5. Paul Strauss focuses on the Tudor queen's image as a nurse of the Church of England in court sermons, see Paul Strauss, "The Virgin Queen as Nurse of the Church: Manipulating an Image of Elizabeth I in Court Sermons," in *Scholars and Poets Talk about Queens*, eds. Carole Levin and Christine Stewart-Nunez (New York: Palgrave Macmillan, 2015), 185–202.

[25] Lena Orlin examines the sibling relationship of Elizabeth with her counterparts, in Lena Orlin "The Fictional Families of Elizabeth I," in *Political Rhetoric, Power and Renaissance Women*, eds. Carole Levin and Patricia A. Sullivan (Albany: Suny Press, 1995), 85–110.

a member of the French royal family and trace the significant changes in the terms that were chosen to accompany this image. Furthermore, the French rulers and their ambassadors developed many other representations of the Tudor monarch—from pirate queen to benevolent ruler—largely in response to the state of diplomatic relations between the two countries.

In some respects, this book's approach is similar to those of two significant works that have touched on foreign perceptions of the Tudor queen. In his essay on the Venetians and Elizabeth, John Watkins looks at their diplomatic relations with a view to establishing how the city state's ambassadors perceived not only Elizabeth but England as a whole.[26] However, the main aim of his article is to explain Spanish influence in Venice in the 1580s, so it lacks a thorough analysis of the ambassadors' written appraisals of Elizabeth. Indeed, Watkins acknowledges that more work needs to be done on this subject.[27]

Nabil Matar's chapter in *The Foreign Relations of Elizabeth I* is perhaps the closest to this study in terms of sources as he explores the diplomatic relations between Elizabeth and Mulay Ahmad al Mansur through detailed analysis of ambassadors' and royal letters. Moreover, he demonstrates that her Gloriana reputation, which stemmed from her victory over the Spanish Armada in 1588, did not reach Morocco.[28] However, his work covers only a short period of time and does not offer a comprehensive analysis of how Elizabeth was perceived by her Moroccan counterpart.

Despite their shortcomings, these two articles show that new facets of Elizabeth's representations and reputations, and therefore a more multifaceted portrait of this most famous English monarch, may emerge through close examination of foreign sources. This study follows their lead and attempts to challenge and counterbalance Anglocentric views of Elizabeth by offering a more analytical exploration of her representations in the correspondence of French rulers and their ambassadors.

---

[26] Watkins, "Elizabeth Through Venetian Eyes," in *Explorations in Renaissance Culture*, vol. 30, 1 (Summer 2004): 121–38, 122–3.

[27] Watkins, "Elizabeth Through Venetian Eyes," 126–8. At the end of his essay, Watkins offers an interesting passage on "Elizabeth's place in the Venetian imagination," 131.

[28] Matar, "Elizabeth through Moroccan Eyes," in *The Foreign Relations of Elizabeth I*, ed. Charles Beem (New York: Palgrave Macmillan, 2011), 145–68, 145–6.

## ANGLO-FRENCH RELATIONS: AMITY,
## INFLUENCE, AND RIVALRY

France and England have a long history of influencing each other. In *Good Newes from Fraunce*, Lisa Ferraro Parmelee explains her interest in the reception and "influence of French ideas on late Elizabethan political thought."[29] Her work provides fascinating French primary sources published in England for both political and religious reasons. It also shows how the two courts exerted significant influence on each other. For instance, we learn that Lord Burghley intervened in contemporary political debates on several crucial occasions through the medium of anonymously authored pamphlets as well as, famously, the royal proclamation of October 18, 1591.[30] Major French thinkers, such as Jean Bodin, were published in English, with the effect that they fashioned and challenged the authorities of both the state and the monarch.[31] In both countries, the monarch's authority and, to some extent, legitimacy were challenged by pamphlets, libels, and books written by both religious and political actors—if it is possible to differentiate between these two groups during the Renaissance period.[32] By focusing on how the French royal family viewed Elizabeth, this study reveals the dynamics of the relationship between the English queen and the French kings, but it also examines how a foreign court perceived England's monarch. Despite the political and religious framework that surrounded their exchanges, Elizabeth and the Valois kings found a way to pursue a relatively positive diplomatic alliance.

[29] Lisa Ferraro Parmelee, *Good Newes from Fraunce: French Anti-League Propaganda in Late Elizabethan England* (New York: University of Rochester Press, 1996), 2.

[30] Parmelee, *Good Newes from Fraunce*, 27. On Burghley's use of a printer, see Elizabeth Evenden, "The Michael Wood Mystery: William Cecil and the Lincolnshire Printing of John Day," *Sixteenth Century Journal* 35 (2004): 383–94.

[31] See Parmelee, *Good Newes from Fraunce* 1, 56–7 and 97.

[32] Rob Content has studied how the royal image was controlled and how the public used "images to criticize Queen Elizabeth," see Rob Content, *"Fair is Fowle*: Interpreting Anti-Elizabethan Composite Portraiture," in *Dissing Elizabeth: Negative Representations of Gloriana*, ed. Julia M. Walker (Durham and London: Duke University Press, 1998), 229–51, 229. On French monarchical representations, Annie Duprat has examined how pamphlets and libels affected Henry III of France's reputation among his fellowmen, see Annie Duprat, *Les rois de papier, la caricature de Henry III à Louis XVI* (Paris: Belin, 2002). On the use of pamphlets in the public sphere, see Joad Raymond, *Pamphlets and Pamphleteering in Early Modern Britain* (Cambridge: Cambridge University Press, 2003). On propaganda and how it affected monarchs' authority and representation, see John Cooper, *Propaganda and the Tudor State Political Culture in the Westcountry* (Oxford: Oxford University Press, 2003).

Historians have long demonstrated a strong interest in Elizabeth's foreign diplomacy, albeit primarily in terms of her relationships and correspondence with Catherine de Medici[33] the first Bourbon king of France, Henry IV. This study attempts to redress the balance by focusing on her relations with his predecessors—the last two Valois kings of France, Charles IX and Henry III.[34] Nate Probasco has explored the Tudor queen's reaction after the St. Bartholomew's Day Massacre,[35] but his essay does not deal in depth with the diplomatic relationship between Charles IX and Elizabeth. Rather, it focuses on the latter's reaction to the massacre and the personal involvement of the French king in the atrocity. Moreover, Probasco cites only English sources, so the French side of the story remains untold.

A handful of scholars have investigated Elizabeth's correspondence with Francis, Duke of Anjou. For instance, Jonathan Gibson and Guillaume

[33] On Catherine de Medici and Elizabeth, see: Susan Doran, "Elizabeth I and Catherine de Medici," in *"The Contending of Kingdoms," France and England 1420–1700*, ed. Glenn Richardson (Aldershot: Ashgate, 2008), 117–32; Elaine Kruse, "The Virgin and the Widow: The political finesse of Elizabeth I and Catherine de Médici," in *Queens and Power in Medieval and Early Modern England*, eds. Carole Levin and Robert Bucholz (Lincoln and London: University of Nebraska Press, 2009), 126–40 and Rayne Allinson, *A Monarchy in Letters: Royal Correspondence and English Diplomacy in the Reign of Elizabeth I* (New York: Palgrave Macmillan, 2012).

[34] Guillaume Coatalen acknowledges the importance of Elizabeth's French correspondence but does not engage with her letters exchanged with the Valois kings, see Guillaume Coatalen, "'Ma plume vous pourra exprimer,' Elizabeth's French Correspondence," in *Representations of Elizabeth I in Early Modern Culture*, eds. Alessandra Petrina and Laura Tosi (New York: Palgrave Macmillan, 2011), 83–104. Even in the collection of essays entitled *Tudor England and its Neighbours*, these two important relationships are left out, see Susan Doran and Glenn Richardson (eds.), *Tudor England and Its Neighbours* (New York: Palgrave Macmillan, 2005). In a chapter, Glenn Richardson analyses the relations of Elizabeth I of England with Henry III and Henry IV of France. He explains how Elizabeth and Henry III used each other in order to defy Spain's domination, and he claims that the death of Anjou is precisely what brought Henry III and Elizabeth together, against Philip II. Even before his death, the two monarchs had developed a friendly rhetoric during the marriage negotiations between Anjou and Elizabeth as well as a shared goal of protecting at all cost their alliance after the death of the king's brother. However, in Richardson's chapter, the focus is more on Elizabeth's relations with Henry IV of France—diminishing somehow Henry III's political importance to the English queen. See Glenn Richardson, "'Your most assured sister': Elizabeth I and the Kings of France," in *Tudor Queenship: the reigns of Mary and Elizabeth*, eds. Alice Hunt and Anna Whitelock (New York: Palgrave Macmillan, 2010), 191–208, 194.

[35] Nate Probasco, Queen Elizabeth's reaction to the St. Bartholomew's Day Massacre," in *The Foreign Relation of Elizabeth I*, ed. Charles Beem (New York: Palgrave Macmillan, 2012), 77–100.

Coatalen have explored the exchange of letters between the queen and the duke during their protracted marriage negotiations.[36] However, they are rather dismissive of what was, in effect, high-level diplomacy. This represents a missed opportunity, because thorough analysis of the communiqués that Charles IX, Henry III, their mother Catherine, the wider French royal family and their ambassadors sent to the English court reveals a series of fascinating perceptions and representations of the final Tudor queen.

Two important works highlight what one might call "the diplomacy of fear." In *Giordano Bruno and the Embassy Affair*, John Bossy focuses on the distrust that existed between France and England from 1582 to Mary Stuart's death. In brief, in the process of trying to identify Walsingham's informant, "Henry Fagot," Bossy reveals a number of complex espionage networks. Although I disagree with some of his conclusions, he amply demonstrates the seriousness of the so-called "Throckmorton conspiracy" and the extent to which the French Embassy in London became a center of sedition.[37] His second work, published ten years later, revisits Walsingham's spy networks in mind-twisting detail, and in particular the flow of information in and out of the French Embassy.[38] Here, also, there are *obiter dicta* about the balance of forces in the Elizabethan polity and the maneuvering of Michel de Castelnau, Seigneur de Mauvissière, Thomas Morgan, Throckmorton, Mauvissière's secretary Courcelles, and the English ambassador at the French court, Edward Stafford.[39] Yet, all of this distrust is just one part of the story. This study examines the importance for both France and England of maintaining reasonable—if not good—diplomatic relations.

[36] See: Jonathan Gibson, "'Dedans la plié de mon fidelle affection': Familiarity and Materiality in Elizabeth's Letters to Anjou," in *Elizabeth I's Foreign Correspondence: Letters, Rhetoric, and Politics*, eds. Carlo M. Bajetta, Guillaume Coatalen and Jonathan Gibson (New York: Palgrave Macmillan, 2014), 63–92 and Guillaume Coatalen and Jonathan Gibson, "Six Holographs Letters in French from Queen Elizabeth I to the Duke of Anjou: Texts and Analysis," in *Elizabeth I's Foreign Correspondence: Letters, Rhetoric, and Politics*, eds. Carlo M. Bajetta, Guillaume Coatalen and Jonathan Gibson (New York: Palgrave Macmillan, 2014) 27–62. On Elizabeth and Anjou, also see: Susan Doran, *Monarchy and Matrimony, the Courtships of Elizabeth I* (London New York: Routledge, 1996).
[37] John Bossy, *Giordano Bruno and the Embassy Affair* (New Haven and London: Yale Nota Bene and Yale University Press, 2002, first published 1991), 9 and 54.
[38] John Bossy, *Under the Molehill: An Elizabethan Spy Story* (New Haven and London: Yale University Press, 2001), 13–15 and 107–10.
[39] This will be discussed further in Chap. 6.

Of course, the great princely families at the French court played pivotal roles in this relationship, and none more so than the Guises. As much as any English historian, Stuart Carroll has traced the ways in which the prominence of this family started to threaten the hard-won peace between France and England.[40] On the basis of this recent scholarship, I examine the two courts' diplomacy and reveal how Elizabeth was perceived by the French royal family and their ambassadors.

## THE FRENCH AMBASSADORS: A WHO'S WHO

The French ambassadors to England played a critical role in how the French royal family understood and perceived Elizabeth. While it is often difficult to tease out the precise motivation and agenda of individual diplomats in this period, it helps to have some understanding of their background. In Chap. 2, I concentrate on three diplomats. The first was Gilles de Noailles, the son of Louis de Noailles and the brother of several other diplomats, notably Antoine de Noailles (1504–1562), who resided at the English court from 1552 to 1556.[41] Gilles was sent to the English court as France's official ambassador from 1559 to 1560, and thereafter he continued to play an important political role both inside and outside the French realm.[42] His successor, Michel de Seure (also known as Sèvre), was a knight of St. John of Jerusalem arrived at the English court in February 1560. He had previously traveled extensively to Algiers, Malta, and the Ottoman Empire, and had been ambassador to Portugal in 1557.[43] De Seure returned to France due to ill health in 1562, whereupon he was replaced by Paul de Foix, who served as French ambassador until July 1566. Born in 1528, the latter was the son of Jean de Foix, Comte de Carmain. A prelate as well as a diplomat, he had studied Greek and Roman literature in Paris and he was on intimate terms with the French royal family, most notably Catherine de Medici.

---

[40] Stuart Carroll, *Martyrs & Murderers: The Guise Family and the Making of Europe* (Oxford: Oxford University Press, 2009), v–viii. Carroll explains that the Guises were enemies of the English crown and of the French royal family, see 232–3 and 242–3. For the Guise network, see Chap. 6 below.

[41] *Ambassades de Messieurs de Noailles en Angleterre*, rédigées par feu M. L'Abbé de Vertot, Tome 1 (Leyden: Dessaint & Saillant Libraires, 1763), 9–10.

[42] *Ambassades de Messieurs de Noailles en Angleterre*, 12–22.

[43] David Potter (ed.), *A Knight of Malta at the Court of Elizabeth I: The Correspondence of Michel de Seure, French Ambassador, 1560–1561* (Cambridge: Cambridge University Press, Camden Series, 2014), 6–9, 13.

He arrived in England as a special envoy in 1561 before acceding to the ambassadorship the following year. He was posted to Italy in 1566 and died in Rome eighteen years later.[44]

De Foix was succeeded as French ambassador to the English court by Jacques Bochetel de La Forest, who in turn was superseded two years later by Bertrand de Salignac de la Mothe Fénélon. The latter was born in Périgord in 1523, the seventh child of Hélie de Salignac and Catherine de Ségur Théobon.[45] However, his parents soon placed him under the protection of a cousin, Jean de Gontaut, who raised Bertrand alongside his own son, Armand. The de Gontauts were an important noble family, and Jean served as special envoy at the courts of Charles V of Spain between 1547 and 1548 and John III of Portugal between 1548 and 1549.[46] Bertrand accompanied his guardian on these missions and gained a good education in the art of diplomacy from him. When Jean died in 1557, Bertrand moved closer to another cousin, Jean Ebrard, Baron de Saint-Sulpice, who held a number of important positions at the French court.

From 1559 to 1561, La Mothe Fénélon was a representative of the nobility in the General Estates. He then served under Michel de Seure at the English court for a year before becoming Ebrard's secretary at the Spanish court, where he garnered high praise from his cousin.[47] Thereafter, he was sent to Scotland in 1566 and the Netherlands a year later. All of this high-level diplomatic experience made La Mothe Fénélon the perfect choice in the eyes of the French royal family when they sought a replacement for Bochetel de La Forest in 1568. The new ambassador did not disappoint: during his embassy, he enjoyed easy access to the queen's councillors and intimate audiences with Elizabeth herself.[48]

---

[44] *Annales Ecclésiastiques du Diocèse de Toulouse*, par un prêtre du diocese (Toulouse: Imprimerie de Bellegarrigue, 1825), 99, 101.

[45] Bertrand de Salignac's biography can be found in the introduction of *Correspondence diplomatique de Bertrand de Salignac de la Mothe Fénélon, ambassadeur de France en Angleterre, de 1568 à 1575*, Tome I (Archives du Royaume: Paris et Londres, 1838) and in Matthieu Gellard, *Une Reine Epistolaire, Lettres et Pouvoir au temps de Catherine de Médicis* (Paris: Classiques Garnier, 2014), 356–9.

[46] For de Gontaut's family, see Francis-Alexandre de La Chenaye-Aubert, *Dictionnaire de la Noblesse*, vol. VII (Paris, 1774).

[47] Gellard, *Une Reine Epistolaire*, 357–8.

[48] Gellard, *Une Reine Epistolaire*, 376–7. And on La Mothe Fénélon's closeness to the queen, see Estelle Paranque, "Queen Elizabeth I and the Elizabethan Court in the French Ambassador's Eyes," in *Queens Matter in Early Modern Studies*, ed. Anna Riehl-Bertolet (New York: Palgrave Macmillan, 2018), 267–86.

Although he was no "Catholic zealot," La Mothe Fénélon's successor certainly had close connections to and relations within the French Catholic League.[49] Michel de Castelnau, Seigneur de Mauvissière, was born in 1520. One of nine children, his parents, Jean de Castelnau and Jeanne Dumesnil, had high hopes for Michel, whom they saw as something of a prodigy. He received an excellent education, having been sent to study in Milan and Naples.[50] A military career followed, during which he forged a friendship with Francis II of Lorraine, duke of Guise, and therefore enjoyed the protection of the Guise family.[51] Later, he became a knight of Malta[52] and played an important role in the Cateau-Cambrésis negotiations of 1559, which earned him the respect and trust of both King Henry II and the Guises.[53]

Mauvissière was sent to Rome during Francis II's reign, then, following Francis's death in 1560, he became France's resident ambassador at the Scottish court, where he acted as mediator between Mary Stuart and her cousin, Elizabeth of England. On returning to France in 1562, he fought with the Guises in the religious wars.[54] More than a decade later, in 1575, Henry III appointed him ambassador to the English court. Over the next ten years, he seemingly made full use of his high-level connections and diplomatic skills in the service of numerous plots and intrigues against the English crown.[55]

Unfortunately, the sources provide scant information on Mauvissière's successor, Guillaume de L'Aubespine, Baron de Chasteauneuf. However, we know that he was the son of a lawyer, Claude de L'Aubespine, and Jeanne Bochetel (Jacques Bochetel de La Forest's sister), and that he followed in his father's footsteps to become a state councillor.[56] In 1572, he was sent as ambassador to the Spanish court with instructions to ascertain

[49] Bossy, *Giordano Bruno*, 9.

[50] *Mémoires de Messire Michel de Castelnau, Seigneur de Mauvissière et de Concressaut, Baron de Jonville*, par M. Petitot (Paris: Foucault Librairie, 1823), 3.

[51] Bossy, *Giordano Bruno*, 13–15.

[52] Bossy, *Giordano Bruno*, 4.

[53] Bossy, *Giordano Bruno*, 6.

[54] Bossy, *Giordano Bruno*, 8–9.

[55] Bossy challenges Mauvissière's implication in the Throckmorton plot, see: Bossy, *Under The Molehill*, 107–10.

[56] *Histoire des Chancelliers et des Gardes des Sceaux de France distingués par les règnes de nos Monarques depuis Clovis Premer Roy Chrétien jusques à Louis Le Grand XIVe du nom, heureusement régnant*, by Francis du Chesne (Paris: Chez l'auteur avec privilège du roy, 1680), 799–800.

Philip II's intentions toward France.[57] Thirteen years later, he was chosen to replace Mauvissière in England. Another strong Catholic, his relations with the English court are best described as "complicated."[58]

## THE SOURCES

The correspondence between the French royal family and their ambassadors is an exceedingly rich but largely untapped resource. When exchanging letters with their ambassadors, Charles IX, Catherine, and Henry III inevitably fashioned their own discrete representations of the English queen. Due to the importance of maintaining royal power and stable alliances, religious beliefs often had to be ignored. In consequence, the French rulers' personal faith had almost no impact on their official views of Elizabeth because they knew they had to preserve the political alliance at all costs, given the events that were unfolding elsewhere in Europe. Therefore, to some extent at least, their letters present an unbiased view of Elizabeth. Furthermore, as Ilona Bell has rightly explained, ambassadors reported rulers' words "more consistently and in more detail than any other extant source."[59] In other words, they were extremely influential in shaping a monarch's reputation in their own homelands.

Although not all of the letters have survived, they remain key sources for this study. Some are available in published anthologies while others are readily accessible in manuscript form. The French ambassadors' reports provide very detailed accounts of the English court, the way of life in the host country, their own experiences, and, of course, their audiences with the queen. They also disclose a good deal of information on the life of a sixteenth-century diplomat, their personal perceptions of the court, and their relationships with their masters in France. Even the briefest glance at this valuable source material reveals that a diplomat's agenda did not necessarily correlate with that of his employer.

David Potter has recently collated Michel de Seure's letters in a comprehensive anthology, which serves as one of the main sources for Chap. 2,[60] while the *Correspondence diplomatique de Bertrand de Salignac de la Mothe*

---

[57] Charles Cauvin, *Henry de Guise, Le Balafré: Histoire de France de 1563 à 1589* (Tours: Alfred Mame et Fils, 1881), 58.

[58] Bossy, *Giordano Bruno*, 54, 58.

[59] Bell, *Elizabeth I: The Voice of a Monarch*, 69.

[60] Potter, *A Knight of Malta at the Court of Elizabeth I*.

*Fénélon, ambassadeur de France en Angleterre, de 1568 à 1575*, which was published in the mid-nineteenth century, provides much of the information for Chaps. 3 and 4.[61] The other ambassadors' letters have never appeared in print, but the reports of Gilles de Noailles, Paul de Foix, and Michel de Castelnau, Seigneur de Mauvissière, are all accessible in manuscript form in either the Bibliothèque Nationale de France or the Archives Etrangères. Unfortunately, those of Guillaume de L'Aubespine, Baron of Chasteauneuf, have proved much more difficult to locate.[62]

As for letters written by or in the names of members of the French royal family, those of Catherine de Medici were published by M. Le Cte Hector de la Ferrière and subsequently by M. Le Cte Baguenault de Puchesse. Among the addressees are the French ambassadors at the English court, Catherine's sons Charles IX and Henry III, and important advisers. Overall, this correspondence provides invaluable information about Elizabeth. Unfortunately, it proved rather more difficult to gain access to Charles IX's and Henry III's letters. Some of the former's correspondence with his ambassadors appears in the final volume of *Correspondence diplomatique de Bertrand de Salignac de la Mothe Fénélon*, but many of his letters seem to have been lost. However, those of Henry III are more accessible, and to some extent they tell us what he wanted people to think about the English queen. Of course, one is inclined to believe that the letters that are written in his own hand or at least signed by him reflect his own opinions. Here, it is important to differentiate between holograph and autograph letters. Although the former are considered more private and personal than the latter, which were written on behalf of the named author, autograph letters still had the direct authorization of the monarch and therefore may be taken to represent his or her views.

Letters, not only as ways to communicate but also as powerful political devices, have intrigued scholars for centuries. Allinson describes the development of "writing technologies" and argues that this "helped to encourage the spread of writing literacy among the ruling elite."[63] Later, he characterizes these rulers' letters as tokens of trust.[64] Dard Hunter explores

---

[61] *Correspondence diplomatique de Bertrand de Salignac de la Mothe Fénélon, ambassadeur de France en Angleterre, de 1568 à 1575*, Books I–VII: *Années 1568–1575* (Paris et Londres: Archives du Royaume, 1838–1840).

[62] This is further discussed in Chap. 6.

[63] Allinson, *A Monarchy of Letters*, 4.

[64] Allinson, *A Monarch of Letters*, 54.

the art and science of papermaking and its roots in European culture,[65] while James Daybell focuses on letters as material objects—from their physical characteristics to how they were sent. The latter's aim is to reveal "the peculiarities of early modern correspondence in all its nuance and complexities from composition to archive."[66] Therefore, I have searched for each and every royal and ambassadorial letter or dispatch that might mention Elizabeth by name and could provide an insight into the sender's true attitude toward her. However, I have also kept in mind the more general context of Anglo-French politics.[67]

Of course, Elizabeth must have had an influence on the French ambassadors' perceptions of her. The latter were duty bound to report the queen's words to their masters, which enabled Elizabeth to fashion her reputation abroad. Moreover, while they are not the primary focus of this book, Elizabeth's own letters—particularly in the 1580s, when relations between the two crowns were especially tense—are pertinent to this historical analysis.

The principal question is: did foreign, and specifically the French court's, perceptions of Elizabeth differ substantially from those of her English subjects? Of course, we know that a sizeable proportion of those subjects viewed her in precisely the same light as some of her foreign critics, especially in the

[65] Dard Hunter, *Papermaking: The History and Technique of an Ancient Craft* (New York: Courier Dover Publications, 1978). Also see Alan Stewart and Heather Wolfe, *Letterwriting in Renaissance England* (Washington: Folger Shakespeare Library, 2004).

[66] James Daybell, *The Material Letter in Early Modern England: Manuscript Letters and the Culture and Practices of Letter-Writing, 1512–1635* (New York: Palgrave Macmillan, 2012), 15. See Daybell, *The Material Letter in Early Modern England*, 148.

[67] See, for examples, some of the other primary sources used: François de Belleforest, *LInnocence de la trèsillustre, très-chaste, et débonnaire Princesse Madame Marie Royne d'Escosse. Où sont amplement refutes les calmonies faulces, & impositions iniques, publiées par un livre secrettement divulgué en France, l'an 1572* (Reims, Jean de Foigny, 1572 & Lyon: Jean de Tournes, 1572); *Continuation des choses plus celebres et memorables advenues en Angleterre, Ecosse et Irlande* (Michel Jove, Lyon, 1570), BNF, Résac. 8 NC 155; Pierre de Lestoile, *Première Partie du Tome Premier, Registre-Journal de Henry III 1574–1589*, edited by MM. Champollion-Figeac and Aimé Champollion fils (Paris: Edouard Proux et Compagnie, 1837); Edit de Nemours, July 7, 1585, in Eugène et Emile Haag, *La France Protestante*, vol. 10 (Paris: 1858); *Le Réveille-Matin des Francis et de leurs voisins*, composé par Eusebe Philadelphe Cosmopolite, en forme de Dialogues, (Edinburgh: Jacques James, 1574); Queen Elizabeth's Armada Speech to the troops at Tilbury, August 9 1588, in *Elizabeth I: Collected works*, 326 and *Hymne sur la naissance de Madame de France, fille du roy très-chrétien Charles IX*, dédié à Jacques Fouyn, prieur et seigneur d'Argenteuil, signé J. S. P. (Lyon: Benoist Rigaud, 1572 et Paris: Mathurin Martin, 1572).

more fraught years of her reign. For instance, English Catholics' criticism sometimes echoed their continental coreligionists' depictions of her as a tyrant. Equally, though, this view should always be set against Elizabeth's generally positive reputation and image at the French court.

Of course, a certain amount of decoding is always necessary when the source material is diplomatic correspondence. As Matthieu Gellard argues, ambassadors were usually unable to express their personal views at the court to which they were sent.[68] On the other hand, early modern diplomatic reports are often rather personal in tone and content, and the ambassadors were frequently willing to pass comment on issues that would never make it into modern-day diplomatic dispatches. Moreover, their relationships with the courts in which they served were also, in some sense, personal. Ambassadors' letters could contain details of everything from the most recent political machinations at court to the state of the weather.[69] More importantly, beyond their own agendas, personal views, and the prevailing political context, their reports contain intriguing information on not only their residence in a foreign country but politics, monarchical representations, and diplomatic dynamics. By reporting on some audiences but not others, and using specific terminology to describe a ruler's personality or reaction to particular events, the ambassadors helped to fashion their host monarch's identity and reputation in their home country.

## Key Diplomatic Periods

This book concentrates on six important episodes that had an impact on Elizabeth and her relations with the Valois royal family. It begins with her accession to the English throne and her nascent regime's fractious relationships with France, Scotland, and Spain.[70] It ends with England's victory over the Spanish Armada in 1588 and how this was viewed within the French court.

---

[68] Gellard, *Une Reine Epistolaire*, 380–3. One thinks here, for example, of the ambassador William Trumbull, a godly Protestant, who was stationed in the early seventeenth century at the archducal court in Brussels.

[69] See e.g. La Mothe Fénélon to the French king Charles IX, 132nd Report, September 10, 1570, in *Correspondence diplomatique de Bertrand de Salignac de la Mothe Fénélon, ambassadeur de France en Angleterre, de 1568 à 1575*, Tome III, Années 1570 et 1571 (Archives du Royaume: Paris et Londres, 1840), 302.

[70] This will be further explained in Chap. 3.

Chapter 2 draws heavily on the letters and diplomatic reports that were sent from 1558 to 1565 to review the state of Anglo-French relations at the beginning of Elizabeth's reign. The initial focus is on the years 1560–1561 and the subsequent Newhaven expedition of 1562–1563.[71] The rest of the chapter concentrates on Elizabeth's marriage prospects, and particularly the first spate of negotiations concerning a possible union with Charles IX of France in 1564 and 1565. As we shall see, Charles was one of three different kings who ruled France in the first seven years of Elizabeth's reign, which not only complicated Anglo-French relations but made it difficult to maintain a stable alliance between the two crowns.

Chapter 3 examines the impact of Mary Stuart's escape to England. Anglo-French relations were thrown into disarray by her flight from Scotland, the subsequent uprising in the north of England, and the eruption of the third French religious civil war. Meanwhile, within England, the Scottish queen posed an imminent threat to the Elizabethan government. Moreover, Elizabeth faced other difficult dilemmas, such as whether to protect the Dutch from Spain and whether to support the Huguenots in France. In these trying circumstances, the correspondence between the French ambassadors and their monarchs contains unusual representations of the English queen—in the sense that they differ markedly from those that are found in the existing historiography.

Chapter 4 studies the aftermath of the St. Bartholomew's Day Massacre and how the French court interpreted Elizabeth's reaction to the mass killing of Huguenots. The reports of Charles IX, Catherine de Medici, and their ambassadors depict the queen as a mutable character. In addition, Elizabeth I and Charles IX not only maintained their amicable relationship but seemed to reinforce it, albeit primarily for appearance's sake. Charles especially strove to ensure that France's alliance with the English crown did not deteriorate.

In Chap. 5, the final years of the extensive marriage negotiations between the Duke of Anjou and Elizabeth provide the political and diplomatic framework for an analysis of the letters that the French royal family exchanged with their representatives at the English court. Perhaps predictably, the perception of Elizabeth changed in this period: as the French

---

[71] See Mortimer Levine, *The Early Elizabethan Succession Question 1558–1568* (Stanford: Stanford University Press, 1966), 203 and Robert Bruce Wernham, *Before the Armada: The Emergence of the English Nation, 1485–1588* (Norton, 1966), 296–7.

royal family's irritation continued to grow, more negative representations of the queen started to seep into their correspondence.

Finally, Chap. 6 covers the years from Anjou's death in 1584 to the assassination of Henry III in 1589. The conflict with the Catholic League escalated in the final year of the latter's reign, meaning that he had little opportunity for regular correspondence with his fellow European monarchs, including Elizabeth.[72] Nevertheless, the letters we have reveal stark contrasts in perceptions of the English queen within the upper echelons of French society at the time.

I believe that studying the way in which a monarch—in this case Elizabeth—is perceived abroad provides a necessary alternative to the familiar policy-led narratives, which are characterized by assumptions of stable diplomacy and business-as-usual among royal ambassadors. The political roles of Charles IX and Henry III were at least as important as that of Catherine de Medici in this period. While the existing historiography tends to rely on English sources, detailed analysis of the corresponding French sources provides a complementary account and enables us to draw rather different conclusions.

---

[72] Henry III was murdered on August 2, 1589, but the Catholic League had seriously challenged and undermined his royal authority since the previous year.

# "her so evil and dangerous will": Long Live the Queen and Diplomatic Games 1558–1565

On November 17, 1558, Elizabeth Tudor succeeded her half-sister, the Catholic Mary, to become Queen of England. However, her reign began in tense circumstances. Between 1554 and 1558, Henry II of France and Philip II of Spain had pursued their quarrel, and the English crown's commitment to Spain had led to reputational damage for the Tudor court. Even worse, arguably, was the looming peace between the two continental European super-powers, which was soon formalized in the Treaty of Cateau-Cambrésis, signed between Elizabeth and Henry on April 2, 1559, and between Philip and Henry a day later.[1]

Elizabeth's accession to the throne was greeted with deep concern all over Europe. In late 1558, Philip II sent one of his closest advisers, Gomez Suarez de Figueroa, Count of Feria, to England to ensure that the transition between the two half-sisters would proceed as smoothly as possible. Both men feared "disturbances [...] given the intrigues and pretensions that some of the enemies of the kingdom and Madam Elizabeth have maintained within the realm."[2] Meanwhile, on hearing the news of Elizabeth's rise to power, Philibert Babou de la Bourdaisière, the newly installed French ambassador in Rome, advised his master, Henry II, to "distract her

---

[1] Cathal J. Nolan (ed.), *The Age of Wars of Religion, 1000–1650: An Encyclopedia of Global Warfare and Civilization*, Vol. 1 (London: Greenwood Press, 2006), 127.

[2] The Count of Feria's Dispatch to Philip II of Spain, November 14, 1558, edited and translated by M.J. Rodrigues-Salgado and Simon Adams, in *Camden Miscellany XXVIII* (London: Camden Fourth Series, Volume 29, 1984), 328.

© The Author(s) 2019
E. Paranque, *Elizabeth I of England through Valois Eyes*, Queenship and Power, https://doi.org/10.1007/978-3-030-01529-9_2

from her so evil and dangerous will."[3] He was undoubtedly referring to her inclination toward the reformed religion and the potential impact of her policy-making on the Catholic Church. De la Bourdaisière was a member of a noble family that had strong links with the Church. His brothers, Jean and Jacques, were *Maître de la garde-robe des Dauphins* and Provost of Tours, respectively, whereas Philibert himself had served as Bishop of Angoulême before his posting to Rome, where he remained until his death in 1570.[4] As a devout Catholic, it is not surprising that de la Bourdaisière perceived Elizabeth as a threat to Henry II. Furthermore, the members of the French royal family themselves and their ambassadors throughout Europe feared that Elizabeth might agree to marry her former brother-in-law, Philip II of Spain, in order to regain control of Calais.[5] For instance, Gilles de Noailles, the French ambassador at the English court until 1560, expressed serious concerns regarding Elizabeth's attitude toward France and the loss of Calais.[6]

The first seven years of Elizabeth's reign were characterized by this difficult political context. Three French ambassadors—Gilles de Noailles, Michel de Seure, and Paul de Foix—attended her court in that period, and each revealed different facets of her personality through their interactions with the queen herself and her court. Moreover, they represented the discrete interests of three successive French kings and one queen regent, all of whom had their own political agendas, especially when it concerned England. While Elizabeth could be seen as a new queen with very little political experience, she was certainly intelligent and sufficiently savvy to learn from the reigns of her half-siblings, and she was well aware that naming a successor too early in her reign would place her in mortal danger.[7]

---

[3] Second Mémoire, Monsieur de la Bourdaisière allant à Rome, c. 1558, BNF MS. Fr. 15,870, fol. 29v.

[4] *Notice sur Philibert Babou de la Bourdaisière et sur le manuscrit qui contient sa correspondance*, M. Henry (ed.) (Reims: Dubois Imprimeurs Libraires, 1859), i–ii; Also see Charles-Martial de Witte, "Notes sur les ambassadeurs de France à Rome et leurs correspondances sous les derniers Valois (1556–1589)," *Mélanges de l'Ecole française de Rome. Moyen-Age, Temps modernes* 83, 1 (1971): 89–121, 95–7.

[5] M. Cardinal de Tournon, special envoy in Venice, to Henry II of France, January 9, 1559, in *Lettres et Mémoires d'Estat des Roys, Princes, Ambassadeurs, et autres Ministres, sous les Règnes de Francis premier, Henry II & Francis II*, Tome II (Paris: Francis Clouzier, 1666), 779.

[6] *Ambassades de Messieurs de Noailles en Angleterre*, by Abbé de Vertot (Paris: Chez Dessaint & Saillant, 1763), 299–301.

[7] Carole Levin, *The Heart and Stomach of a King*, 5–9.

This chapter engages with these contrasting voices and views in a period when Anglo-French relations were deeply unstable. First, it analyzes how France pursued peace with England in the aftermath of the latter's recent loss of Calais and notwithstanding the English military incursion into Scotland. We learn that the French rulers and their ambassadors repeatedly expressed their willingness to be good neighbors in their efforts to forge a strong and stable alliance with England. Next, the chapter examines how the French royal family had to adapt to Elizabeth's unprecedented status as an independent female ruler and considers their perceptions of her as a young, inexperienced queen. Perhaps predictably, we find that their perceptions were tinged with suspicion.

## A QUEST FOR PEACE

When Elizabeth became Queen of England, it may have seemed that the French and Spanish courts were finally prepared to refrain from military conflict for the first time in decades. However, the death of Henry II in 1559 meant that France was suddenly plunged into a regency. Moreover, the new French king Francis II's consort was Mary Stuart, and her mother, Marie de Guise, was Mary's regent in Scotland. Yet, initially, Henry's successors and their ambassadors were profoundly amicable in their diplomatic communications with England.

In the midst of the political upheaval in England, Gilles de Noailles, ambassador at the English court, wrote to Henry II informing him that the new Tudor queen was pleased to be assured of Henry's "perfect friendship" and that she had "always hoped for the natural goodness" of his majesty.[8] However, on June 30, 1559, barely six months after Elizabeth's coronation, Henry was fatally injured during a jousting tournament that was held to celebrate the double marriage of Elisabeth of Valois to Philip II of Spain and Marguerite of France (Henry's sister) to Emmanuel Philibert, Duke of Savoy. The unexpected demise of France's monarch marked a significant shift in European diplomacy and politics.[9]

---

[8] Gilles de Noailles to Henry II of France, June 7, 1559, Archives des Affaires Etrangères (hereafter AE) MD Angleterre, Register IV, fol. 250, "toute seurté de vostre amitié parfaicte qu'elle ne s'en peust assez louer, ny promettre ce qu'elle a tousiours espéré du bon naturel de votre majesté."

[9] Jean-Francis Dreux du Radier, *Tablette anecdotes et historique de rois de France depuis Pharamond jusqu'à Louis XV* (Paris: Couturier, Lamy et Laporte, 1781), 189.

Upon receiving news of the king's accident, Elizabeth I invited Gilles
de Noailles to her chamber, and "apart, close to a window far away from
any company," the French ambassador handed over letters written by
Anne of Montmorency, Constable of France (1493–1567).[10] Montmorency
had been one of the most prominent French political figures for decades,
as well as a close friend of both Francis I and Henry II, which had made
him a major figure at court.[11] Therefore, it is not surprising that de Noailles
informed him directly that the English queen "showed a great displeasure
and sorrow" regarding the injury that had befallen the king. He reported
that she was hoping "with a good heart that on this day there had been no
spear in France, or that she had been carried to his chamber, or even
because it had already happened, that she had been a good surgeon so that
his recovery could be in her hands." With this declaration, and despite the
fact that she only used the term "recovery," Elizabeth showed her desire
to be seen as the savior not only of Henry himself but of France. She continued to "talk about the great virtues and beauties that she had been told
about the said king," and asserted that ever since her accession "to this
crown, she had always promised herself that she would renew [the alli-
ance] between them, even more perfect."[12]

While these claims seem somewhat theatrical and their veracity cannot
be assessed, Gilles de Noailles explained that his private audience with the
queen "lasted more than hour," and he believed her comments "seemed to
be all accompanied with lots of affection." He insisted that Elizabeth had
demonstrated genuine sorrow over the misfortune that had befallen a man

[10] Gilles de Noailles to Monsieur Le Connestable, July 10, 1559, AE MD Angleterre,
Register IV, fol. 272, "elle me fist assez tost après venir en sa chambre en laquelle m'ayant
meyné à part en une fenestre fort loing de toute compaignie."

[11] See Francis Decrue de Stoutz, *Anne de Montmorency: Grant-Maître et Connétable de
France, à la cour, aux armées et au conseil du roi Francis Ier* (Paris: Eugène Plon, Nourrit et
Cie, 1885); Francis Decrue de Stoutz, *Anne, duc de Montmorency, connétable et pair de
France sous les rois Henry II, Francis II et Charles IX* (Paris: Eugène Plon, Nourrit et Cie,
1889) and Brigitte Bedos Rezak, *Anne de Montmorency: seigneur de la Renaissance* (Paris:
Edition Publisud, 1990).

[12] Gilles de Noailles to Monsieur Le Connestable, July 10, 1559, AE MD Angleterre,
Register IV, fol. 272 "souhaitant de bon Coeur que de tout ce jour (qui lui avoit esté si
malheureuse) il ne se fust trouvé de lance en France, ou que sa personne eust esté portée là
en sa Chambre, ou bien puisque cela estoit advenu, qu'elle fust si bonne sirurgienne que la
guérison peust estre en sa main"; "Puis, se mit à parler des grandes vertus et beautéz qu'on
lui avoit tousiours dict du Roy" and "depuis son advènement à ceste couronne, elle s'estoit
tousiours promise qu'elle se renouvelleroit entre eux deux, aultant en plus parfaicte."

whom she viewed as "such a great and virtuous prince, who was to her a perfect friend, brother, and neighbor."[13] While Henry II could hardly be considered a true ally of England, it is important to note that, having just acceded to the throne the previous year, Elizabeth could not be held personally responsible for initiating war with France. Moreover, despite the loss of Calais, she did not wish to harm her chances of establishing a strong Anglo-French alliance. Therefore, while her sincerity may be doubted, she certainly seemed to convince the French ambassador, who subsequently devoted significant effort to conveying Elizabeth's profound concern for "her good brother" to one of France's most important politicians.[14]

On July 10, Elizabeth wrote directly to Henry and once again expressed her "great sorrow" regarding his injury.[15] She also sent a special envoy, Charles Howard, "with her most affectionate recommendations" to the king and assured him of her "true friendship."[16] Her desire to appear as a friend and "good sister" to the French king was dutifully reported by de Noailles, demonstrating the importance of such language in difficult times and reinforcing the need for France and England to overcome their differences and become allies.

After ten agonizing days, the forty-year-old Henry died and his eldest son Francis became King of France. In an emotional letter, the latter informed de Noailles of the tragic death of his father, and expressed his desire to secure the alliance that Henry and Elizabeth had promised to pursue. He affirmed:

> she can be assured to have in myself a best brother and unreserved friend forever [...] make her know that I desire nothing more than the continuation and sure establishment of our said mutual friendship and the maintenance of the good Peace lastly done and sworn between them [Elizabeth and Henry II].[17]

---

[13] Gilles de Noailles to Monsieur Le Connestable, July 10, 1559, fol. 273, "tous cest honneste langaige, Monseigneur, dure plus d'une heure [...] lesquels contes me semblèrent tous accompagnez de beaucoup d'affection [...] qu'elle avoit grande occasion de porter ennui du mal d'un si grand et veruteux Prince, qui luy estoit si parfaict amy, frère et voysin."

[14] Gilles de Noailles to Monsieur Le Connestable, July 10, 1559, fol. 273, "son bon frère."

[15] Elizabeth I of England to Henry II of France, July 10, 1559, TNA, SP 70/5, fol. 109, "grand ennuy."

[16] Elizabeth I of England to Henry II of France, July 10, 1559, "noz tresaffectueuses recomandations" and "vraye amitié."

[17] Francis II of France to Gilles de Noailles, July 12, 1559, AE MD Angleterre, Register IV, fol. 275, "qu'elle se peult asseurer de m'avoir tousiours pour le meilleur frère et entier

After an audience with de Noailles during which the ambassador assured Elizabeth of Francis's good intentions toward England, the queen reiterated her desire to pursue an alliance with France in a letter to the young king. She expressed the hope that their friendship "continues in strength" and added that she wished to maintain Sir Nicholas Throckmorton as her ambassador at the French court.[18]

In another report, de Noailles once more conveyed Elizabeth's sincere grief over Henry II, claiming that "she bore a great regret and sorrow in the heart" and "had received an extreme pain" when she heard about his death.[19] According to the French ambassador, Elizabeth did not hide her tears and even stopped eating due to her distress at the news.[20] These words echo those de Noailles chose to describe the Tudor queen's pain upon first hearing of the accident. Again, it is impossible to determine the sincerity of her feelings, but such demonstrations of sorrow and grief certainly helped Elizabeth secure an alliance between the two crowns. To some extent, then, the demise of Henry actually enabled Elizabeth to forge better diplomatic relations with France.

Interestingly, de Noailles's report gives the impression that he felt Francis was a diplomatic pawn who was not yet his own master. While the ambassador insisted that Elizabeth wanted "a true correspondence of friendship to be continued from father to son," he suggested that the new French king

> always loved, followed, and embraced his [Henry II's] wills, his ways, including his actions, that there would only be years that separate them to perceive the difference which could exist between the father and the son and that the true love and obedience that he [Henry II] and the queen, your mother, had always found in you [Francis II] had made them hope to see in you one of the greatest accomplished, virtuous, and benevolent

amy […] luy faire congnoistre que je ne desire rien plus que la continuation et seur establissement de nostre dicte mutuelle amitié, et l'entretement de la bonne Paix dornierement faicte et jurée entre eulx."

[18] Elizabeth I of England to Francis II of France, July 23, 1559, TNA, SP 70/5, fol. 163, "quelle continue en force."

[19] Gilles de Noailles to Francis II of France, July 19, 1559, AE MD Angleterre, Register IV, fol. 276, "elle en portoit ung merveilleux regret et ennuy dans le Coeur."

[20] Gilles de Noailles to Francis II of France, July 19, 1559, fol. 277, "qu'elle avoit reçeu une extresme doulleur par la nouvelle de sa mort, ayant esté contraincte de faire plus grande demonstration et de larmes et d'abstinence de manger."

princes that has ever lived. To which the said lady infinitely praised, and taken by a new affection toward you, said and swore three times, the hand on the stomach, that she would completely keep and honor her faith and promise of peace.[21]

Preserving the tenuous alliance that Henry and Elizabeth had just forged was paramount. In this letter, de Noailles demonstrated his own key role in the maintenance of this new relationship by highlighting that it was Francis's responsibility to realize his parents' goal of establishing a good rapport with England. Of course, the inference is that he viewed Francis as a rather weak king who should merely follow Henry's wishes, whereas he considered Elizabeth as a powerful, independent monarch who swore her good intentions toward the French with her "hand on the stomach" to signal her sincerity and honesty.

A few weeks later, Elizabeth sent a special envoy, Sir Peter Mewtas, to the French court to express her condolences directly to Francis II and his mother Catherine de Medici. In a subsequent letter, Francis admitted to feeling "great discontent and sorrow," thanked Elizabeth for her kind gesture, and revealed that he needed "all the support and comfort from all our friends,"[22] while repeating his willingness to maintain the alliance that his father had forged with the queen and highlighting the "mutual and perfect affection" that now existed between the two crowns.[23] Similarly, Catherine was deeply touched by "this wise and prudent consolation that you are giving to us,"[24] because

---

[21] Gilles de Noailles to Francis II of France, July 19, 1559, fol. 278, "aviez tousiours tant aymé, suivy et embrassé ses volontéz, ses façons, jusques à ses exercises, qu'il n'y auroit que les seuls ans qui nous fissent maintenant appercevoir la difference qui pourroit estre du père au filz, et que la vraye amour et obeisance que luy et la Royne vostre mère, avoient tousiours trouvé en vous, nous avions fondé certaine espérance de vous voir l'ung des plus grand accompli, plus vertueux, et benings Prince qui ayent jamais esté. Ce que la dicte Dame se mit à louer infiniment, et comme esprise de nouvelle affection envers vous, dict et jura pas trois fois, mettant la main sur l'estomach, qu'elle nous garderoit et tiendroit inviolablement la foy et promesse de Paix."

[22] Francis II of France to Elizabeth I, August 30, 1559, TNA, SP 70/6, fol. 148, "un fort ennui et desplaysir [...] nous avons en bon besoing de la soutien et confort de tous nos amys."

[23] Francis II of France to Elizabeth I, August 30, 1559, "mutuelle et parfaicte affection."

[24] Catherine de Medici to Elizabeth I, September 11, 1559, in *Lettres de Catherine de Médicis*, (later referred as *LCM*) publiées par le Ct Hector de la Ferrière, Tome 1 (Paris: Imprimerie Nationale, 1880), 125, "si saige et prudente consolation que vous nous donnez."

the pain that we are feeling from the loss that we have had of the late king
our very honored lord and husband has been so recent and deplorable and
we are bearing such an extreme trouble, regret, and displeasure that we very
need that God who has inflicted this to us gives us the strength to be able to
bear it.[25]

She concluded her letter by explaining that she aimed to strengthen the
nascent alliance in the interests of "the peace and tranquility of our realms,
states, and countries."[26] Catherine was not yet acting as Queen Regent of
France, but Elizabeth was well aware of her influence in the French court,
so she was determined to forge good relations with her.[27]

In early 1560, Michel de Seure, a knight of Malta,[28] replaced Gilles de
Noailles as French ambassador at the English court. Elizabeth received
him "with a very good face and other words full of good will."[29] De
Seure's role was to ensure that Anglo-French relations remained stable. In
the midst of growing tension between Scotland, France, and England, he
reported that Elizabeth expressed "sincere friendship and a true desire to
maintain it."[30] During another audience with de Seure in 1561, the queen
reportedly asserted that

[25] Catherine de Medici to Elizabeth I, September 11, 1559, 125, "la douleur que nous
ressentons de la perte que nous avons l'aide du feu Roy nostre tres honoré seigneur et mary
nous est si récente et si lamentable et en portons ung si extreme ennui, regret et desplaisir
que nous avons bon besoing que Dieu qui nous a visité de ceste affection nous donne la force
de pouvoir supporter."
[26] Catherine de Medici to Elizabeth I, September 11, 1559, 126, "accroiste et augmenter
au commun bien, repoz et tranquillité de noz royaumes, estatz et pays."
[27] Kathleen Wellman explains that "after Henry's death, Catherine emerged as a political
force, although her position was initially ambiguous." This statement demonstrates that the
queen mother had to be taken into consideration when dealing with France. See Kathleen
Wellman, *Queens and Mistresses of Renaissance France* (New Haven and London: Yale
University Press, 2013), 236.
[28] Francis II of France to Gilles de Noailles, January 5, 1560, AE MD Angleterre, Register
IV, fol. 359.
[29] Gilles de Noailles to Francis II of France, January 20, 1560, AE MD Angleterre, fol.
352, "avec ung for bon visaige, et autres paroles pleines de toute bonne volunté."
[30] Michel de Seure to Francis II of France, September 24, 1560, in David Potter (ed.), *A
Knight of Malta at the Court of Elizabeth I: The Correspondence of Michel de Seure, French
Ambassador, 1560–1561* (Cambridge: Cambridge University Press, Camden Fifth Series),
59, "elle me respondit premièrement que l'on cognoistroit tousjours de son costé une sin-
cérité d'amytié et vrray désir de la conserver."

she has never had anything more inestimable than peace and friendship with
the kings her neighbors, as the most precious thing that God can send to
them when they are worthy of his grace that war is for the poor and the
needy, and not for those who have such beautiful states.[31]

The new ambassador therefore portrayed a queen who valued peace and
did not wish to engage in unnecessary wars with her continental
neighbors.

In 1559, de Noailles had reported Elizabeth's desire to

plant [friendship] in your heart, Sir, who is his [Henry II's] son and his successor, where she expects to see it so rooted that it will produce all the good
and mutual effects that are required for the safety and maintenance of the
Peace and good intelligence between your two majesties.[32]

This language of friendship and goodwill was echoed five years later by
Elizabeth herself in a letter to Charles IX. She expressed the hope that
their friendship had

already taken good root in your heart so that it may not be easily shaken and
undermined, on which hope we rely as we have already started planting in our
heart the same plant of true friendship toward you [...] [W]e hope with God's
help these two plants will last for a long time and produce such fruits that not
only we but also our realms, countries, and people will benefit from them.[33]

[31] Michel de Seure to Charles IX of France, January 23, 1561, in *A Knight of Malta*, 68,
"qu'elle n'avoit jamais rien de si cher que la paix et l'amitié des Roys ses voysins, comme la
chose plus precieuse que Dieu leur peust envoyer quant ilz sont dignes de sa grace que la guerre
estoict le propre des pauvres et necessiteulx et non de ceulx qui ont tant de si beaulx estatz."
[32] Gilles de Noailles to Francis II of France, July 19, 1559, fol. 277, "de ce qu'il luy avoit
pleu establir une si ferme et seure amitié avec Elle, qu'en si extrémité mesme il avoit eu sou-
venance de la planter dans le coeur de vous, Sire, qui estes son filz et son successeur, où elle
s'attend de la veoir si vifrement enracinée, qu'elle produira tous les bons et mutuelz effectz
qui sont requis pour la seureté et entretenement de la Paix, et bonne intelligence d'entre vos
deux majestez."
[33] Elizabeth I of England to Charles IX of France, December 29, 1564, BNF MS. Fr. 6613,
fol. 70, "fonder vostre amitié qui vous semble d'avoir déjà prins si bonne racine en vostre
cueur que ne se pourra aisément esbranler ny diminuer, sur laquelle espérance entendons et
aussy avons déjà commence de planter en nostre cueur la mesme plante de vraye amitié
envers vous, si que nous espérons que avec l'aide de Dieu ces deux plantes seront de longue
durée et produisent tels fruits que oultre les plaisirs qui en viendront à nous memes, nos
royaulmes pays et peuples en recepvront aussy grand profit."

Strikingly, in this letter Elizabeth revealed that her hopes and expectations extended far beyond "true friendship." On two occasions she used the word "heart" to emphasize her determination to maintain good relations with France, while the "plant" and its "fruits" were at the foundation of what she believed to be good diplomacy. The fact that this personal letter to Charles IX corresponded so closely with de Noailles's report to Francis II in 1559 demonstrates that the English queen adopted an identical approach toward the two brothers, and reveals that powerful tropes, such as nurturing a plant in someone's heart, were used repeatedly to reinforce this fragile alliance.

Catherine was equally keen to engage in the quest for peace. In March 1560, Francis II sent a special envoy, Jean de Monluc, Bishop of Valence, to the English court to discuss the Scottish situation. Catherine informed Elizabeth that she did not want the bishop to arrive "without this letter from me,"[34] yet the message that the envoy delivered was very brief and did not contain any information regarding the nature of his visit beyond the fact that he had been appointed by Catherine herself and enjoyed her trust.[35]

A month earlier, Catherine had insisted that an alliance with England was "one of the things of this world that we most desire."[36] She had more of an opportunity to pursue that goal in subsequent years because Francis died unexpectedly at the age of sixteen in December 1560, nine-year-old Charles acceded to the French throne, and Catherine acted as regent. In the summer of 1562, she wrote to Elizabeth and praised "the good inclination and the singular affection that you have regarding the welfare of this realm through the honest words, good and amicable actions that you use toward us."[37] Two years later, when Charles came of age, Catherine's regency officially ended, but she continued to exert great influence over her young son and insisted, "as the intention of the king, our very honored lord and son, and ours are fully inclined to everything that requires

---

[34] Catherine de Medici to Elizabeth I of England, March 1560, in *LCM*, Tome 1, 33, "sans ceste lettre de moy."

[35] Catherine de Medici to Elizabeth I of England, March 1560.

[36] Catherine de Medici to Elizabeth I of England, February 20, 1560, in *LCM*, Tome 1, 170, "c'est une des choses de ce monde que plus nous désirons."

[37] Catherine de Medici to Elizabeth I of England, July 27, 1562, in *LCM*, Tome 1, 366, "Nous cognoissons tousjours de plus en plus l'inclination bonne et singulière affection que vous avez au bien de ce royaulme par les honnestes propos, bons & amyables depportemens dons vous usez envers nous."

our duty of our mutual friendship that is between us, for being something we singularly respect."[38]

These letters reveal that every member of the French royal family, as well as their ambassadors, employed the language of amity and goodwill in their dealings with the English court. Yet, there is scant evidence of true affection and friendship; instead, their correspondence is dominated by formal salutations such as "very high and very excellent princess, our very dear and loved sister and cousin."[39]

Later chapters will explore what the exchange of letters between monarchs reveals about the state of bilateral affairs and the stability of the Anglo-French alliance. Here, it suffices to say that the quest for peace was a necessary step for the French if they ever wanted to develop and maintain strong ties with the English queen.

## NEGOTIATING WITH A QUEEN: A POTENTIAL BRIDE

As noted earlier, the twenty-five-year-old Elizabeth was viewed as a rather inexperienced ruler at the start of her reign. In a letter to Monsieur de Gondran, *Garde des Sceaux* (Keeper of the Seals) of Dijon, who was instructed to pass the missive on to Henry II and Anne of Montmorency, de Noailles explained that "the secretary Cecil has the greatest voice, and his Mistress relies mostly on him regarding affairs of State."[40] However, while the importance of Elizabeth's councillors should not be ignored, many letters written by successive French ambassadors reveal a more complex balance of power, portraying a queen who enjoyed control over her own affairs, including her potential marriage negotiations.

---

[38] Catherine de Medici to Elizabeth I of England, November 9, 1564, in *Lettres de Catherine de Médicis*, (later referred as *LCM*) publiées par le Ct Hector de la Ferrière, 1563–1566, Tome II (Paris: Imprimerie Nationale, 1885), 233, "Nous cognoissons tousjours de plus en plus l'inclination bonne et singulière affection que vous avez au bien de ce royaulme par les honnestes propos, bons & amyables depportemens dons vous usez envers nous."

[39] Catherine and Francis II used such greetings—marking somehow a certain distance between them and Elizabeth, see letters mentioned above. For a specific example, see Catherine de Medici to Elizabeth I of England, November 9, 1564, 233, "Très haulte et très excellente princesse nostre très chère et amée seur et cousine."

[40] Gilles de Noailles to Monsieur de Gondran, Garde des Sceaux de Dijon, pour faire entre au Roy et à Monsieur Le Connestable, June 15, 1559, AE MD Angleterre, Register IV, fol. 251, "le secrétaire Cecil y a plus grande voix, et que aussy sa Maistresse se repose le plus en luy de tous affaires d'Estat."

Elizabeth's future husband had been a topic of great interest among the French monarchs and their ambassadors since the very start of her reign. Of course, at the time, it was inconceivable that a woman would remain unmarried and rule on her own. Elizabeth's predecessor, Mary I, who was also queen regnant in her own right, had married Philip II of Spain in an effort to provide England with an heir. The French court was well aware that Philip would not cede his alliance with England easily, and potential unions with members of the Swedish and Austrian royal houses, as well as Elizabeth's style of rule, dominated the French ambassadors' correspondence, which in turn framed their opinions of Elizabeth as a potential queen consort of the French king.

As early as 1559, de Noailles noted that "the said queen has no intention to marry," which worried her subjects to such an extent "that they cannot stop complaining about it."[41] Yet, as the French ambassadors continued to report to their masters, this did not prevent countless suitors from arriving at court and attempting to seduce Elizabeth. In September 1559, de Noailles observed that some lords from the duchy of Saxony had recently proposed "marriage of the said princess with one of the Saxon princes, named Frederick."[42] He then explained that the Duke of Finland was also expected at the English court "for the marriage of his older brother with the said princess, and comes by sea with six beautiful ships, so highly accompanied of gentlemen and servants that we can count five hundred men at least."[43]

These meetings seemed to be of great interest to the French, as de Noailles continued to provide detailed reports on them. A month later, he revealed that "this last Wednesday, the Duke of Finland, second son of the King of Sweden, arrived in this city [...] [The] queen sent her Master of the Horse [Robert Dudley] to receive him two or three miles from here."[44] De Noailles

---

[41] Gilles de Noailles to Monsieur de Gondran, fol. 251, "la dicte Dame n'a aucune envie de se marier: pour le moings, tous ses parens en ont telle paour, qu'ils ne se peuvent garder de s'en plaindre."

[42] Gilles de Noailles to Francis II of France, September 10, 1559, AE MD Angleterre, Register IV, fol. 311, "mariaige de la dicte Princesse avec l'ung des Princes de Saxe, nommé Frédéric."

[43] Gilles de Noailles to Francis II of France, September 10, 1559, fol. 311, "L'on attend icy en brief le Duc de Finelant, second filz du Roy de Suedde pour le mariaige de son frère aisné avecque cette dicte Princesse, et vient par mere en six beaulx navires, si grandement accompaigné de gentilshommes et serviteurs, qu'on faict compte de cinq cent hommes pour le moing."

[44] Gilles de Noailles to Francis II of France, October 6, 1559, AE MD Angleterre, Register IV, fol. 320, "mercredy dernier arriva en ceste ville le Duc de Finelan, second filz du Roy de

explained that Elizabeth would not see the duke before Sunday, and while "no one is able to judge these things, as there are so many uncertainties and little resolution from the said Queen," he believed that "it will not be as he wishes."[45] Therefore, it seems that the French ambassador was still of the opinion that Elizabeth preferred to remain single, at least for the time being.

In November 1559, it was the turn of the ambassadors from Spain and the Holy Roman Empire to propose a union with Charles II, Archduke of Austria:

> [L]ast Friday the said lady gave them an audience throughout the morning in her garden, walking with them for three hours, and we think that this party would be concluded, given that all the lords of the said Council, and some of the nobles, give it much honor and favor to the said ambassador of the Emperor.[46]

De Noailles seemed to interpret this private audience as proof that Elizabeth was about to enter serious marriage negotiations with the Habsburg court in Vienna. Although he did not attend the meeting himself, he was keen to highlight not only its unusual length but also the rumors that started to circulate in its aftermath. Given the amount of detail that the French ambassador was able to relay to his master, it may have been that the court had spies everywhere, including in the queen's garden. On the other hand, this episode could be viewed as an early example of Elizabeth's mastery of the art of diplomacy. It is possible that she had no intention of keeping the audience private, because she felt that she could utilize the subsequent rumors and gossip about an impending marriage to secure better terms in her political and diplomatic alliances.

---

Suedde, ayant ceste Royne envoyé au devant de lui son Grand Escuyer pour le recepvoir à deux ou trois mile d'icy."

[45] Gilles de Noailles to Francis II of France, October 6, 1559, fol. 320, "Dimanche prochain, il verra la dicte Dame avec laquelle je ne sçay comme il fera: mais on a une grande opinion que ce ne sera comme il desire […] y a personne qui puisse bien juger de ces choses, tant il se voiet encores d'incertitude, et peu de resolution en la dicte Royne."

[46] Gilles de Noailles to Francis II of France, November 2, 1559, AE MD Angleterre, Register IV, fol. 339, "Les Ambassadeurs de l'Empereur et du Roy Catholicque sollicitent par ensemble et fort vifvement le Mariaige de M. l'Archiduc avec ceste Princesses; et vendredy dernier la dicte Dame leur donna Audience toute la matinée dans son Jardin se promenant entre eux deux l'espace de trois heyres, et pense l'on que ce party soit pour recepvoir conclusion, faisans tousles Seigneurs de ce dict Conseil, et les plus Grandz de deça beaucoup d'honneur et faveur au dict Ambassadeur de l'Empereur."

However, if that were the case, de Noailles was not fooled. He did not believe that she would agree to marry the archduke or indeed anyone else, and expressed the opinion that

> she will want to temporize again, although if she feels in danger or in necessity, it would appear that she could easily let herself be convinced to choose this party in the hope to have more help and assistance from it than from others.[47]

In short, the French ambassador knew exactly what Elizabeth was doing—delaying, negotiating, exploiting potential marriage arrangements for her own ends. But this did not prevent him from engaging in extensive dialogue with her. For instance, following an audience in December 1559, de Noailles reported the queen's interest in the marriage of Philip II of Spain and Elisabeth of Valois, Henry II's eldest daughter. In particular, she expressed concern over the young princess's upcoming, arduous journey to Spain. The French ambassador answered that "the difficulty and long journey, and even more the separation from her dear parents, could cause her some sadness and regret, but everything will be easily borne with the pleasure of finding the King of Spain, her husband."[48] In other words, the joy of marriage would trump all of the sadness the young French princess, Elisabeth, might feel on leaving her country and family. The ambassador then described Elizabeth I's reaction to this comment, reporting that, "laughing, she retorted if there was some pleasure in finding the husband[;] for her part, she believed she could not find one unless she was praying for one."[49] Therefore, it seems that the queen was far from con-

[47] Gilles de Noailles to Francis II of France, November 2, 1559, fol. 339, "Toutesfois, j'ose croyre qu'Elle n'est encore preste à se resouldre d'estuy-cy ny d'aultre, et qu'Elle vouldra encore temporizer, bien que si Elle se croit en affaires et nécessité, il seroit à estimer qu'elle pourroit aysément se laisser aller à ce party pour l'espérance d'en avoir plus de secours et appuy que d'autre qui se présente."

[48] Gilles de Noailles to Francis II of France, December 9, 1559, AE MD Angleterre, Register IV, fol. 341, "la dicte Royne s'enquist du partement de la Royne d'Espaigne, et dict que ce temps luy sembloit mal propre pour ung si long voiaige. Je luy repondis que la difficulté et longueur du chemin, et encores plus, la separation de ses très chers parents luy pourroient donner quelque pensement et regrect, mais que tout cela se supporteroit plus aisément, pour le Plaisir d'aller trouver le Roy d'Espaigne son Mary."

[49] Gilles de Noailles to Francis II of France, December 9, 1559, fol. 341, "A quoy, en riant, Elle réplicqua si'l y avoir Plaisir d'aller chercher le mary, et que de sa part, Elle cuydoit n'en pouvoir trouver ung, si Elle ne l'alloit prier."

vinced that a husband was sufficient to guarantee a woman's happiness. Moreover, by laughing at de Noailles's prediction, she left little doubt that she would not welcome such a union for herself.

It is revealing that Elizabeth took the danger of naming a successor much more seriously. As early as 1561, she confessed to Michel de Seure that she

> did not want at all to start that matter of declaring her successor, which is the only point that could trouble more her own peace for many reasons that she has known to plead, among which is counted the inconstancy of this nation and the proof that she has seen for herself during the reign of Queen Mary her sister for this desire that many had in changing depending on their inclination.[50]

Although she was supposedly a naive young queen, here Elizabeth proved that she had learned from her half-sister's mistake and knew that she had to remain wary of people who proclaimed their unequivocal loyalty toward her.[51] She demonstrated that she was well aware of the potential consequences of naming a successor so early in her reign, and indeed of marrying a foreign prince or a lord from her own country. Doing so always ran the risk that the heir apparent (or the husband) would start to command more allegiance than the current ruler—a situation that Mary I had allowed to develop by acknowledging Elizabeth as her successor. In addition, Elizabeth's status as a single woman made her both weak and powerful at the same time. More importantly, her Protestantism made it difficult to secure dynastic alliances with European Catholic states. De Seure's report of this meeting also reveals that the French ambassador never shied away from reporting the facts. There was no point in cultivating false optimism in the French court, so he told Charles IX in no uncertain terms that

---

[50] Michel de Seure to Charles IX of France, November 4, 1561, in in *A Knight of Malta*, 99, "la dicte dame Royne d'Angleterre ne vault aulcunement entrer en ceste matiere de declarer son successeur qui est le seul poinct qui lui pourroict plus troubler son repos pour beaucoup de raisons qu'elle a sçeu alleguer, entre lesquelles est comptée l'inconstance de ceste nation et la prevue qu'elle en a veue en son endroict vivant la Royne Marie sa soeur pour ce desir que plusieurs avoient de changement selon leur inclination."

[51] Historians such as Susan Doran and Carole Levin have mentioned and analyzed Elizabeth's reluctance to marry on this basis: see Susan Doran, *Monarchy and Matrimony: The Courtship of Elizabeth I* (London and New York: Routledge, 1996); Carole Levin, *The Reign of Elizabeth I* (New York: Palgrave, 2001) and Carole Levin, *The Heart and Stomach of a King*.

it would take a great deal of effort to persuade Elizabeth to accept a proposal of marriage.

While many scholars have focused on the marriage negotiations between Elizabeth and Francis, Duke of Alençon (which continued after he became the Duke of Anjou in 1576), Catherine de Medici actually offered all of her remaining sons as potential grooms to the English queen following the death of Francis II in 1560.[52] Most strikingly, as we shall see in Chap. 3, she attempted to forge a union between Charles and Elizabeth on two separate occasions: first between 1564 and 1565, then between 1568 and 1569.

It was de Seure's successor as French ambassador at the English court, Paul de Foix, who first raised the possibility of a marriage to Charles IX with the English queen. He began his audience with Elizabeth by assuring her that she was greatly respected among the French people for "her greatness," to which Elizabeth evidently responded that she was pleased to hear of "the good affection that was mutual."[53] She then asked for details of the meeting between the French rulers and the Queen of Spain, Elisabeth of Valois, which had taken place in the south-west of France earlier in the year. Elizabeth commented on "the great graces that your Majesty has received from God, to see together a king of France and a queen of Spain, your children, elected to such a high degree of honor that there is none higher in Christianity."[54] De Foix took the opportunity to interrupt the queen at this point and expressed the thought that Catherine's "grace would be increased if we would see the king accompanied by a great and virtuous queen such as her."[55] He insisted that "Monsieur Cecil came to talk to me about it and found it suitable for them [*leurs personnes*, meaning Charles and Elizabeth], pleading only some inconvenience for

[52] For more references on Elizabeth's marriage negotiations with the Duke of Anjou, see Chap. 5.

[53] Paul de Foix to Catherine de Medici, March 3, 1564, BNF MS. Fr. 6613, fol. 13, "elle pourroit clairement cognoitre combien Votre Majesté cherchoit sa grandeur [...] la bonne affection qu'elle vous rendoit."

[54] Paul de Foix to Catherine de Medici, March 3, 1564, "Et commença à discourir des grandes grace que Votre Majesté avoit reçeues de Dieu, s'estant veue femme du plus grand et premier Roy de la Chrétienté, mère de deux Roys, à present veoir ensemble un Roy de France et Royne d'Espaigne, vos enfans esleuz en si hault degré d'honneur qu'il ny'en a point de plus en la Chrétienté."

[55] Paul de Foix to Catherine de Medici, March 3, 1564, "Et je luy dis que ces graces prandroit grand accroissement si vous voiez accompaigné le Roy avec une Royne si grande et vertueuse qu'elle."

the subjects."[56] The queen then interrupted the ambassador to explain that "the said Cecil had written down some difficulties, which she had not wished to be revealed to me [de Foix] because they were only excuses, and she found only one to be relevant: the difference of age."[57] This report reveals a complex balance of power between the queen and her councillors, but also between the queen and her French counterparts. Flattery and praise were insufficient to convince her to subordinate her realm—and herself—to France: she would be the one to decide. Indeed, she showed de Foix that she was in full control of her personal affairs; even her most eminent adviser, Cecil, had no say in this area.

This first round of marriage negotiations continued for several months. De Foix proved persistent, reflecting the interests of his mistress, Catherine, who had conceived the idea. In January 1565, the latter issued a direct instruction to her ambassador to offer her son in marriage to the English queen. The words she used in her letter would be repeated in the correspondence between Elizabeth and Catherine in later years. Expressing her eagerness to reinforce her friendship with Elizabeth through "a closer bond," Catherine asserted that she would "be the happiest mother on earth if one of my children from a well-loved sister had made her a very dear daughter, to the great honor, wealth, and greatness of our States."[58] Obviously, such a marriage would bring the two countries closer together. However, as the final sentence reveals, Catherine believed that it would also strengthen both of them. Perhaps she felt that it would enable them to become genuine rivals to the Habsburg Empire, which at the time was considered a very real threat to the other European nations. Catherine also told her ambassador to remind Elizabeth that their two countries "were such close neighbors that it takes only three hours to go from one to

---

[56] Paul de Foix to Catherine de Medici, March 3, 1564, "Adjoustant que Monsieur Cecil estoit venu sur ces propos parler à moy et en fin avoir trouvé toutes les commoditez pour leurs personnes, alléguant seulement quelques incommodité des subjetz."

[57] Paul de Foix to Catherine de Medici, March 3, 1564, "Et la dicte Royne interrompant ce propos me dit: que le dict Cecil avoit drssé par escript certaines difficultez, lesquelles Elle n'avoit point voulu qu'elles me fussent baillées parcequ'elles estoient recherchées de trop loing, et qu'elle n'en y trouvoit qu'une qui estoit l'inégualité de l'aage."

[58] Catherine de Medici to Paul de Foix, January 24, 1565, BNF MS. Fr. 15,888, fol. 234, "désirerois avec elle d'estraindre ceste nostre amitié d'ung plus étroit lien, et me sentirois la plus heureuse mè du monde, si ung de mes enfans d'une bien aimé seur m'en avoit faict une très chère fille, au grand honneur, bien et grandeur de nos Estatz."

another."[59] Elizabeth had previously advanced the idea of meeting Charles in person, and this was probably Catherine's way of agreeing to her request. (No doubt the queen was reluctant to agree to marry a total stranger, given her father's famous disappointment on seeing Anne of Cleves for the first time.)

A few weeks later, de Foix informed Elizabeth of Catherine's desire to become her mother-in-law. However, the queen's reaction was unexpected:

> the said lady's color and countenance changed several times, like that of a person feeling joy mixed with genuine shame, and after the reading, [she] said that while the Queen had given her a great honor, she did not feel worthy of it, and, whatever happens, she will continue to reciprocate her [Catherine's] affection throughout her life, as if she had been born her daughter.[60]

The French ambassador then explained that Elizabeth had expressed major reservations about the age difference between herself and Charles:

> if it had pleased God, she [wished that she] had been ten years younger, as this would have enabled her to participate in such a great [union], but she feared that the Queen and the King had been misinformed about her age and would eventually be displeased with her, especially in light of the King's great youth, which would leave her feeling old and unattractive and alienated from him, just as the late queen Mary her sister had been from the King of Spain.[61]

Here, once again, Elizabeth revealed that she had learned a great deal from her predecessor's errors. She used her age not only ever to decline

[59] Catherine de Medici to Paul de Foix, January 24, 1565, "Mais, Dyey mercy, noz pays sont si voisins, qu'il ne fault que trois heures de passer l'un à l'aultre."
[60] Paul de Foix to Catherine de Medici, February 14, 1565, BNF MS. Fr. 15,888, fol. 235, "Ladicte dame changera plusieurs fois de couleur et de contenance, comme une personne enprinse de joye, meslée à une honneste vergogne, et, après avoir oy la lecture, dist que par le grand honneur que la Royne luy faisoit, elle s'en sentoit tant redevable, que, quoy qu'il advient, elle lui rendroit toutte sa vie pareille affection que sy elle lui estoit née fille."
[61] Paul de Foix to Catherine de Medici, February 14, 1565, "Disaoit que pleust à Dieu qu'elle fust plus jeune de dix ans pour pouvoir participer à ung si grand bien, mais qu'elle pensoit que la Royne n'eust pas esté bien informée de son age, qui estoit tel. qu'elle craignoyt que enfin il n'en advent raproche à la Royne et au Roy et à elle beaucoup de mécontentement, d'aultant que en la grande jeunesse du Roy elle se trouveroit ja vieille et partant mal agréable et délaissée de luy comme la feue royne Marie sa soeur avoyt esté du roi d'Espagne.

Catherine's proposal, but also to demonstrate that her sister's unhappy marriage had taught her a valuable lesson.

Four months later, de Foix was forced to inform Catherine that there was now little prospect of a marriage between Charles and Elizabeth. Apparently, the English nobility feared that "the greatness of the King [Charles IX] [...] threatened this realm [England] with servitude and oppression," and felt that an alternative union with Charles II, Archduke of Austria would be less dangerous.[62] Furthermore, while de Foix assured Catherine that "the queen of England has declared many times that she would not marry someone from her realm,"[63] he had noticed that "she had become colder" on the topic of marrying the French king.[64] This observation proved well founded, as Elizabeth continued to reject Charles IX's proposals.

Nevertheless, Catherine refused to abandon her plan and became increasingly fierce in her exchanges with her ambassador. For instance, her impatience and irritation are obvious in a letter of July 1565 in which she urged de Foix to obtain a definitive answer from Elizabeth. Catherine claimed that the English queen had always shown genuine interest in her son as a potential husband, so she was puzzled by Elizabeth's stalling tactics (an art that she would master in later years) and the lack of agreement on the terms of the union.[65] She accused the English queen's council of focusing unnecessarily on the age difference, and insisted that the monarchs looked no more than three or four years apart. Moreover, she instructed her ambassador to remind the members of the council that they were endangering their own positions, not to mention England itself, by adopting a policy that was likely to leave Elizabeth without an heir.[66] Next, returning to a familiar theme, she declared that her son was willing to

---

[62] Paul de Foix to Catherine de Medici, June 4, 1565, "La grandeur du roy [...] menace ce royaulme avec servitude et oppression [...] Et pour ce que ces soupzçons et crainctes cessent en la personne de l'archiduc Charles, ils trouvoient le mariaige avecques luy moins dangereux pour cela."

[63] Paul de Foix to Catherine de Medici, June 4, 1565, fol. 32v, "la Royne d'Angleterre aye déclarée plusieurs fois qu'elle ne se vouloyt marier à aucun de son royaume."

[64] Paul de Foix to Catherine de Medici, June 4, 1565, fol. 33v, "Je trouvoys en ses propos et en sa parole qu'elle s'estoyt beaucoup refroidye."

[65] Catherine de Medici to Paul de Foix, July 31, 1565, in *LCM*, Tome II, 307.

[66] Catherine de Medici to Paul de Foix, July 31, 1565, "c'estoit se mettre en danger de laisser son royaume sans postérité descendue d'elle, qui leur estoit plus que necessaire pour le bien et le repos du royaume."

agree to the marriage despite the age difference, so Elizabeth should show "the same contentment as him" and accept the union.[67]

Later in the same letter, Catherine suggested that Mary, Queen of Scots, "would be called to the crown of England without any difficulty" if Elizabeth refused to marry Charles and failed to produce an heir.[68] However, she then tempered this obvious threat with a promise that she and Elizabeth "would not remain lesser good and assured friends" even if the English queen rejected Charles's latest proposal. She also insisted that there would be no "diminution or alteration to our common and perfect friendships."[69] Nevertheless, her final instruction to de Foix reveals that she still expected her plan to come to fruition: "Regarding your leave, you will be able to [depart] once we have seen that the marriage of the said queen of England succeeds, for which I deem your attendance and presence no less useful and necessary than it has been until now."[70] Clearly, then, Catherine wanted de Foix to remain at the English court until he concluded the marriage negotiations to her satisfaction, notwithstanding his warnings about Elizabeth's and the court's feelings on the matter and his own desire to return to France. Yet, there was nothing he could do, and he was eventually allowed to relocate to Italy the following year.

Elizabeth's continued single status meant that she remained the center of attention, and the incessant marriage negotiations fueled speculation among the ambassadors at her court and the countless special envoys who beat a path to her door. From Sweden to Austria, Elizabeth attracted a wealth of interest in her dynastic future, not least from Catherine de Medici, who sensed a unique opportunity to tighten the bonds between England and France and make future conflict between the two nations unthinkable. Yet, from the very beginning of her reign, Elizabeth showed

---

[67] Catherine de Medici to Paul de Foix, July 31, 1565, "le mesme contantement que luy mesme."

[68] Catherine de Medici to Paul de Foix, July 31, 1565, 308, "venant la royne d'Angleterre à décéder sans enffans, elle [Mary Stuart] et le conte de Roze son mary feussent appellez à la couronne d'Angleterre sans aucune difficulté."

[69] Catherine de Medici to Paul de Foix, July 31, 1565, "elle se pourroit asseurer que le Roy mondict sieur et filez et moy ne luy demeurerions moings bons et seurs amys [...]n'advint diminution ny altercation de nos communes et parfaictes amitiez."

[70] Catherine de Medici to Paul de Foix, July 31, 1565, 310, "Quant à vostre congé, vous ne le pouvez avoir que nous n'ayons premièrement veu ce qui réussira du faict du mariage de ladicte royne d'Angleterre, pour lequel je n'estime vostre demeure et presence par dela moings utile et necessaire qu'elle a esté jusque à present."

little interest in marrying a foreign prince, and, despite all of her potential suitors' best efforts, they soon realized that they would have to deal with the Queen of England as a sole ruler.

## POWER AND POLITICS: ELIZABETH, THE QUEEN OF GAMES

The nature of Elizabeth's queenship and how she might approach political matters with her European counterparts were issues of enduring fascination for the French court. Successive French ambassadors reported interesting audiences with the queen as well as candid assessments of her ability as a monarch. Their letters therefore offer valuable insights into the young queen's rapid mastery of the political game.

Praise for Elizabeth began as early as 1560 with de Noailles's and de Seure's reports on her queenship. For instance, the latter told a special envoy, Jacques de la Brosse, Cupbearer to the King, who had been sent to Scotland to resolve a delicate diplomatic issue, that Elizabeth was well disposed toward both Scotland and France "as a virtuous and good princess."[71] He seemed convinced that the English queen would not be an enemy to the French. Yet, by then, de Noailles had already alluded to the power she wielded at court, shaping the Valois family's perception of Elizabeth as a true monarch of England and, as such, someone who needed to be handled carefully.

As England and France drifted closer to war over Scotland, Elizabeth warned de Noailles that, "knowing well that her realm was small, it was therefore much easier to protect it, and that, although she was a woman, she was nonetheless the daughter of predecessors who had known [how] to protect it until now."[72] Some scholars, such as Susan Frye, have questioned the veracity of Elizabeth's famous speech of 1588: "I know I have the body but of a weak and feeble woman but I have the heart and stomach of a king and of a king of England too,"[73] whereas others, such as Carole Levin and Leah Marcus, see no reason to question it (see Chap. 6 for further discus-

---

[71] Michel de Seure to Jacques de la Brosse, March 7, 1559–1560, in *A Knight in Malta*, 41, "elle en parle en vertueuse et bonne princesse."

[72] Gilles de Noailles to Francis II of France, February 1, 1560, AE MD Angleterre, Register IV, fol. 358, "sçachant bien que si son Royaulme estoit petit, il en estoit d'autant plus ayse à garder, et que bien qu'Elle fust femme, Elle estoit neantmoings fille des Prédecesseurs qui l'avoient sçeu conserver jusques icy."

[73] Queen Elizabeth's Armada Speech to the troops at Tilbury, 9 August 1588, in *Elizabeth I: Collected Works*, 326.

sion of Elizabeth's Tilbury speech).[74] I believe that Levin's and Marcus's case is strengthened by the fact that de Noailles reported Elizabeth referring to herself in very similar terms almost thirty years earlier. The Tudor queen was well aware of her unique status as a sole female ruler and the modest size of her realm.[75] Yet, it seems that she utilized these apparent shortcomings to shape her royal authority, viewing her gender as a strength when everyone around her perceived it as a weakness.

Throughout the course of her reign, the queen held audiences with de Noailles and countless other ambassadors in her private chamber, the court's galleries, and even, as we have seen, the palace gardens. These intimate meetings allowed her to discuss important matters of state in confidence but also to shape foreign perceptions of her via the ambassadors' reports. According to the French dispatches, quite delicate matters could be discussed in these audiences, with de Noailles recording one that took place "in a gallery where she [Elizabeth] was walking accompanied by only four or five ladies."[76]

In August 1559, the French royal family grew concerned that England might assist rebellions against the Scottish and French crowns. After delaying an audience with de Noailles, Elizabeth finally received him in the house of her lord admiral in Horsley, Surrey. The ambassador was escorted to a private chamber, where Elizabeth, who was "wearing a furred gown," greeted him and explained that she had suffered "three big bouts of fever" and "feared a fourth."[77] She then asked de Noailles to sit next to her near

[74] See the discussion regarding if Elizabeth actually said these words or not: see *Elizabeth I: Collected Works*, 325 where Leah S. Marcus, Janel Mueller, and Mary Beth Rose expressed "little doubt that her speech was actually delivered." Also see, Carole Levin, *The Heart and Stomach*, 144–7.

[75] See Estelle Paranque, "Queen Elizabeth I and the Elizabethan Court in the French Ambassador's Eyes," in *Queen Matters in Early Modern Studies*, ed. by Anna Riehl Bertolet (New York: Palgrave Macmillan, 2017), 267–84. Also see, Kevin Sharpe's compelling analysis of the Tilbury Speech, Kevin Sharpe, *Selling the Tudor Monarchy: Authority and Image in Sixteenth Century England* (New Haven and London: Yale University Press, 2009), 337.

[76] Gilles de Noailles to Francis II of France, February 1, 1560, fol. 357, "trouvé la dicte Royne en une gallerie où elle se promenait accompaignée de quatre ou cinq Dames seullement."

[77] Gilles de Noailles to Francis II of France, August 22, 1559, AE MD Angleterre, Register IV, fol. 299, "Sire, je revins bientost de Horsley où est encores ceste Royne en une maison de son Admiral, distant 24 mil d'icy, en laquelle assez tost après, on me mena en la chambre privée de la dicte Dame, où je ne la trouvay, mais elle y survint aussy tost, vestue d'une robe fourrée [...]elle avoit esté bien mallade de trois gros accès de fièvre, dont les premiers avoient esté en deux jours consécutifs, et ce tiers deux aultres jours après, de sorte qu'elle se craignoit d'une quarte."

a window from which she could see her knights and gentlemen, including her Master of the Horse, Robert Dudley, race for "the Ring."[78] This was an organized spectacle in which the queen's courtiers competed for a token of her affection. With her eyes still firmly fixed on the race, Elizabeth "asked me what news I had from France."[79]

At the heart of de Noailles's report of this meeting were his master's concerns regarding England's attitude towards Scotland. Yet, he spent the first page describing the setting and strikingly revealed that the queen was more interested in the games that were taking place outside than the threat of war with Scotland and France. He tried to explain that France was determined to maintain the peace, despite the trouble in Scotland, and that Francis's interests were wholly compatible with those of Elizabeth herself.[80] She answered that Francis was a "good brother and friend to inform her" of that fact,[81] but then immediately "looked again at the race and talked to me about something else about her knights and their best attempts to win," instantly undermining the French king's message.[82]

By receiving the French ambassador at the very moment when her gentlemen were racing for her favor, Elizabeth displayed the sharp political acumen that would characterize her reign. First, she demonstrated that she would decide which matter was of paramount importance: her gentlemen's race or the message that the French ambassador wished to convey from his master. Second, by holding the meeting in a private setting, she knew that she could ensure that she remained in full control of the discussion. She insisted that the ambassador must sit on the floor with her, with cushions under their knees, "or else she would never allow me to talk to her."[83] This threat of exclusion demonstrates that Elizabeth was

[78] Gilles de Noailles to Francis II of France, August 22, 1559, "d'alla asseoir près d'une fenestre, au devant de laquelle son Grand Escuyer, et dix ou onze aultres Gentilshommes se tenoient prestz pour luy donner du Plaisir à voir courre la Bague."

[79] Gilles de Noailles to Francis II of France, August 22, 1559, "me demanda quelles nouvelles j'avois de France."

[80] Gilles de Noailles to Francis II of France, August 22, 1559, fol. 300.

[81] Gilles de Noailles to Francis II of France, August 22, 1559, "Vostre dicte Majesté l'en avoit bien voulu advertir saichant assy qu'elle auroit Plaisir de veroi qu'il se pourreust ainsi à vos affaires, estimant que les vostre et les siens, n'estoient entre vos majestés qu'une mesme chose. Elle me dict que c'estoit faict en bon frère et amy que de luy donner cest advertissement."

[82] Gilles de Noailles to Francis II of France, August 22, 1559, "et après ce elle se remit à veoir courre et me parler d'autre chose que des Chevaliers et de leurs meilleurs coups."

[83] Gilles de Noailles to Francis II of France, August 22, 1559, "se leva de sa Chaise et demanda des carreaulx pour s'asseoir bas, disant que la chaise lui faisoit mal: puis me pria de

willing and able to assert her royal authority over foreigners as well as her own subjects, and she was clearly not afraid to reveal her strong will to anyone. All of this helped her to shape her image as a powerful monarch. In addition, allowing ambassadors to "catch" her in a jovial moment while she enjoyed a game was actually a calculated device that enabled her to assert complete control over diplomatic negotiations.

A week later, de Noailles informed Elizabeth that a traitor to the French crown, James Hamilton, third Earl of Arran, had recently landed in England. The son of the second earl, who had been regent of Scotland in 1542, Arran was considered of dynastic importance, to such an extent that Henry II had briefly offered him the hand in marriage of his daughter Elisabeth. He had campaigned alongside the French on the continent but eventually converted to Protestantism. Then, in February 1559, he founded a Protestant congregation at Châtelherault and Henry II summoned him to court. Arran was viewed as a serious threat to France and the Scottish throne, so Henry (and later Francis II and Mary, Queen of Scots) intended to imprison him. However, he fled to Switzerland and then to England with the help of the English ambassador at the French court, Sir Nicholas Throckmorton.[84] Elizabeth and Cecil both held meetings with him after his arrival in England.[85]

However, de Noailles reported that the queen "popeyed, pretending not to know nor to have heard anything about [Arran] [...] and after reminding her again, she answered she did not know where he was."[86] She then swore that if she learned anything that might help the French authorities to track him down, she would tell them immediately, "not only because she was obliged by the terms of the treaty, but also because of the honesty and friendship" that she was keen to preserve between herself and Francis.[87]

m'approcher et de vouloir prendre la peyne de me baisser, me prétendant ung carreau pour mettre soubz le genouil mais l'ayant plié, comme je fis aussy tost sur la natte seullement, elle me commanda par deux fois de le prendre, ou que aultrement me permettrait jamais que je parlasse ainsy à Elle."

[84] ODNB, James Hamilton, third earl of Arran, (1537/8–1609), Rosalind K. Marshall. Accessed on 18 April 2018.

[85] Elizabeth to Throckmorton, August 28, 1559, SP 70/6 fol. 142; and Cecil to Throckmorton, August 29, 1559, SP 70/6 fol. 144.

[86] Gilles de Noailles to Francis II of France, August 28, 1559, fol. 304, "comme esbahye, feignant ne congnoistre ny entendre de qui je parlois, après le luy avoir derechef bien remontré, me respondit qu'elle ne sçavoit où estoit le dict Comte."

[87] Gilles de Noailles to Francis II of France, August 28, 1559, "non seulement par l'obligation du Traicté, mais par honnesteté et amitié."

Less than six months later, however, she again appeared "popeyed and ignorant" when de Noailles informed her that another traitor to the French crown had taken refuge in England. In a letter to Francis, the ambassador admitted that he found it strange that the queen was so ill-informed about the important events that were happening within her realm:

> the said lady took some time to think and, with a little sally, told me the truth[.] I reminded her that she had heard something the evening before when she was rolling dice with many of her lords but that she could not believe that the servants and ministers whom she holds inside this border could have known of this affair.[88]

Elizabeth often used this mask of ingenuousness to deflect the French ambassador's more delicate questions. She pretended to be unaware of many of the issues he raised, and frequently adopted a playful attitude when confronted with the seriousness of the situation that allowed her to ward off further enquiries. In short, she developed a highly effective technique for playing—and winning—political games against much more experienced opponents.

Five years later, Paul de Foix reported that the queen still loved games.[89] He found her "in her private chamber playing chess and [...] heard that she was furious that the Queen of Scotland had married the son of the Earl of Lennox [Henry Stuart, Lord Darnley]."[90] Seizing the opportunity to offer some avuncular advice, de Foix reminded the queen that the game of chess was "an image of speech and foresight and not men's actions, in which when someone loses a pawn it might seem like no big deal, but it often brings with it the loss of the entire game."[91] The queen replied that

---

[88] Gilles de Noailles to Francis II of France, January 20, 1560, fol. 354, "la dicte Dame fit au comment l'estonnée et ignorante [...] Ce que entendant la dicte Dame le print ung peu à penser et puis avec une petite saillie, me dict que à la vérité, je luy faisois recorder d'en avoir ouy parler le soir precedent ainsy qu'Elle jouait au detz avec autens de ses Seigneurs mais qu'Elle ne pouvoit penser ne croire que les serviteurs et ministres qu'Elle en tient en ceste Frontière eussent aulteure intelligence de ceste menée."

[89] Jackie Eales discussed the importance of chess as diplomatic and political tool. She presented a paper at Queen's House Conference 2018: Elizabeth I: The Armada and Beyond, 1588–2018, entitled "Chess, Court Culture, and Queenship in the Age of the Armada."

[90] Discours de Paul de Foix, 6 June, 1565, BNF MS. Fr. 15,888, fol. 325, "trouvant la dicte dame en sa chamber privée, qui jouoyt aux eschetz, et pour ce qu'il avoit entendu qu'elle estoyt fort faschée de ce que la reine d'Escosse se marier avec le filz du comte de Lenos."

[91] Discours de Paul de Foix, 6 June, 1565, "luy dist que le jeux des echetz esttoyt une ymage du discours et prevoiyances et aulcunes des actions des hommes, où quand l'un per-

"the son of the Earl of Lennox was nothing more than a pawn, but if she was not careful, he could harm her."[92] Elizabeth was clearly well aware of what the marriage represented and that people felt that Mary, rather than Elizabeth herself, was securing the future of her dynasty.

Yet, receiving the French ambassador while playing chess once again demonstrated the Tudor queen's tactical ability. Although it seemed that Mary and Darnley had made a decisive political move by marrying each other, Elizabeth was determined to prove them wrong and show that she was the true, legitimate ruler of England. De Foix concluded his report by informing the French court that "she greatly complained about the disloyalty of the Earl of Lennox and his son, showing her willingness to do the worst she could to them."[93] This thirst for vengeance reflected the development of a more scheming and warlike persona that the French court could not afford to ignore.

## Defiance Persists: Elizabeth, Warrior Queen

When she ascended to the English throne, Elizabeth's legitimacy was contested both within and outside the borders of her realm. Many Catholics did recognize Henry VIII's marriage to Anne Boleyn and therefore viewed Elizabeth as a bastard. However, the debate over young queen's legitimacy reached new heights when Francis II and his consort Mary Stuart succeeded to the French throne in 1559. Both Elizabeth and Mary were granddaughters of King Henry VII of England, but there was no doubt about Mary's legitimacy. Moreover, she had been raised as a devout Catholic, like the previous Queen of England, Mary I, and on her mother's side she enjoyed the support of a very powerful French noble family: the Guises. Elizabeth had displayed considerable discontent over Francis and Mary's pretentions to the English throne prior to their accession to the French throne,[94] and her irritation only grew once they became rulers.

doyt un pion il sembloit que ce feust peu de choses, toutefois bien souvent il apportoyt la perte de tout le jeu."

[92] Discours de Paul de Foix, 6 June, 1565, "A quoy la dicte dame respondit qu'elle entendoit bien que le filz du comte de Lenos n'estre que ung pion, mais qu'il seroit bien pour luy donner mal sy elle n'y prenoit garde."

[93] Discours de Paul de Foix, 6 June, 1565, "elle se plaignoit grandement de la desloyaulté dudict comte de Lenos et son filz, monstrant avoir vollunté de leur faire le pire qu'elle pourroyt."

[94] Gilles de Noailles to Monsieur de Gondran, Garde des Sceaux de Dijon, pour informer le Roy et Monsieur le Connestable, June 15, 1559, AE MD Angleterre, Register IV, fol. 253,

In January 1560, de Noailles informed Francis that Elizabeth and her ministers viewed the fact that "the queen [Mary] has taken the coat of arms and title of England" as an "act of hostility."[95] Two months later, in one of his first dispatches since replacing de Noailles as ambassador, Michel de Seure raised this delicate issue with Marie de Guise, Queen Regent of Scotland and Mary's mother. He informed her that her daughter's decision to take "the coat of arms and title of England" was liable to generate enmity between Scotland and England.[96] Elizabeth's concern was understandable, as Mary's claim to the English throne in the context of the strong alliance between Scotland and France posed a significant threat to the Tudor queen's authority.

Thereafter, the issue cropped up regularly in Elizabeth's audiences with de Seure. In September 1560, having explained that Elizabeth had been reluctant to see him,[97] the ambassador reported that he "endeavored to soften her as much as [...] [he] could"[98] and reassured her of Francis's good intentions toward England. However, she feared that she would be forced to "protect her realm and reputation" and asserted that she would not allow her friendship to be abused, as it had been in the past.[99] Elizabeth continued to raise the issue even after Francis's death. For instance, in January 1561, de Seure informed Charles IX that Elizabeth remained unhappy that "the queen your sister [Mary] still carries her [Elizabeth's] coat of arms" and felt that the matter was likely to undermine Anglo-French relations.[100]

---

"Que toutesfois la dicte Royne et tous ceux de son Royulme ne laissent d'estre en continuelle peyne et craincte du cousté de France pour doubte qu'ils ont que de ceste part, il ne leur doit reserve quelque mauvaise pensée à cause des pretentions des Roy et Royne Daulphins."

[95] Gilles de Noailles to Francis II of France, January 12, 1560, AE MD Angleterre, Register IV, fol. 350, "c'est que la Royne a prins ses armes et Tiltre d'Angleterre, prétendans ester une forme d'hostilité."

[96] Michel de Seure to Marie de Guise, March 8, 1559/1560, in *A Knight of Malta*, 44, "du tiltre que la Royne vostre fille a pris de ce roiaume, et des armories qu'elle en porte."

[97] Michel de Seure to Francis II of France, September 24, 1560, in *A Knight of Malta*, 58.

[98] Michel de Seure to Francis II of France, September 24, 1560, 60, "Je cherchay de l'adoulcir le plus qui me feust possible."

[99] Michel de Seure to Francis II of France, September 24, 1560, "elle avoict esté contraincte d'entrer pour conserver son royaume et sa reputation [...] quand l'on vouldroict abuser de son amitié comme elle l'avoict faict au passé."

[100] Michel de Seure to Charles IX of France, January 23, 1561, in *A Knight of Malta*, 70–73, "la Royne vostre soeur portoict encores ses armoiries."

It was in the best interests of the English and French courts to preserve the peace established by the Treaty of Cateau-Cambrésis in 1559. However, the French had no experience of engaging and working with a sole female ruler, and this contributed to the persistence of strong elements of distrust and defiance on both sides. The growing tension, which was rooted in France's religious civil wars and Elizabeth's support of the Huguenots, resulted in the introduction of passports and the refusal of permission to cross borders as well as the imprisonment of several key French political figures. In the summer of 1561, Elizabeth complained to de Seure that one of her squires, Sir Livingston, had been refused safe conduct. She expected Charles IX to address the matter immediately and instructed the ambassador to inform her of its resolution as soon as he received word from Paris.[101]

Granting passports and safe conduct to the envoys who shuttled between England and France was a significant aspect of the alliance. In September 1562, Sir Nicholas Throckmorton (1515/16–1571), the English ambassador at the French court, asked for a passport for one of his men to return safely to England. Catherine de Medici affected puzzlement at the request, given "the freedom you have always had to send to the said country everything and as many times as you wished."[102] Moreover, she felt that it "harmed the sincere and perfect friendship that lies between the queen of England, my good sister, and ourselves," because he should know that no diplomat needed anything more "than the name of the princess that your serve and the title that you hold as ambassador of this realm, which will always be respected and honored from us until the end."[103] Catherine concluded the letter with a stark warning that Throckmorton's unjustified apprehension regarding the envoy's safe passage had the

---

[101] Michel de Seure to Charles IX of France, August 21, 1561, in *A Knight of Malta*, 93.

[102] Catherine de Medici to Sir Throckmorton, September 21, 1562, in *LCM*, Tome I, 405, "fait bailler à vostre homme, suivant la requeste que vous m'en avez faicte, un passeport pour le voyaige qu'il va faire en Angleterre, non qu'il luy soit aulcunement necessaire, pour la liberté que vous sçavez bien avoir tousjours eue d'envoyer audict pays toutes et quants fois que bon vous a semblé."

[103] Catherine de Medici to Sir Throckmorton, September 21, 1562, 406, "vous faictes tort à la sincere et parfaite amytié qui est entre la royne d'Angleterre, ma bonne seur, et nous, de me demander un sauf-conduit pour me venir trouver; car, comme je vous ay déjà escript, il ne vous en fault point de meilleur ny plus seur que le nom de la princesse que vous servez et le lieu que vous tenez en ce royaume de son ambassadeur, qui sera toujours respecté et honoté de nous jusqueus au bout."

potential to weaken the alliance with England.[104] Nevertheless, the ambassador repeated his request a few days later. Once again, though, Catherine refused to issue a passport, reiterating her assurance that such a document was unnecessary.[105] This and a number of similar incidents undermined the queen regent's relations not only with Throckmorton but also, to some extent, with Elizabeth herself.

Anglo-French relations were also strained by brigands' incessant attacks on the merchant fleets of both countries, including one striking example in the later summer of 1562.[106] Catherine wrote directly to Elizabeth to assure her that she would address the issue of French pirates' attacks on English ships "in the interests of the maintenance of the good peace and perfect friendship that lies between us."[107] A month later, having heard of "some English ships being arrested in Brittany and injury caused to [your] subjects,"[108] the queen regent promised Throckmorton that the English traders would receive compensation.[109]

However, a few days later, pirates stole a number of the ambassadors' own letters and dispatches. He complained to Catherine, but she merely replied that she had already proven her intention to maintain good relations with England. Moreover, she insisted she had heard nothing of the stolen package, but pledged that its contents would be returned to him immediately if she ever did. Thereafter, the row escalated. It seems that the ambassador accused Catherine of sending Monsieur de Vieilleville to England before safe conduct had been granted. Angrily, the queen regent responded that Throckmorton himself could come and go as he pleased between the two countries, so she did not understand why one of her trusted advisers could not do the same. Once again, she concluded with a general warning that Throckmorton's behavior was endangering the alliance, then added the specific threat that he was making the restitution of

---

[104] Catherine de Medici to Sir Throckmorton, September 21, 1562, 406.

[105] Catherine de Medici to Sir Throckmorton, October 8, 1562, in *LCM*, Tome I, 415.

[106] For other complaints regarding good being stolen and ships being vandalized, see the following letters: Catherine de Medici to Paul de Foix, January 15, 1564, in *LCM*, Tome II, 139; Catherine de Medici to Elizabeth I of England, January 10, 1565, 251 and Catherine de Medici to Elizabeth I of England, September 16, 1565, 317.

[107] Catherine de Medici to Elizabeth I of England, August 2, 1562, in *LCM*, Tome I, 367, "pour le respect de l'entreténement de la bonne paix et parfaicte amitié qui est entre nous."

[108] Catherine de Medici to Sir Throckmorton, September 5, 1562, in *LCM*, Tome I, 395, "j'ay aussi entendu la plaincte que la reyne d'Angleterre ma bonne seur vous a faicte d'aucuns navires anglois arrestés en Bretaigne et déprédations faictes sur ses subjects."

[109] Catherine de Medici to Sir Throckmorton, September 5, 1562, 396.

Calais to England much less likely.[110] In July 1563, Elizabeth finally recalled Throckmorton and replaced him with Thomas Smith. Catherine seized the opportunity to tell the new ambassador that his predecessor had been a poor representative of England, which had caused her to expect "nothing good from his [Smith's] arrival." Indeed, she had even considered "sending a man to him to observe his actions."[111]

Elizabeth proved to be equally intractable on the issue of piracy. In July 1562, she ordered the seizure of all ships on the Thames "near this city of London, both English and foreigners, including French, Spanish and Flemish."[112] This command infuriated the French, who openly wondered why their ships had been targeted. Elizabeth assured the new French ambassador, Paul de Foix, that all of the non-English ships were simply inspected and released, then offered a justification for the order:

> God has put the safety and lives of her subjects in her hands, and [she feels she must] obviate everything that might threaten them, which she will do while God allows her to live, using diligence to compensate for the weakness and recklessness of her sex, and even more so in light of the wars in France that endanger them [Elizabeth's subjects], given that the troops are nearby, in Normandy.[113]

Here, Elizabeth was at pains to remind the French that she not only ruled by divine right but had a moral obligation to protect her subjects.[114]

---

[110] Catherine de Medici to Sir Throckmorton, September 17, 1562, *LCM*, Tome I, 400–2.

[111] Catherine de Medici to Thomas Smith, July 26, 1563, in *LCM*, Tome II, 74–75, "pour sçavoir certainement les maulvais offices qu'il a faicts en ce royaulme pendant qu'il y a esté. Ne pouvant pour ceste cause riens espérer de bon de sa veneue, j'ay, pour soubçon, délibéré envoyer un homme près de luy pour observer ses actions."

[112] Paul de Foix to Catherine de Medici, July 24, 1562, BNF MS. Fr. 6612, fol. 105, "l'on arresta tous les navires qui sont trouvez sur la rivière de Thamize près ceste ville de Londres, tant des Anglois, que Estrangers, Francis, Espagnolz et flamans."

[113] Paul de Foix to Catherine de Medici, July 27, 1562, BNF MS. Fr. 6612, fol. 110, "disant que Dieu luy avoit mis ses subjects soubz sa charge, pour estre soigneusement de leur bien et salut, et obvier à tout ce qui sembleroit les menasser d'aucung danger, ce qu'elle feroit tant que Dieu luy donneroit vie, récompensant par sa diligence ce qu'il pourroit estre de faulte en elle pour l'infirmité et imprudence du sexe, et d'autant qu'il sembloit que les guerres de France les menacent de quelques dangers, estans les forces si proches en Normandie."

[114] On Elizabeth's father figure, see Estelle Paranque, "Royal Representations Through the Warrior and Father Figures in Early Modern Europe," in *History of Monarchy*, Elena Woodacre (ed.) (London: Routledge, forthcoming 2019).

The case of Antoine de Duprat, Sir de Nantouillet and Provost of Paris since 1553, who had been sent to the Tower of London after the signing of the Treaty of Cateau-Cambrésis, also highlighted the fragility of Anglo-French relations at this time. Catherine took a personal interest in de Duprat's predicament and wrote directly to Elizabeth in the hope of securing his release.[115] However, Elizabeth replied that she found both the letter and the request "rather strange."[116] She assured Catherine that the provost had been "favorably treated, as he is living in the house of one of the principal merchants and counselors in our city of London, so we thought and expected to be thanked rather than criticized."[117] Elizabeth signed off with another assertion of her royal authority: "we do not know anyone superior to us apart from God."[118] Although she had not yet gone to war at this point in her reign, such demonstrations of power enabled the Tudor queen to fashion a warlike image far beyond the borders of her realm.

The refusal of safe conduct, seizing and stealing goods from foreign vessels, and Elizabeth's unwillingness to free hostages all fueled the antagonism between the two realms. Indeed, relations deteriorated to such an extent that the French court and its ambassadors feared that Elizabeth might soon declare herself their enemy. As early as June 1559, Gilles de Noailles had reported that the English queen had ordered extra fortifications and doubled the garrisons in Jersey and Guernsey.[119] Moreover, two weeks later, he informed Henry II that "this queen has diligently armed and equipped three great new vessels that have not yet been at sea."[120] Finally, in November, he warned Henry's successor, Francis II, that people

[115] Catherine de Medici to Elizabeth I of England, January 25, 1563, in *LCM*, Tome I, 486–7.

[116] Elizabeth I of England to Catherine de Medici, February 7, 1563, in *LCM*, Tome I, 486, "bien estrange, et aussi les requestes tells que ne les pouvons pas accorder en la manière qu'elles sont faictes et fondées."

[117] Elizabeth I of England to Catherine de Medici, February 7, 1563, "Quant à son emprisonnement il a été si favorablement traité, n'estant en autre lieu qu'en la maison d'un des principaux marchands et conseillers de nostre ville de Londres, que nous pensions et attendions plus tost en estre remerciée que blasmée."

[118] Elizabeth I of England to Catherine de Medici, February 7, 1563, 487, "que nous ne cognoissons sauf Dieu aucun supérieur."

[119] Gilles de Noailles to Monsieur de Gondran, Garde des Sceaux de Dijon, pour informer le Roy et Monsieur le Connestable, June 15, 1559, AE MD Angleterre, Register IV, fol. 253.

[120] Gilles de Noailles to Henry II of France, July 1, 1559, AE MD Angleterre, Register IV, fol. 259, "Ceste Royne faict armer et esquipper en toute diligence trois grands vaisseaulx neufs qui n'ont encores esté sur mer."

all over England were discussing the prospect of war, while English merchants were sending envoys to their representatives in Normandy, Brittany,
and even Bordeaux and instructing them to return home.[121]

Elizabeth usually justified her actions on the basis of national self-
defense, although sometimes the line between legitimate protection of her
realm and overt aggression toward her southern neighbor was rather
blurred. For instance, in November 1559, de Noailles informed Francis
that she had ordered some twenty ships to start patrolling the Channel,
ostensibly because she feared an attack from the French king.[122] A few
months later, Michel de Seure was forced to assuage her concerns about
the presence of some French galleys near the coast by explaining that they
were en route to the Levant.[123]

The first religious civil war to ravage France erupted on March 1, 1562
with the Massacre of Vassy. Thereafter, the French feared that Elizabeth
was supporting and arming the Huguenots, and in June 1562 Paul de
Foix informed Catherine de Medici that she might be preparing an invasion force.[124] Three weeks later, he reported that the Privy Council had
ordered "twelve ships to go to sea under the command of Master Winter,
Vice-Admiral of the North, who is one of this country's most renowned
mariners."[125]

In the ensuing conflict, the English supported the Huguenot leader,
the Prince of Condé. His forces took possession of Le Havre, which was
known as Le Havre-de-Grace at the time, in the autumn of 1562. Condé
agreed that the English should occupy the port as a means of pressuring
the French royal family to restore Calais to English rule. However, other
Huguenots were more patriotic and a siege began on May 22, 1563. Five
days earlier, Catherine had written to Paul de Foix in London. Her letter
insisted that Elizabeth had promised to relinquish Le Havre on condition

[121] Gilles de Noailles to Francis II of France, November 22, 1559, AE MD Angleterre,
Register IV, fol. 339.

[122] Advis d'Angleterre envoyez au Roi par l'Ambassadeur Gilles de Noailles, November 9,
1559, AE MD Angleterre, Register IV, fol. 334.

[123] Michel de Seure to Charles IX of France, January 23, 1561, in *A Knight of Malta*,
67–68.

[124] See Paul de Foix to Catherine de Medici, June 6, 1562, BNF MS. Fr. 6612, fol. 54 and
Paul de Foix to Catherine de Medici, June 13, 1562, BNF MS. Fr. 6612, fol. 59v.

[125] Paul de Foix to Catherine de Medici, July 1, 1562, BNF MS. Fr. 6612, fol. 84, "il a esté
ordonné par le Conseil de la Royne d'Angleterre, douze navires pour se mettre en mer soubz
la conduit de Maistre Winther Vis-Admiral de North, qui est ung des plus entendus de ce
pays au faict de la Marine."

that Calais was returned to the English crown, but now the English queen seemed to be reneging on that pledge. Moreover, the English ambassador's "imprecise, ambiguous, and confusing words" were hindering resolution of the crisis.[126] Catherine concluded with the explicit threat that she was prepared to use force to regain her city.[127]

The French finally entered Le Havre a few months later and thereafter the port remained French. Under the terms of the Treaty of Troyes, which was signed on April 11, 1564, Elizabeth agreed to relinquish any claim to Le Havre in return for 120,000 gold crowns. There was no mention of Calais.

Despite Elizabeth's defeat at Le Havre, the French ambassadors' reports did not depict her as a spent force. As early as July 1559, less than one year into her reign, Gilles de Noailles told Francis II that she was in full control of England's armed forces. He reported that she had recently intended to travel to the Isle of Sheppey but "felt a little unwell at the house of Millord Cobam after a great feast had been taken, which caused her to interrupt her journey[. However,] she was happy to go to Gillingham to see her sailors, on twenty-eight vessels."[128] Therefore, although Elizabeth was forced to abandon the planned trip to Sheppey, the French ambassador portrayed her as a warrior queen who took the opportunity to boost her troops' morale with a personal visit. She also granted them some time off.

Later in the same dispatch, de Noailles reported that the queen had subsequently visited her lords in "Heltan, de Nonchis, and Hampton Court," and that she had spent fifteen days in Richmond.[129] After finally arriving in Watford, she held a two-and-a-half-hour meeting with her council, during which the state of the country's armed forces was high on the agenda. De Noailles reported that the queen asked

---

[126] Catherine de Medici to Paul de Foix, May 17, 1563, in *LCM*, Tome II, 39–40, "les propoz de sondict ambassadeur, que parolles incertaines, ambigues et confuzes."

[127] Catherine de Medici to Paul de Foix, May 17, 1563, 40–41.

[128] Gilles de Noailles to Francis II of France, July 29, 1559, AE MD Angleterre, Register IV, fol. 281, "ceste Royne s'acheminan vers l'Isle de Choppet s'est trouvé ung peu mal en la maison du Millord Cobam après ung grand festin qui luy avoit esté là prepare, de sorte que cela a esté cause d'interrompre son voyage, s'estant contentée d'avoir esté jusqu'à Gerlingam voir son equipage de mer, qui s'est trouvé de 28 vaisseaux."

[129] Gilles de Noailles to Francis II of France, July 29, 1559, "ayant donné pour quelques jours congé à la pluspart du reste des Mariniers, et Gens qui estoient sur les autres navires, et faict ressser l'equipage, elle s'est rapprochée à Houatford à huict mil de ceste ville, et se dict que de là, ira passer par des maisons de Heltan, de Nonchis et Hontoncourt, et se render dans quinze jours à Richmont, pour y faire quelque residence."

the Treasurer of the Navy and the Master Provider of naval food supplies
and weapons [...] how long it would take to equip twenty [ships] for war,
with two months' supplies for three thousand men, and finally ordered the
Master Provider to buy, kill, and salt six hundred head of cattle on her
account, in order to ensure that the vessels and the men would be ready
within fifteen days of receiving the said queen's order.[130]

Here, once again, de Noailles depicted a warrior queen who issued direct
orders to her admirals, generals, and other officers with a view to preparing England for war. Therefore, it was hardly surprising that Anglo-French
relations remained tense throughout this period. Despite repeated expressions of good intentions and affection on both sides, the French ambassadors perceived and depicted Elizabeth as a strong ruler who might well
become a serious threat to the French crown in the near future.

The first seven years of Elizabeth's reign are traditionally characterized
as a time when France and England strove to establish a strong and stable
alliance. Yet, elements of distrust and defiance caused the French side to
develop an image of Elizabeth as a rather deceitful and belligerent queen.
Although she was still viewed as a potential bride for any number of
European princes, dukes, and other lords, there was no doubt that she was
also a powerful monarch in her own right who was willing and able to
assert her royal authority both within and beyond the borders of her realm.

## CONCLUSION

As this chapter has amply demonstrated, Elizabeth's reputation as a shrewd
politician is entirely justified. She dominated and even toyed with the
ambassadors, special envoys, and courtiers who competed with one
another to secure audiences. Her relations with the French court were
sometimes strained, yet Catherine de Medici, Henry II, Francis II, and

---

[130] Gilles de Noailles to Francis II of France, July 29, 1559, "la dicte Dame entra en son
conseil, où elle n'avoit encores esté, et y fus deux heures et demye ... j'ay eu advis, Sire, que
audict Conseil où la dicte Dame assista, avoient esté mandez le Trésorier de la Marine, et le
Maistre Pourvoyeur des vietuailles et munitions de navires pour sçavoir dans quell temps ilz
en pourroient avoir appresté vingt, esquipez en guerre, avec l'avituellement de deux mois
pour trois mille hommes et enfin tout ordonner audict Maistre Pouvoyeur, d'achepter six
cens boeufs sur son credit et les faire tuer et saller, au reste qu'il seroit mis ordre que les
navires et hommes fussent prests, quand ilz serotine commandé par la dicte Dame dans 15
jours de l'advertisemment."

Charles IX, as well as their ambassadors, were desperate not to alienate her in any way. Indeed, it is fair to say that they all had grudging respect for her queenship.

Elizabeth was just twenty-five years old when she acceded to the English throne. However, thanks in part to her stepmother, Katherine Parr, she had received an excellent education that gave her all the skills she needed for her future role. In their meticulous reports to their masters, the French ambassadors portrayed a queen who was interested in securing a harmonious alliance with her Valois counterparts yet remained determined to defend her country and retain control over her own affairs, including her marriage negotiations.

The following chapter continues this exploration of the French royal family's rather ambivalent attitude toward Elizabeth by focusing on the emergence of increasingly strident representations of the Tudor queen as she entered the second decade of her reign.

# "a rock": Between Peace and Conflict—An Intriguing Queen, 1568–1570

In May 1568, Mary Stuart's flight from Scotland took her across Elizabeth's northern border and almost immediately into captivity, triggering a diplomatic and political crisis in England and, arguably, throughout Europe.[1] The English government—and particularly Elizabeth herself—rightly feared that her cousin's presence in England would encourage Catholics to challenge the Protestant queen's authority and legitimacy.[2] Meanwhile, that August, continuing tension between France's Huguenots and Catholics erupted into a third religious war, just five months after the Peace of Longjumeau had brought the second to an end.[3] As we have seen, nine years earlier, Philip II of Spain had married Elisabeth of Valois, daughter of Henry II of France and Catherine de Medici, with the aim of improving relations between the two nations. By and large, the strategy had succeeded,

---

[1] The situation of the Scottish Queen worried the French royal family who begged Elizabeth to help her, as seen in a letter from Catherine de Medici to Queen Elizabeth, 26 May 1568, BL, Cottonian Library, Caligula, C.1, Plut XX D, fol 74: "that she will receive the aid, favour, shelter, and friendship that she has the right to expect from you as a distressed princess," ("qu'elle recevra toute l'ayde, faveur, secours et amitié qu'une princesse affligée comme elle est. doibt espérer de vous").

[2] Shenk, *Learned Queen*, 22.

[3] As Arlette Jouanna explains, the formation of the Protestant "Holy Alliance" between the Prince of Orange of the Netherlands and the Huguenot leaders, Louis I, Prince of Condé and Gaspard de Coligny, made Philip II of Spain and Charles IX of France more determined than ever to fight heresy in all of Europe. See Arlette Jouanna, *La France du XVIe siècle, 1483–1598* (Paris: PUF, 1996), 449–51.

© The Author(s) 2019
E. Paranque, *Elizabeth I of England through Valois Eyes*, Queenship and Power, https://doi.org/10.1007/978-3-030-01529-9_3

and France and Spain had become firm allies against the Protestant threat. Moreover, the alliance survived Elisabeth's death on 3 October 1568.[4]

Later that month, Charles IX of France (who had recently celebrated his eighteenth birthday) and his still-influential mother, Catherine de Medici, appointed a new ambassador to the English court: Bertrand de Salignac de la Mothe Fénélon, a member of the king's religious order.[5] No specific reasons were given for his appointment, but in light of the religious turmoil that was engulfing Europe, it is safe to assume that the French rulers expected La Mothe Fénélon, a man of strong faith, to become a fierce defender of not only French but Catholic interests at the English court.

Elizabeth has long been depicted as a Protestant heroine who embodied Protestant ideals.[6] For instance, Linda Shenk has demonstrated that Elizabeth was portrayed as a sort of "Queen Solomon."[7] This image partially stemmed from *Christian Prayers and Meditations in English, French, Italian, Spanish, Greeke, and Latine*, which John Day published in London in 1569,[8] and Shenk argues that it enabled Elizabeth to project "transnational Protestant leadership." However, while the prayer book portrayed the queen "as multilingual," its impact on the wider European scene is far from certain.[9] Therefore, it is worth exploring whether this representation of Elizabeth, which undoubtedly became prevalent in her home country, contrasted with foreigners' perceptions of the Tudor queen.

La Mothe Fénélon's reports and the letters of Catherine de Medici and Charles IX, particularly between 1568 and 1570 when the balance of power was less favorable to England, reveal a much more complex and rather ambivalent attitude toward Elizabeth. As England's principal goal was to counter the supremacy of Spain in Europe, it could not afford to jeopardize its alliance with France. By contrast, remaining on good terms

[4] Catherine de Medici to Philip II of Spain, November 13, 1568, *Lettres de Catherine de Médicis*, publiées par M. Le Cte Hector de la Ferrière, Tome III, 1567–70 (Paris: Imprimerie Nationale, 1887), 207.

[5] Catherine de Medici to Queen Elizabeth, October 1568, BL Cottonian Library, Caligula E, vol. VI, fol. 60 and see Catherine de Medici to Earl of Leicester, October 18, 1568, BL, Add. MS n° 19,398.

[6] See the works of John E. Neale *Queen Elizabeth I* (London, 1934) and Roy Strong, *The Cult of Elizabeth: Elizabethan Portraiture and Pageantry* (1999) and the discussion in the introduction which explains the complexities behind such a representation.

[7] Shenk, *Learned Queen*, 35.

[8] *Christian Prayers and Meditations in English, French, Italian, Spanish, Greeke, and Latine* (London, published by John Day: 1569, STC 6428).

[9] Shenk, *Learned Queen*, 24 and 21.

with England was not so critical for Charles and Catherine while their own relations with Spain remained largely peaceful and strong.[10] Furthermore, there was a degree of mistrust in the correspondence between Elizabeth and the French king as suspicions persisted that she was offering clandestine support to the French Huguenots and the Prince of Orange in his battle against Spanish dominion in the Netherlands.

Hence, Elizabeth had a multifaceted reputation in the late 1560s: peacemaker and loyal ally of the French royal family, but also scheming queen who was secretly aiding Charles's enemies. To some extent, both of these characterizations were justified as Elizabeth was a chameleon who adapted her behavior to meet the challenges of constantly shifting and complex political events. However, her French counterparts eventually recognized that she was a unique source of sage advice and wise counsel. As this chapter explains, La Mothe Fénélon played a pivotal role in reassuring the French royal family that Elizabeth remained loyal to the Anglo-French alliance and wished to preserve good relations with them. Moreover, he defended her legitimacy and portrayed her as at least the equal of any other European monarch, regardless of gender. Nevertheless, the image of a more defiant and warlike queen gradually emerged in his reports as well as Catherine's and Charles's responses. All three had no doubt that she was prepared to defend her interests both inside and outside the borders of her realm by asserting her royal authority right across the European political scene, if necessary. Detailed analysis of their correspondence sheds new light on Elizabeth's complex reputation at a time when—according to the French ambassador—every prince of Europe was keeping a close eye on every move and decision she made, especially in relation to Mary, Queen of Scots.[11]

---

[10] An alliance remained between France and Spain. However, from 1567, their relations deteriorated slowly. See Bertrand Haan, *L'Amitié entre princes. Une alliance franco-espagnole au temps des guerres de Religion (1560–1570)* (Paris: PUF, 2011), 125–64; Alain Tallon, "Les puissances catholiques face à la tolérance religieuse en France au XVIe siècle; droit d'ingérence ou non intervention," in *L'Europe des traités des Westphalie. Esprit de la diplomatie et diplomatie de l'esprit*, Lucien Bély (ed.) (Paris: PUF, 2000), 22–23 and Barbara Diefendord, *Beneath the Cross: Catholics and Protestants in Sixteenth Century Paris* (Oxford: Oxford University Press, 1991), 82–83.

[11] La Mothe Fénélon to Catherine de Medici, December 5, 1568, in *Correspondence diplomatique de Bertrand de Salignac de la Mothe Fénélon, ambassadeur de France en Angleterre, de 1568 à 1575*, Tome I, Années 1568 et 1569 (Archives du Royaume: Paris et Londres, 1838), 34, "je luy dis que les yeux de toutz les gens de bien du monde estoient tournez sur les déportemans dont elle useroit au soulagemant des afflictions et adversités de ceste princesse".

## THE GOOD RELATIVE AND THE PEACEFUL QUEEN

When La Mothe Fénélon arrived as French ambassador to the English court in late 1568, his first mission was to secure France's alliance with the English queen.[12] Scholars have paid considerable attention to the virtual family bond that was used to perpetuate good relations between the two monarchies. Yet, their works have failed to examine the impact of this rhetoric on the participants' reputations or indeed the specific goals the two sides hoped to achieve.[13] In the previous chapter, we saw that Elizabeth and the French rulers employed rather formal greetings when corresponding with one another. However, this started to change between 1568 and 1570, as both sides adopted the personas of members of a fictional family.

One major feature of the correspondence between the two courts was their concern for each other's wellbeing. For example, in a letter dated July 1568, Catherine thanked Elizabeth for her enquiries about her health, then insisted that the English queen "will never meet anyone who loves you or longs for your wellbeing as much as I do."[14] The intention is obvious: both parties included declarations of affection and concern in their letters in the hope of creating a strong personal bond that would help to preserve the Anglo-French alliance. Specifically, the French rulers and their ambassadors increasingly addressed Elizabeth as if she were an honorary member of the Valois family and she responded in similar vein.

Meanwhile, La Mothe Fénélon's reports consistently portrayed the English queen as a peaceful, benevolent, and just ruler. For instance, in his first report, dated November 16, 1568, the French ambassador assured

[12] La Mothe Fénélon to the French king Charles IX, 1st Report, November 16, 1568, in *Correspondence diplomatique*, Tome I, 3.

[13] See the works of Susan Doran, "Elizabeth I and Catherine de Medici," in *The contending kingdoms: France and England 1420–1700*, ed. Glenn Richardson (Aldershot: Ashgate, 2008); Elaine Kruse, "The Virgin and the Widow: The political finesse of Elizabeth I and Catherine de Médici," in *Queens and Power in Medieval and Early Modern England*, eds. Carole Levin and Robert Bulcholz (Lincoln and London: University of Nebraska, 2009) and in Glenn Richardson, "'Your most assured sister': Elizabeth I and the Kings of France," in *Tudor Queenship: the reigns of Mary and Elizabeth*, eds. Alice Hunt and Anna Whitelock (New York: Palgrave Macmillan, 2010), the author focuses on the image of a "good sister" of the English queen.

[14] Catherine de Medici to Queen Elizabeth, July 1568, in *Lettres de Catherine de Médicis* publiées par M. Le Cte Hector de la Ferrière, Tome III, 1567–70 (Paris: Imprimerie Nationale, 1834), 153, "que n'aymerez jamais personne qui vous y corresponde myeulx et qui désire plus vostre bien et contentement que je fais."

Charles IX of Elizabeth's "friendship and sincerity as a true good sister."[15] His use of this appellation indicates that it was not just the members of the French royal family who understood that the cultivation of strong—albeit virtual—familial bonds had a crucial role to play in preserving the peace between the two nations. However, as in a real family, the "relatives" were not averse to exploiting these bonds in the hope of gaining an advantage and asserting their authority. Elaine Kruse has highlighted Catherine de Medici's attempts to establish a "mother–daughter relationship" between herself and Elizabeth. However, in the early years of Elizabeth's reign, their relationship was usually expressed in traditional, sisterly terms,[16] with Catherine generally referring to Elizabeth as "our dearest and dearly loved good sister and cousin" and signing her letters "your good sister and cousin, Caterine."[17] There was a shortlived shift in early 1572 amid discussions over a possible marriage between Elizabeth and Francis, Duke of Alençon, during which Catherine started to briefly address Elizabeth as her "daughter." Later in the decade, however, the "mother–daughter" relationship was fully established when the marriage negotiations entered a new phase.[18]

The relationship between Charles IX and Elizabeth was more consistent. In November 1568, La Mothe Fénélon reported that the English queen viewed herself as Charles's "main ally and confederate sister,"[19] and the following month, after the death of Elisabeth of Valois, he reported that Elizabeth "grieved her death as if it were her own sister."[20] Elizabeth's strong desire to remain on intimate, sisterly terms with her French counterpart are self-evident in these reports. Four months later, the ambassador informed Charles IX: "she was happy, as your true sister, and true

---

[15] La Mothe Fénélon to the French king Charles IX, 1st Report, November 16, 1568, in *Correspondence diplomatique*, Tome I, 6.

[16] See Orlin "The Fictional Families of Elizabeth I," 85–110.

[17] Catherine de Medici to Queen Elizabeth, August 15, 1569, in *LCM*, Tome III, 267, "noslre très chère et très amée bonne soeur et cousine", "Vostre bonne soeur et cousine, Caterine." It is also important to note that these references were usual between princes—hence the importance to study shifts in the use of them and how this influenced diplomatic relations between crowns.

[18] Elaine Kruse, "The Virgin and the Widow," 129.

[19] La Mothe Fénélon to Catherine de Medici, November 16 1568, in *Correspondence diplomatique*, Tome I, 35, "votre principale alliée et confédérée bonne seur."

[20] La Mothe Fénélon to the French king Charles IX, 5th Report, December 10, 1568, in *Correspondence diplomatique*, Tome I, 8, "quant à l'inconveniant de la Royne d'Espaigne, qu'èle la regrétoit de tout son cueur, et en portoit deuil comme si c'eust esté sa propre seur."

daughter of the Queen, to hear of your success, and wishes you as much prosperity as she wishes for herself."[21] If she did indeed identify herself as Catherine's "true daughter," Elizabeth's intention may have been to signal that she valued their relationship and recognized the older woman's authority, even though Catherine was not of royal blood and was no longer queen regent.[22] More importantly, by including these familial terms in his report, La Mothe Fénélon cultivated the image of an English queen who wished to be considered part of the Valois family.[23]

On the other hand, the ambassador also hinted that Elizabeth may have had an ulterior motive for these displays of familial affection: she wished to counsel the French king.

> [S]he wanted to give her opinion openly about what I told her, as, being Queen, as she is, she was unable not to feel so involved or interested in the causes of others as she is in those of your Majesties […] [and] you may believe that she proceeds with many good intentions and righteousness, as if she has the honor to be a second mother to the king.[24]

As we have seen, Elaine Kruse argues that Catherine de Medici attempted to establish her superiority over Elizabeth by adopting the maternal role during their marriage negotiations in the late 1570s.[25] Here, ten years earlier, we see Elizabeth herself employing a similar tactic with respect to eighteen-year-old Charles, albeit while acknowledging Catherine's preeminence by identifying herself as his "*second* mother." This revealed not only the English queen's desire to increase her influence over the French

---

[21] La Mothe Fénélon to the French king Charles IX, 29th Report, April 12, 1569, in *Correspondence diplomatique*, Tome I, 310, "qu'elle se resjouyssoit, comme votre propre seur, et comme propre fille de la Royne, du bon acheminement de voz affères, esquelz elle desiroit semblable prospérité que aulx siens propres."

[22] Catherine's regency ended in 1563. However as Fanny Cosandey argues, she continued to exercise power during her son's reign, in Fanny Cosandey, *La Reine de France. Symbole et Pouvoir, XVe et XVIIIe siècle* (Paris: Gallimard, 2000), 321.

[23] It is difficult to assess La Mothe Fénélon's motivation here. He may have had his own reasons to highlight Elizabeth's affection for the French royal family, but what they may have been must remain a matter of speculation.

[24] La Mothe Fénélon to Catherine de Medici, December 5, 1568, in *Correspondence diplomatique*, Tome I, 32, "mais qu'elle m'avoit tout ouvertemant voulu dire son opynion sur ce que je luy avois proposé, bien qu'estant Royne, comme elle est., elle ne pouvoit en rien se sentir si conjointe ne si intéressée en la cause des autres, comme elle faisoit en celle de Vos Majestez, en laquelle vous pryoit croire qu'elle procèderoit, avec autant de bonne intention et de droicteure, comme si elle avoit l'honneur d'estre une segonde mère du Roy."

[25] Elaine Kruise, "The Virgin and the Widow," 129.

king by offering him maternal words of wisdom but also her determination to assert the superior position that she felt was hers by right. The sentiment was reiterated in May 1570, when La Mothe Fénélon told his master that Elizabeth craved "the honor that you would be her own son."[26] Moreover, other letters echoed this tone of maternal benevolence, such as when the French ambassador informed Catherine of Elizabeth's declarations of "singular affection for the King" in April 1569.[27]

In these dispatches from the English court, La Mothe Fénélon consistently presents Elizabeth as a sincere and loyal relative of the French king and his mother, and signals her affection for them through repeated use of such terms as "true sister" and "second mother." Moreover, his use of the latter term indicates that the ambassador recognized Elizabeth's right to participate in French affairs and give "her opinion openly" without any fear that this might compromise her reputation as a peace-loving and firm ally of the French nation.

As noted earlier, La Mothe Fénélon's principal task was to preserve the alliance with England in the midst of his country's ongoing difficulties with the Huguenots and the eruption of the third religious civil war. In a report to the French king dated December 21, 1568, he remarked that when the Spanish ambassador, Guerau de Espés, who had a difficult relationship with the queen,[28] questioned Elizabeth's sincerity regarding her alliance with France, she had replied that "she was your absolute good sister and great friend who desired prosperity [...] for your affairs and wanted neither to harm you nor to declare herself against you."[29] A month later, Catherine instructed La Mothe Fénélon to ask Elizabeth to prove her loyalty to the French crown, given that English ships had recently attacked French vessels, and asserted that "the good peace and friendship

---

[26] La Mothe Fénélon to the French king Charles IX, 110th Report, May 27, 1570, in *Correspondence diplomatique de Bertrand de Salignac de la Mothe Fénélon, ambassadeur de France en Angleterre, de 1568 à 1575*, Tome III, Années 1570 et 1561 (Archives du Royaume: Paris et Londres, 1840), 165, "l'honneur que vous fuissiez son propre fils."

[27] La Mothe Fénélon to Catherine de Medici, April 17, 1569, in *Correspondence diplomatique*, Tome I, p. 317, "la singulière affection qu'elle portoit au Roy."

[28] See James Anthony Froude, *History of England from the Fall of Wolsey to the Defeat of the Spanish Armada* (London: John W. Parker and Son, West Strand, 1856).

[29] La Mothe Fénélon to the French king Charles IX, 7th Report, December 21, 1568, in *Correspondence diplomatique*, Tome I, 55, "estre tout entièremant votre bonne et grande amye, desirant la prospérité et establissemant de voz affaires, et qu'elle n'avoit garde de nuyre ny se déctairer contre vous."

between the two realms will not be maintained unless you can make her hear our case."[30]

With the alliance suddenly under threat, the French ambassador convinced Elizabeth to demonstrate her good intentions by publishing a proclamation that England was still France's official ally, so English ships should not attack or steal from French vessels:

> [S]everal French [ships] have been violently attacked and harassed [...] Her Majesty does not believe that such deeds were done by her subjects as this would compromise and ruin the good relationship that exists between the French king, her good brother, and herself [...] [P]rinted in London on 29 January 1569.[31]

Elsewhere, the proclamation instructed Elizabeth's subjects to return any stolen goods to the French authorities. By quoting the document in full, La Mothe Fénélon highlighted not only the queen's desire to preserve the peace with France but also her determination to safeguard her reputation among her French counterparts. In his next report, he again insisted that her intentions were entirely peaceful:

> I received a declaration from her that she wishes to preserve the alliance that she has developed since her coronation with the late king your father, and with You and the Queen, your mother [...] She is resolved to remain loyal to the treaties and accords of good peace that exist between Your Majesties and your countries and subjects.[32]

---

[30] Catherine de Medici to La Mothe Fénélon, January 13, 1568, in *LCM*, Tome III, 219, "la bonne paix et amitié d'entre ces deux royaumes, ne se feraient, executions sans lui en faire entendre les justes causes."

[31] La Mothe Fénélon to the French king Charles IX, 15th Report, January 30, 1569, in *Correspondence diplomatique*, Tome I, 175, "comme plusieurs Françoys, ses subjectz, ayant esté violentement prins, avec leurs navyres et biens, par gens de guerre sur mer [...] Sa Majesté n'entend point qu'il soyt faict ny usé de telz déportemens par ses subjectz, au préjudice et nuysance de la bonne amytié, qui est. entre le dict Roy de France, son dict bon frère, et elle [...] printed A Londres le 29 janvier 1569."

[32] La Mothe Fénélon to the French king Charles IX, 22nd Report, March 8, 1569, in *Correspondence diplomatique*, Tome I, 222, "j'ay eu ceste déclaration d'elle que pour le desir de conserver l'amytié qu'elle a contractée, dez son avènement à sa couronne, avecques le feu Roy vostre'père, et continuée avecques Vous et avec la Royne vostre mère, elle est. résolue de demeurer entièrement aux trettez et capitulations de la bonne paix, qui est. entre Voz Majestez et voz pays et subjectz."

Reminding Charles IX that his father had signed the treaty that secured peace between the two nations back in 1559 allowed Elizabeth (and possibly La Mothe Fénélon) to highlight that her loyalty to and good relations with the French royal family had endured over many years, despite occasional outbursts of religious tension and even civil war.[33]

Nevertheless, suspicions that England was providing aid to the Huguenots persisted, and in December 1569 Elizabeth once more felt compelled to inform the French court of her peaceful intentions. La Mothe Fénélon reported:

> she vehemently rejected two offers she received: the first was to initiate actions with your subjects for the advancement of their religion, and the other was to pursue and instigate war in your realm [...] [S]he decided that neither of these two actions befitted her honor and conscience, judging with her heart that Your Majesties could not hold grudges against your subjects, and that it was your subjects who provoked and irritated you [...] [S]he refused to support their cause and does not desire the perpetuation of war in your realm, so she welcomes pacification [...] [S]he will not consider helping them now, nor will her subjects be allowed to do so, at the risk of losing their heads.[34]

In this report, the French ambassador seemed convinced that Elizabeth wanted to preserve the peace not only between the two crowns but within the borders of France itself. He viewed her as a strong ally of the French king, but even more importantly as a peace-loving and fair ruler in her own right:

---

[33] On the importance to maintain peace between the two crowns and how the 1559 Peace of Cateau-Cambrésis and the 1572 Treaty of Blois shaped French relations, see Wallace T. MacCaffrey, "The Newhaven Expedition, 1562–1563," *The Historical Journal*, vol. 40, 1 (1997): 1–21.

[34] La Mothe Fénélon to the French king Charles IX, 78th Report, December 17, 1569, in *Correspondence diplomatique*, Tome III, 395, "qu'elle avoit fermement rejecté deux très véhémentes persuasions qu'on s'estoit esforcé de luy donner; l'une d'entreprendre la devance de voz subjectz travaillez pour la religion, et l'aultre de nourrir et foumanter la guerre en vostre royaulme, affin qu'elle ne passât au sien car n'avoit estimé que l'une ny l'aultre de ces deux praticques peult convener à son honneur ny à sa conscience, jugeant en son cueur que Voz Majestez Très Chrestiennes n'avoient peu vouloir mal à leurs subjectz, et que c'estoient plustost voz subjectz qui vous avoient provoquez et irritez lesquelz nonobstant qu'on leur fit empeschement en leur religion, debvoient, plustost que de mouvoir les armes, s'en estre allez hors du royaulme; par quoy avoit renuzé d'estre pour leur cause, et n'avoit non plus desiré'la continuation de la guerre en vostre royaulme, ains d'y veoir de bon cueur une paciffication; et que de leur envoyer maintennant du secours elle ne le feroit ny permettroit à ses subjectz, sinon au péril de leurs testes."

the said Lady told me that I was her witness, and that […] she has always
wanted peace in your realm, and she hoped your subjects would not defy
you by rejecting your pact, as long as the terms were indeed as I had told her
they were.[35]

Clearly, Elizabeth's goal was to convince the French royal family that she
was a just and benevolent queen, which would enable her to continue to
speak her mind on important issues.

Traditionally, English-language literature has consistently presented
Elizabeth as a paragon of justice and benevolence. For example, in
1559, John Aylmer published a work that praised the young queen's
virtue and clemency.[36] Moreover, Elizabeth was not averse to crediting
herself with similar attributes. For instance, in 1586, when the English
Parliament urged her to reach a decision over the fate of Mary Stuart,
she declared: "I have pardoned many traitors and rebels."[37] Interestingly,
given the political context of the late 1560s—specifically the eruption of
a third religious war in France, the Dutch revolt, and Mary Stuart's
unexpected arrival in England—it also made sense for the French
ambassador to help Elizabeth to project this positive, benign image to
her Valois counterparts, because increasing the trust between the two
sides was sure to benefit the alliance. Therefore, it is hardly surprising
that he repeatedly cast her as a peacemaker. However, he went further
and insisted that she had a *right* to offer opinions and advice on important matters, including religion. In April 1569, he informed Charles IX
that "she does not support the justice of those who declared war to you
[French king] nor that she can accuse them [the Huguenots] of great
injustices." Moreover, while she insisted that it was wrong to persecute
the Huguenots for their religious beliefs, she could not condone their
refusal to attend

[35] La Mothe Fénélon to the French king Charles IX, 121st Report, July 14, 1570, in
*Correspondence diplomatique*, Tome III, 238, "la dicte Dame m'a respondu que je luy estois
tesmoing, que, entre ses meilleurs désirs, elle avoit toutjours heu bien expécial celluy de la
paix de vostre royaulme, et qu'elle espéroit que voz subjectz ne se diffameroient tant que de
la rejetter, si les condicions estoient telles que je disoys."
[36] John Aylmer, *An Harborowe for faithful and trewe subjects* (London, 1559), N4v.
[37] "Queen Elizabeth's second reply to the parliamentary petition urging the execution of
Mary, Queen of Scots, November 24 1586," in *Elizabeth I: Collected Works*, 197.

Mass and other Catholic ceremonies or their decisions to launch an uprising against their sovereign and to kill their neighbors [...] [The queen] urged me to convey to you, your Most Christian Majesties, that she [...] wants only a good outcome for the king's cause, so she is delighted by your success, and desires it as much as she desires her own.[38]

In other words, according to La Mothe Fénélon's account of their meeting, while Elizabeth denounced any unprovoked persecution of her coreligionists in France, her ultimate sympathy lay with the king. She refused to support those who committed atrocities but also, crucially, those who did not respect their rulers' religion as well as those who challenged royal authority in any way. If correctly reported, these sentiments are unsurprising. After all, Elizabeth was facing religious divisions inside her own borders, and she desperately wanted to avoid an uprising among her Catholic subjects. Moreover, there was no hypocrisy in her linking of justice and benevolence to the maintenance of royal authority because there had been no persecution of England's Catholics in the first decade of her reign.

The previous December, in another meeting with La Mothe Fénélon, the queen had explained her religious policy. She reminded the French ambassador—and of course, through him, the French royal family—that she had not abolished Catholicism in her realm, "though they are more numerous and from noble families."[39] Furthermore,

moved only by the zeal of God's honor and her own conscience, she has established without contradiction her religion in her realm, her subjects live in peace, with no concern for all the storms that erupt around them, and if

---

[38] La Mothe Fénélon to the French king Charles IX, 31st Report, April 20, 1569, in *Correspondence diplomatique*, Tome I, 318, "Il m'a semblé, par les derniers propos que j'ay eu avec ceste Royne, qu'elle n'est. tant pour la justice de ceulx qui vous mènent la guerre en votre royaulme qu'elle ne les accuse de beaulcoup d'injustice; car, ayans discouru ensemble assés ongtems, et quelque foys avec contraire opinion l'ung à l'autre, du jugement qu'il a. pieu à Dieu d'en fère par les armes, elle en fin m'a dict que, comme elle eust bien vollu que vous, Sire, et la Royne, eussiez esté escrupuleux à ne vous laysser persuader de fère ny souffrir que voz subjectz fussent persécutez [...] d'aller à la messe et aulx ceremonies de l'esglize romaine qu'ilz n'en ont vollu fèrede s'eslever contre leur Roy et de'thuer leurs prochains, me priant de fère bien entendre à Voz Majestez Très Chrestiennes qu'elle ne peult, en façon du monde, vouloir que tout bien à la cause des Roys, et que, partant, elle se resjouyt de votre prospérité, et la désire comme la siienne propre."

[39] La Mothe Fénélon to Catherine de Medici, letter, December 5, 1568, in *Correspondence diplomatique*, Tome I, 29, "d'oster aux catholiques la leur, bien qu'ilz fussent en plus grand nombre et des plus grands de son royaulme."

possible your Majesties should follow her example in the [situation] you are currently facing, as it has never crossed her mind to change the laws of her country or her religion.[40]

With this declaration, Elizabeth candidly differentiated herself from her French counterparts by explaining that her constancy in religious affairs had helped her to maintain peace in her own realm. Indeed, she was so certain that she had followed the best path that she presented it as an example for Charles and Catherine to follow. The obvious implication was that she was just and fair, which had enabled her to maintain royal authority and preserve peace in England for more than ten years, whereas her French counterparts were unjust, which had caused their nation to descend into chaos and civil strife. The lesson concluded as follows:

> [Elizabeth] advised that, if God is invoked in both religions and you allow only one […] she is of the opinion that, as wise people say, although the law might be harsh, you should still support it and not break it in order to please some of your people without having previously pleased the others, even in times of war.[41]

Once again, then, La Mothe Fénélon gave Elizabeth a platform on which she was able to pass judgement on French domestic affairs. On this occasion, he allowed her to proffer unsolicited advice to the French royal family regarding how to safeguard Catholicism while also granting the Protestants religious freedom. In her view, this was the only means through which they might achieve some peace and reconciliation among the French people. Moreover, she spoke with authority, because she herself had reaped

---

[40] La Mothe Fénélon to Catherine de Medici, letter, December 5, 1568, 30, "estant meue du seul zcte de l'honneur de Dieu, et de sa consciance, elle eust estably, sans aulcung contradict, le règlemant de sa religion dedans son royaulme, souz lequel ses subjectz avoient despuys vescu en grand repoz, sans rien sentir de. ces orages qui s'estoient eslevez tout à l'entour d'eulx, si ne pouvoit, à son advis, quadrer son exemple à celui don't Voz Majestez aviez présentemant uzé, car ne luy estoit jamais advenu de changer ces édictz, ny en la religion."

[41] La Mothe Fénélon to Catherine de Medici, letter, December 5, 1568, 31, "conseillé que, puys que Dieu estoit invoqué en l'une et en l'autre relligion, que vous n'en eussiez jamais permis que l'une […] elle avoit opynion que, sellon le dire des anciens, encor que la loy en fust ung peu dure, que vous la debviez néanmoings avoir supportée quelque temps, et ne la rompre ainsi à l'appétit des ungs, sans avoir premièremant pourveu à l'intéretz des autres, mesmes en temps que les armes estoient desjà prinses."

the benefits of the great benevolence she had displayed toward her Catholic cousin, Mary Stuart.

Historians have long been fascinated by this image of justice and benevolence. Indeed, Mary Villeponteaux has cataloged countless references to Elizabeth's supposed kindness and mercy over the course of five centuries of English literature.[42] To some extent, La Mothe Fénélon helped the Tudor queen to establish herself as the personification of justice and grace initially among her French counterparts and ultimately for posterity, especially in his reports on her attitude toward Mary Stuart. As previously mentioned, when Mary arrived in England, he informed the French court that Elizabeth undoubtedly had her cousin's best interests at heart. Indeed, in December 1568, he reported that

> She [Elizabeth] wants to give all the help she can to the Queen of Scotland, in all good conscience and without staining her reputation [...] [N]othing in the world will stop her keeping her word on this matter, and she will keep the promises she has made to her [Mary].[43]

However, Elizabeth's actions—including imprisoning Mary in a variety of castles in the north of England—were hard to reconcile with these public declarations of care and concern for her Scottish cousin. Charles IX and Catherine de Medici had good reason to worry about their former sister- and daughter-in-law.

Nevertheless, La Mothe Fénélon continued to reassure them of Elizabeth's good intentions toward Mary, writing that she felt it was "her royal duty" to help the Queen of Scotland. Indeed, he had been moved to defend Elizabeth's honor when her enemies "wrote and said nasty things against their sovereign."[44] At the end of 1568, he shared another of Elizabeth's assurances regarding her benevolence toward her cousin:

---

[42] Mary Villeponteaux, *The Queen's Mercy: Gender and Judgement in Representations of Elizabeth I* (New York: Palgrave Macmillan, 2014).

[43] La Mothe Fénélon to Catherine de Medici, letter, December 5, 1568, 33, "qu'elle délibéroit certaynemant donner tout le secours, qu'en bonne consciance et sans la maculer, elle pourroit à la Royne d'Escoce, et qu'elle ne voudroit, pour chose du monde, que ses paroles en cela vinssent a estre démentyes de ces etfectz, et qu'elle accompliroit les promesses qu'elle luy avoit faictes."

[44] La Mothe Fénélon to the French king Charles IX, 5th Report, December 10, 1568, in *Correspondence diplomatique*, Tome I, 39, "le debvoir de sa royale grandeur [...] trop escript, et trop prononcé demal contre leur souverayne."

> No one else on earth cares so much about her [Mary's] person, her state and her reputation as she does, being her blood and niece [in fact, Elizabeth was Mary's first cousin, once removed] [...] she has gladly forgotten all the disputes that happened between them, and she does not wish to avenge herself now that she has sought refuge and help in her realm.[45]

Three weeks later, the French ambassador rammed the point home by informing his master, "she [Elizabeth] is always ready to do everything she can for the said Lady, without offending her own conscience."[46] This reference to Elizabeth's conscience—by which she probably meant her religious beliefs as well as her own safety—was surely included to remind her French counterparts that they should be similarly careful.

Throughout 1569, although Elizabeth and La Mothe Fénélon continued to assure the French king and his mother of the goodwill she felt toward Mary, the queen's audiences with the French ambassador suggested a rather different attitude. The Scottish queen had been accused of complicity in the murder of her husband. Indeed, it was this that had caused her to take the fateful decision to flee across the border. Now, though, rather than offering her unconditional support, Elizabeth repeatedly insisted that it was her duty to secure "justice for the murder of the late King of Scotland, who was her subject" as well as her kinsman.[47] "[T]he said Lady [Elizabeth] indicated that she had not been offended or irritated by her [Mary]," but the implication was clear: Mary was a suspect and she would be treated as such.[48]

---

[45] La Mothe Fénélon to Catherine de Medici, letter, December 28, 1568, in *Correspondence diplomatique*, Tome I, 66, "qu'il n'y avoit personne, souz le ciel, qui heust tant de soing de la personne, de l'estat et de la réputation d'elle, qu'elle avoit, estant de son sang et sa niepce, et qu'elle avoit de bon cueur oblyé toutes les querelles, qui avoient esté entre elles, n'ayant garde de s'en venger maintenant qu'elle estoit venue à recours en son royaulme."

[46] La Mothe Fénélon to the French king Charles IX, 13th Report, January 20, 1569, in *Correspondence diplomatique*, Tome I, 134, "qu'elle seroit toutjour preste de fère, sans offencer sa conscience, tout ce qu'elle pourroit pour la dicte Dame."

[47] La Mothe Fénélon to the French king Charles IX, 39th Report, June 3, 1569, in *Correspondence diplomatique de Bertrand de Salignac de la Mothe Fénélon, ambassadeur de France en Angleterre, de 1568 à 1575*, Tome II, (Archives du Royaume: Paris et Londres, 1838), 7, "la justice du murtre du feu Roy d'Escoce, qui estoit son subject."

[48] La Mothe Fénélon to Catherine de Medici, August 22, 1569, in *Correspondence diplomatique*, Tome II, 172, "la dicte Dame a monstré qu'elle estoit aucunement irritée et offancée contre elle."

During the summer of 1569, the French court started to pressurize Elizabeth to make a decision and offer public support to Mary's bid to regain her throne. She answered their requests with a patient explanation of the complexity of the situation, as La Mothe Fénélon reported:

> The said Lady replied that no one on earth wanted to help with the restoration of the Queen of Scotland more than herself, without exposing her to the danger that her enemies represented [...] [T]here are four ways to rescue her and restore her: one through force, another through counsel, another through money, and the fourth through an agreement [...] [Elizabeth declared that] the said Queen of Scotland has not shown any sign of contempt regarding the peace of her realm and the blood of her subjects, she has always preferred to regain her crown through the agreeable consent of her subjects rather than through the violence of war.[49]

Both Elizabeth herself and the French court must have known that this portrait of a peace-loving Mary was far from accurate. In a letter to the Spanish queen, Elisabeth of Valois, Mary had declared that she needed to be rescued in order to "punish my rebels" and asserted that she would

> risk every danger to re-establish the ancient and good faith throughout this whole island. I beg you will keep this secret, for it might cost me my life; yet whatever you hear, be assured that I shall never change my opinion, however I may be compelled to accommodate myself to circumstances.[50]

As Mary had asked Elisabeth to lobby both her husband and her French family for help, it is safe to assume that Charles and Catherine knew of her desire for vengeance.

---

[49] La Mothe Fénélon to the French king Charles IX, 55th Report, September 1, 1569, in *Correspondence diplomatique*, Tome II, 211, "La dicte Dame m'a respondu « que nulle aultre personne du monde ne desiroit plus soigneusement pourvoir au restablissement de la Royne d'Escoce qu'elle faisoit, pourveu que ce fût sans l'exposer au dangier de ses ennemys [...] Qu'il y avoit quatre sortes de secours pour la remettre, l'ung, de force; l'aultre, deconseil; l'aultre, d'argent et le quatriesme, par ung bon accord; et que la dicte Royne d'Escoce n'avoit monstré tant mesprizer le repoz de son royaulme et le sang de ses subjectz, qu'elle n'eust toutjour préféré son retour a sa coronne par l'agréable consentement de ses subjectz que par la violence d'une guerre."

[50] Queen of Scots to the Queen of Spain, Elisabeth, wife of Philip, September 24, 1568, in *Letters of Mary, Queen of Scots, and documents connected with her personal history*, ed. Agnes Strickland, vol. 1 (London: Henry Colburn Publisher, 1842), 86–87.

By including Elizabeth's depiction of Mary as a queen who wanted to spare the lives of her subjects and avoid war in his report, it seems that La Mothe Fénélon wanted to cast Elizabeth as the ultimate peacemaker and mediator between the Queen of Scotland and the rest of the world. To some extent, this role, as defined by the French ambassador, allowed the English queen to justify her treatment of Mary, whatever it may be, and acknowledged that she had every right to assert her royal authority. It also placed her in a position that demanded respect from her French counterparts. However, objective analysis of Elizabeth's behavior suggests that she was not a peacemaker but a monarch who used her diplomatic skills and talent for self-promotion to deflect criticism and avert disaster.

## A Demonstration of Strength

La Mothe Fénélon referred to Elizabeth's "grandeur" in the very first report he sent to Charles IX in November 1568.[51] The following year, he declared that "she has shown that she is a true Queen, daughter of a King, sister of a King, and from all royal birth" and that God had always "differentiated the good and legitimate princes, legitimately blessed by God's approbation, from the evil and iniquitous tyrants." He also stressed the importance of maintaining good relations with her, because "the good and legitimate princes, with good consciousness, act kindly toward the other princes, neighbors, and allies."[52] Although this statement could be viewed as mere diplomatic rhetoric, it reveals a French ambassador who was more than willing to lobby his master on behalf of his host. His self-appointed mission was to convince Charles to think of Elizabeth as his equal and the legitimate Queen of England. Given that her legitimacy had been controversial since the day she had been declared a bastard at just three years of age, the French ambassador's reference to her "royal birth" may be construed as a deliberate attempt to end the debate once and for all.

---

[51] La Mothe Fénélon to the French king Charles IX, 1st Report, November 16, 1568, in *Correspondence diplomatique*, Tome I.

[52] La Mothe Fénélon to the French king Charles IX, 55th Report, September 1, 1569, in *Correspondence diplomatique*, Tome I, 3, "elle avoit monstré qu'elle estoit vrayment Royne, fille de Roy, et seur de Roy, et de toute royale extraction [...] différancé des bons et légitimes princes, légitimemant béniz par approbacion de Dieu, aux meschans et iniques tirans [...]les bons et légitimes princes avoient droictemant, et en bonne consciance, toujours procédé en auaires des autres princes, leurs voisins et allez."

Scholars have explored this notion of Elizabeth's "grandeur" and her representation as the equal of any king. Indeed, Carole Levin has pointed out that English writers perceived her as *both* the King and the Queen of England, especially in the last few years of her reign.[53] La Mothe Fénélon did not go that far, but he never wavered from his conviction that she had just as much right to rule as any other monarch, including his own master. As we shall see, however, French pamphleteers did not share his deferential attitude toward the English queen.

In September 1569, the French ambassador wrote that he had "been sent by a great King to a great Queen," and therefore accorded the two royal houses equal status.[54] In another dispatch, he insisted that it was important to maintain "royal correspondence between a true Queen and a great King."[55] Although La Mothe Fénélon invariably used feminine terms when referring to Elizabeth, from the very beginning of his tenure he depicted her as a powerful monarch and asserted that, "though her sex is weak, I think she is however a rock who will not bend in any direction."[56] After just a couple of weeks in her court, the French ambassador was already convinced that Elizabeth was at least as strong as any other ruler (including Charles IX himself) and could not be bullied into submission. If the French royal family wanted to deal with England, they would have to treat Elizabeth as an equal, not try to dominate her.

To some extent, the term "rock" alluded to Elizabeth's solid royal pedigree,[57] but it also hinted at her granite will and implied that she was unlikely to bow to external pressure. It was the French ambassador's way of reminding his master that Elizabeth was stubborn, tenacious, and immune to manipulation, regardless of her sex. Ten years into her reign, she was an experienced ruler who not only enjoyed supreme royal authority

---

[53] Carole Levin, *The Heart and Stomach of a King*, 121–48.

[54] La Mothe Fénélon to the French king Charles IX, 55th Report, September 1, 1569, in *Correspondence diplomatique*, Tome I, 4, "d'estre envoyé de la part d'ung grand Roy à une grande Royne."

[55] La Mothe Fénélon to the French king Charles IX, 47th Report, July 11, 1569, in *Correspondence diplomatique*, Tome II, 90, "royalle correspondance de vraye Royne avecques ung grand Roy."

[56] La Mothe Fénélon to the French king Charles IX, 1st Report, November 16, 1568, in *Correspondence diplomatique*, Tome I, 5, "le sexe duquel elle estoit fut estimé léger, je la trouverois toutefois ung rocher qui ne se plieroyt à tous sens."

[57] For Carole Levin, Elizabeth was "both woman and man in one, both king and queen together, a male body politic in concept while a female body natural in practice." in Carole Levin, *The heart and stomach of a King*, p. 121.

in her own realm but also felt that her voice should be heard throughout Europe.

As we saw earlier, Elizabeth's advice to the French royal family was frequently couched in terms of justice, peace, and benevolence, but she employed similar tropes when her mind turned to the exercise of royal authority. For instance, in August 1569, La Mothe Fénélon reported:

> regarding the trust that your Most Christian Majesties have in her with respect to your affairs, in communicating them to her privately, she felt obliged to wish you prosperity [...] and to beg you to believe that, regarding the religion in which she believes, and which is implemented in her state, she wishes that your crown, your greatness and authority, as well as that of your Mother, the Queen, remain total and undiminished, as she wishes for herself.[58]

Elizabeth firmly believed that subjects had to respect and obey their monarch's authority—no matter which religion they practiced—and the allusion to royal authority in this report was designed not only to convince her French counterparts of her solidarity in the third religious civil war but also to remind them that she expected similar support in return, if necessary. In other words, Charles should not even consider taking the side of England's Catholics should they decide to rebel against Elizabeth. According to La Mothe Fénélon, the queen was concerned about "the authority that was due to you [Charles] from your subjects as if it were a question of preserving her own authority over her subjects."[59]

The French ambassador's reports of his audiences with Elizabeth reveal a self-assured monarch who was determined to fight her corner and shape her French counterparts' opinion of her. For instance, in response to the

[58] La Mothe Fénélon to the French king Charles IX, 51st Report, August 10, 1569, in *Correspondence diplomatique*, Tome II, 147, "La dicte Dame me respondit que, pour la confiance que Voz Majestez Très Chrestiennes monstriez avoir d'elle en voz affaires, en les luy faisant ainsy privéement communiquer, elle se sentoit obligée d'en desirer la prospérité., comme certes elle faisoit, et vous prioyt de croyre que, demeurant la religion, de laquelle elle estoit, en son estat, elle desiroit au reste que vostre coronne et vostre grandeur et authorité, ensemble celle de la Royne, vostre mère, demeurassent aussi entiers et sans diminution comme elle le desiroit pour elle mesmes."
[59] La Mothe Fénélon to the French king Charles IX, 97th Report, March 27, 1570, in *Correspondence diplomatique*, Tome III, 92, "qu'elle y procèderoit avec aultant de considération de l'authorité qui vous est. deuhe sur voz subjectz, comme s'il estoit question de saulver la sienne sur les siens."

bull of excommunication that Pope Pius V issued against her in January 1570, she declared that "every Christian crown is in bad shape," given the Huguenots' unconscionable rebellion against the French crown and the Pope's unjustified condemnation of "any state that he considers heretical or schismatic."[60] By equating the head of the Catholic Church with the Protestant rebels who were in the process of challenging Charles IX, Elizabeth stressed that the preservation of monarchical authority was of paramount importance, so all rulers should stand together as one whenever it was challenged. Therefore, she expected her French counterparts to refuse any requests for aid and support from Catholic plotters in England, just as she wanted them to believe this is what she had done when France's Huguenots had asked her for assistance.

Six months later, the French ambassador revealed that Elizabeth remained indignant about her excommunication:

> Twice, she told me that the Holy Roman Emperor used to write to her often and showed her affection and benevolence; by contrast, the Pope strove to be unpleasant in his bull by naming her *flagitiorum serva* [servant of crime], but she was not worried about this.[61]

Irrespective of whether the English queen was genuinely unconcerned about the terminology that was used in the papal bull, she clearly felt that it was worth raising the issue with the French ambassador and, therefore, with his master Charles IX. She yet again signaled that royal authority trumped religious authority by drawing a contrast between the Pope's

---

[60] La Mothe Fénélon to the French king Charles IX, 81st Report, January 4, 1570, in *Correspondence diplomatique*, Tome III, 4, "Et luy ayant seulement répliqué ce mot « c'est. qu'il est. fort à craindre que, tant que la division de la religion » durera, que l'on sera toutz les ans a recommancer, elle m'a soubdain respondu qu'a la vérité puisque les Protestans commancent de proposer entre eulx, assavoir s'il y a aucune cause pour laquelle l'on puisse sellon Dieu et conscience, se soubstraire de l'obéyssance d'ung prince et le démettre de son estat; ainsy que le Pape, de son costé, déclaire aussi les estats de ceulx, qu'il tient pour scismatiques ou.hérétiques, toutz comis et vacquans; elle estime que toutes les couronnes de la Chrestienté sont assez mal."

[61] La Mothe Fénélon to the French king Charles IX, 115th Report, June 19, 1570, in *Correspondence diplomatique*, Tome III, 199, "par deux foys, à propos de me dire que l'Empereur luy a naguières escript avec aultant d'abondance, d'affection et de bienveuillance comme au contraire le Pape s'est. esforcé de luy donner ung bien mauvais salut par une sienne bulle, en laquelle il l'appelle flagiciorum serva mais que c'est. chose de quoy elle ne se soucye guiere."

impulsive, unreasonable behavior and the Holy Roman Emperor's affection, perhaps with the aim of garnering a declaration of support from another benevolent ruler, Charles, in expectation of an upsurge of Catholic hostility against her.

Elizabeth's royal authority was inextricably linked to her refusal to marry, as her single status ensured that she remained the sole and primary royal authority in England. Her French counterparts surely understood this, yet they seemed unable to believe that the queen had no interest in securing a husband and instructed La Mothe Fénélon to keep them abreast of any marriage negotiations.

On November 27, 1570, Charles IX married the Emperor Maximilian II's daughter, Elizabeth of Austria. However, prior to this union, during the summer of 1569, Catherine had once again raised the possibility of a marriage between Charles and Elizabeth of England.[62] After receiving Catherine's instructions, La Mothe Fénélon wrote to Charles to extol the English queen's "great qualities that God has invested in her—beauty, knowledge, virtue, and the greatness of a state."[63] This time, Elizabeth had no hesitation in dismissing Charles's (or rather his mother's) advances. However, La Mothe Fénélon's report of her refusal returned to a familiar theme:

> the King would not want her, as he would be ashamed to enter Paris with a queen for his wife who looks as old as she is, and she is not at an age when she can leave her country, as the Queen of Scotland did when she arrived so young in France.[64]

[62] Catherine de Medici proposed all her sons to Elizabeth I of England, even Henry d'Anjou, future Henry III of France, as a letter to La Mothe Fénélon demonstrated: Catherine de Medici to La Mothe Fénélon, May 4 1570, in *LCM*, Tome III, 314, "Sur quoy ledict ambassadeur me fit response que, si je parlois pour mon fils le duc d'Anjou, qu'il en escriroit vollontiers, etqu'il pensoit que sa maîtresse aurait bien agréable d'en ouïr parler."
[63] La Mothe Fénélon to the French king Charles IX, 48th Report, July 27, 1569, in *Correspondence diplomatique*, Tome II, 117, "grandes qualité, que Dieu avoit miz en elle, de beaulté, de sçavoir, de vertu et de grandeur d'estat, pour ne vouloir laysser aulcune belle postérité après elle pour y succéder."
[64] La Mothe Fénélon to the French king Charles IX, 48th Report, July 27, 1569, 118, "que le Roy ne vouldroit poinct d'elle, et qu'il se tiendroit tout honteux de monstrer, à une entrée à Paris, une Royne pour sa femme, qui parût si vieille qu'elle feroit, et qu'elle n'estoit plus en eage pour sortir de son pays, comme avoit faict la Royne d'Escoce, quant on la porta bien jeune en France."

As in 1565, then, Elizabeth used the age difference between herself and Charles as a convenient excuse to decline the offer without offending Catherine's and Charles's sensibilities. More significantly, though, she made an important point by comparing herself with Mary Stuart, who had traveled to France in 1548, before her sixth birthday. The implication was clear: Elizabeth was not a pliant, obedient child who was prepared to relinquish her crown to become the consort of a French king, as Mary had been. Rather, she was a powerful ruler who had no intention of abandoning her country and losing her royal authority. She, and she alone, would rule England until the day she died. At the end of his report, La Mothe Fénélon asserted: "the private councillors of this realm are resolved that their Queen will never marry, and if she seems to entertain the prospect it will be merely to keep the world occupied so her subjects will not urge her to announce a successor to her crown."[65]

This determination to remain unmarried and, consequently, maintain her royal authority forced the French court to perceive Elizabeth as Charles IX's equal. Her subjects continued to pressurize her to marry and produce an heir, but she remained resolute, as La Mothe Fénélon reported in November 1569:

> She replied that if her subjects loved her and wished to see her live and have descendants, they needed to give her the freedom to choose to marry or not [...] [R]egarding the convocation of her parliament, none of her predecessors had ever convoked it more than three times in their reign, whereas she has already had four of them, and during the last one she was tormented over the marriage issue, so she is resolved on two matters: the first is that she will never summon parliament again, and the other is that she will never marry, and she has decided to die with that opinion.[66]

---

[65] La Mothe Fénélon to the French king Charles IX, 48th Report, July 27, 1569, 119, "Les principaulx de ce royaulme tiennent pour résolu que leur Royne ne se mariera jamais, et quant bien elle en feroit quelque semblant ce ne seroit que pour amuser le monde afin que ses subjectz ne la pressent de déclairer son successeur à la couronne."

[66] La Mothe Fénélon to the French king Charles IX, 74th Report, November 25, 1569, in *Correspondence diplomatique*, Tome III, 355, "elle a respondu que, si ses subjectz l'aymoient et desiroient la veoir vivre ou avoir lignée d'elle, qu'ilz debvoient la laysser en sa liberté de se maryer ou non [...] quant à convoquer son parlement, que nul de ses prédécesseurs n'en avoit jamais tenu que trois en sa vie, et elle en avoit desjà tenu quatre, dont, en ce dernier, ôn l'avoit tant tourmentée de ceste matière de mariage, qu'on l'avoit faicte résouldre à deux choses l'une, ne tenir jamais plus parlement, et l'autre, de ne se marier jamais, et qu'elle delliberoit mourir en ceste opinion."

This account echoes a speech Elizabeth delivered to Parliament in 1566, during which she declared: "I will deal therein for your safety and offer it unto you as your prince and head, without request. For it is monstrous that the feet should direct the head."[67] A year later, she dissolved Parliament on account of the members' incessant hectoring over her single status and the succession. Dismissing them, she stated, "as to liberties, who is so simple that doubts whether a prince that is head of all body may not command the feet not to stray when they would slip? God forbid that your liberty should make my bondage."[68] These two speeches revealed the English queen's firm intention to defend her royal authority and legitimacy as an unmarried woman and sole ruler.

She used the word "head" in both speeches to draw attention to the "male" side of her royal identity. This suggests that she was familiar with John Knox's famous aphorism "the head should not follow the feet"[69]— that is, men should not be guided by women. Elizabeth positioned herself not as a woman but as England's only legitimate monarch, which meant she was the "head" while the Members of Parliament were "the feet." Two years later, notwithstanding a challenge to her royal authority in the form of the Northern Rebellion, she displayed the same stubbornness and determination to rule alone during her frequent audiences with La Mothe Fénélon.

Although the French ambassador had depicted Elizabeth as "a true sister" and a peaceful queen in his first report to Charles IX, at the time she had warned him of her temper, declaring that she was "of the species of lions that soon relent if they are not browbeaten, but anger quickly when provoked."[70] Here, Elizabeth not only reminded the ambassador of her legitimate right to rule England—which had featured lions on its coat of arms since the twelfth century—but also indicated that she was fully prepared to defend herself if attacked or "provoked." Interestingly, although she was happy to project this rather fearsome, masculine image

---

[67] Queen Elizabeth's Speech to a Joint Delegation of Lords and Commons, November 5, 1566, in *Elizabeth I: Collected Works*, 98.

[68] Queen Elizabeth's speech dissolving Parliament, January 2, 1567, in *Elizabeth I: Collected Works*, 105.

[69] John Strype (ed.), *Annals of the Reformation and Establishment of Religion* (Oxford: Clarendon Press, 1874), 7.

[70] La Mothe Fénélon to the French king Charles IX, 1st Report, November 16, 1568, in *Correspondence diplomatique*, Tome I, 5, "qu'èle estoit de race de lion, qui s'adoulcissoit bien tost s'il n'estoit rudoyé, mais estant provoqué, il s'irritoit incontinant."

to her French counterparts, English gentlemen tended to view her rather differently, at least at the beginning of her reign. For instance, in 1559, John Aylmer focused on the queen's feminine attributes, claiming that "she commeth in lyke a lambe, and not lyke a Lyon."[71] Nine years later, however, there was no sign of lamb-like compliance as she faced the prospect of an uprising in the north of her realm. In November 1568, La Mothe Fénélon informed Charles that

> tomorrow, in Hampton Court, she will assemble the Duke of Norfolk and other major earls and barons of her court [...] to resolve what we believe to be the affairs of the Queen of Scotland [...] [T]here are many Catholics in this county who could, because of this princess, attempt to launch a rebellion in the country.[72]

This fear proved well founded twelve months later when a group of Catholic nobles from the north of England—including Charles Neville, Earl of Westmorland, and Thomas Percy, Earl of Northumberland—occupied Durham and celebrated Mass in the city's cathedral. These nobles had nurtured the hope of replacing Elizabeth with her cousin Mary ever since the latter's flight from Scotland in May 1568. They planned to arrange her marriage to Thomas Howard, the Duke of Norfolk—a powerful noble—before deposing and killing Elizabeth.[73]

---

[71] John Aylmer, *An Harborowe for faithful and trewe subjects*, (London, 1559), N4v.

[72] La Mothe Fénélon to the French king Charles IX, 2nd Report, November 22, 1568, in *Correspondence diplomatique*, Tome I, 11–13, "convoque demain à Hantoncourt les ducs' de Norfoc, et les contes et principaulx barons de sa court [...] pour résouldre cepandant, ainsi qu'on dict, les affères de la Royne d'Escoce [...] souz prétexte qu'il y a beaucoup de catholiques en icelle contrée, qui pourroient, a cause de ceste princesse, attempter quelque rébellion dans le pays." Also see Krista Kesselring, *The Northern Rebellion of 1569: Faith, Politics, and Protest in Elizabethan England* (New York: Palgrave Macmillan, 2010), 46–47.

[73] Charles IX was well aware of this proposed marriage and encouraged it secretly. In letters to La Mothe Fénélon, he showed his desire to see the marriage happening, see Charles IX to La Mothe Fénélon, July 27, 1569, in *Correspondence diplomatique*, 35, "Au demeurant, m'en m'a adverty que la Royne d'Escosse est. bien avant en propoz de mariage avec le duc de Norfolc, et que l'on espère que les choses s'en pourront mener à quelque bonne fin; ce que j'ai occasion de desirer beaucoup plustost qu'il se fasse." Furthermore, Charles IX ordered in a coded letter that his ambassador played a role in the potential marriage, Charles IX to La Mothe Fénélon, September 20, 1569, in *Correspondence diplomatique*, Tome VII, 53, "Chiffré, j'ay sceu ce qui a esté mis eh avant pour le faict du mariage de la Royne d'Escosse, mabettesoeur, avec le duc de Norfolc, lequel j'ay occasion de desirer qu'il s'effectue pour beaucoup de grands respectz et considérations, et mesmes pour l'affection

As she formulated her response to the plotters, Elizabeth knew that the French royal family would be watching her closely, and they would expect her to justify all of her actions toward Mary. Before long, French pamphleteers added to the pressure on the English queen with accusations that she had mistreated Mary and Norfolk.[74] For instance, one pamphlet printed by Nicolas Chesneau—a devout and militant Catholic who had connections at the French court[75]—held Elizabeth personally responsible for Mary's imprisonment and labeled her a defender of Protestantism.[76] Given Chesneau's contacts with elite French society, his diatribe may well have attracted the attention of the royal family. If so, they may have thought that it did not diverge too far from La Mothe Fénélon's recent depictions of a more belligerent queen.

Moreover, Elizabeth was not averse to displaying this aspect of her personality when responding to the French court's repeated requests for information about Mary. As noted above, she had previously emphasized her commitment to justice and benevolence when offering advice to Charles or justifying her own maintenance of royal authority. Now, though, she seemed determined to demonstrate that she was indeed a "lion," and a rather vexed one at that. In February 1569, La Mothe Fénélon expressed his master's concern over Mary's continuing imprisonment, to which Elizabeth replied, "a bit angry, that she had not used force or violence against the Queen of Scotland, and that she had put her in a place where she would be better treated than where she had stayed before."[77]

que j'ay tousjours cognue que le dict duc de Norfolc a porté à l'entretènement de la paix entre ce royaume et celuy d'Angleterre, et aussy que je croy qu'il ne se pourroit présenter aucun autre party, du quel ma dicte belle soeur puisse recepvoir plus de bien, proffit et advantaige, pour son particullier, que de celluy là; et à ceste cause, je veux que vous vous employés dextrèment en cest affaire, et le favorisiés de si bonne façon qu'il en puisse réuscyr quelque bon-effect."

[74] For example see *Continuation des choses plus celebres et memorables advenues en Angleterre, Ecosse et Irlande* (Michel Jove, Lyon, 1570), BNF, Résac. 8 NC 155 and *Discours des troubles nouvellement advenuz au royaume d'Angleterre* (Chez Nicolas Chesneau, Paris, 4 October 1570), BNF, Résac. 8 NC 154 A.

[75] Luc Racaut, "Nicolas Chesneau: Catholic Printer in Paris during the French Wars of Religion, 1558–1584," *Historical Journal* 52, (2009): 23–41 and Luc Racaut, "'Une juste moitié de vos livres': Le rôle de la propagande religieuse dans la production pamphlétaire," in *Médialité et interprétation contemporaine des premières guerres de Religion*, eds. Gabriele Haug-Moritz et Lothar Schilling (Paris: De Gruyter Oldenbourg, 2014), 39.

[76] "the Queen of Scots was imprisoned by order of the Queen of England" in *Discours des troubles nouvellement advenuz au royaume d'Angleterre*, 16.

[77] La Mothe Fénélon to the French king Charles IX, 17th Report, February 10, 1569, in *Correspondence diplomatique*, Tome I, 188, "ung peu en collère, qu'elle n'avoit point faict

The English queen exercised admirable self-control during most of her audiences with the French ambassador, but sometimes her temper got the better of her. For instance, in September 1569, La Mothe Fénélon informed Charles that "some wicked people had upset her [Elizabeth's] heart against the Queen of Scotland" regarding Mary's claim to the English crown.[78] Then, a few days later, he reported Elizabeth's fierce reaction upon hearing the news that the Duke of Norfolk intended to marry Mary:

> the Queen of England and the Duke of Norfolk exchanged intense words [...] and I hear that she is furious that he was considering, without her knowledge, marrying the Queen of Scotland, and expressly forbade him from persisting with his plan in any way.[79]

This account demonstrates that Elizabeth was willing and able to intervene in the marriage plans of any and all of her subjects. As such, her royal authority equaled or exceeded that of any male monarch in Europe. Nevertheless, La Mothe Fénélon reported that the uprising in northern England left her demoralized: "it is said that the Queen of England bears a true pain in her heart about the uprising in the North, tearfully saying that she has never deserved this from her subjects."[80] This unprecedented display of emotion at court was testament to the fact that Elizabeth considered respect for her royal authority of paramount importance. In September 1569, the French ambassador found her "more jealous and

---

force ny violence à la Royne d'Escoce, et qu'elle l'avoit faicte venir en ung lieu pour estre mieulx trettée que là où elle estoit au paravant."

[78] La Mothe Fénélon to the French king Charles IX, 56th Report, September 5, 1569, in *Correspondence diplomatique*, Tome II, 219, "Je viens d'entendre que quelques mauvaises personnes luy ont merveilleusement soublevé le cueur contre la Royne d'Escoce par ung aultre nouveau moyen, après qu'ilz ont veu que celluy de la cession du tiltre de ce royaulme demeuroit convaincu par les amples déclarations de Vostre Majesté; c'est. qu'ilz luy ont persuadé que, n'ayant ta dicte Royne d'Escoce peu parvenir au premier et plus eminent lieu de ceste coronne."

[79] La Mothe Fénélon to Catherine, September 14, 1569, in *Correspondence diplomatique*, Tome II, 236, "il y avoit eu de grosses parolles entre la Royne d'Angleterre et le duc de Norfolc, [...] j'entendz qu'elle s'estoit corroucée fort asprement à luy de ce qu'il trettoit, sans son sceu, de se maryer avec la Royne d'Escoce, lui deffendant fort exprésséement de n'y prétandre plus, en quelque façon que ce soit."

[80] La Mothe Fénélon to Catherine, November 30, 1569, in *Correspondence diplomatique*, Tome II, 371, "L'on dict que la Royne d'Angleterre porte ung merveilleux ennuy dans son cueur de ceste esiévation du North, disant avecques larmes qu'elle n'a, rien moins mérité que cella de ses subjectz."

defiant than ever toward the Queen of Scotland and demanded that her watch must be doubled." She was also still "extremely furious toward the Duke, and infinitely toward the Queen of Scotland."[81]

To some extent, such statements were consistent with contemporary prejudice against women, as espoused by the influential Scottish clergyman John Knox in his infamous book *The first blast of the trumpet against the monstruous regiment of women*, in which he claimed that they "lack prudence and right reason to judge the things that be spoken."[82] Yet, while the French ambassador had no hesitation in depicting a "furious" and "angry" queen in some of his dispatches, he never once described Elizabeth as foolish or irrational in her policies toward Mary and the Northern Rebellion. Instead, he attributed her occasional displays of anger at court to the exercise of traditional monarchical—and therefore predominantly male—authority rather than feminine weakness. Moreover, he reinforced this representation with frequent references to her "heart," and indeed the suggestion that it "might be too hard,"[83] because the heart was popularly associated with the most courageous aspects of kingship (e.g., Richard the Lionheart).

The reference to Elizabeth's hard heart implied that she would not be moved by appeals for clemency in the case of Mary Stuart. On another level, it suggested that she was well up to the task of ruling as the undisputed monarch of England, and was prepared to vent her anger in the interests of asserting her monarchical authority. In one report, La Mothe Fénélon described her furious reaction to some English lords who attempted to excuse the Duke of Norfolk's involvement in the Northern Rebellion:

> One of them dared to say that, according to the laws of the realm, they [the rebels] were guilty of nothing. "Mad men," she replied, "what the laws of this realm cannot do to his head, my authority will" [...] The next day the

---

[81] La Mothe Fénélon to the French king Charles IX, 60th Report, September 23, 1569, in *Correspondence diplomatique*, Tome II, 246, "plus grande jalousie et deffiance qu'elle n'avoit encores esté de la Royne d'Escoce, et a vollu que, oultre le redoublement des gardes" and La Mothe Fénélon to the French king Charles IX, 66th Report, October 18, 1569, 289, "elle estoit grandement courroucée contre le dict duc, et infinyement contre la Royne d'Escoce."

[82] John Knox, *The first blast of the trumpet against the monstruous regiment of women* (Geneva, J. Poullain and A. Rebul, 1558), STC 15070, 24.

[83] La Mothe Fénélon to the French king Charles IX, 62nd Report, October 3, 1569, in *Correspondence diplomatique*, Tome II, 257, "pour luy en esmouvoir le cueur, si elle ne l'a trop dur."

Duke was sent to the Tower, and immediately his house was searched, his mail opened, his papers seized, and Norfolk's gentlemen were brought in for questioning and to testify against him.[84]

Here, yet again, Elizabeth demonstrated her strong will and preeminence over all of her subjects, and especially anyone who dared to challenge her authority. Furthermore, according to La Mothe Fénélon, she openly challenged Parliament and even went so far as to place her own authority above the laws of the realm. This particular display of autocratic power may have been a reaction to the precarious situation in which she found herself in 1569, but she never lacked the wherewithal to intimidate and overpower her foes.

As we have seen, the French ambassador felt that Elizabeth's monarchical authority rested on various aspects of her personality. From likening herself to a lion to her open displays of anger at court, Elizabeth demanded respect as an equal to her male counterparts, while La Mothe Fénélon dutifully recorded every last detail of a ruler whom he held in great esteem. Nevertheless, as time went on, his accounts contained ever more warnings of the difficulties the French royal family might encounter in their future dealings with Elizabeth, which helped to sow the seeds of tension and mistrust in Anglo-French relations.

## THE SCHEMING PROTESTANT QUEEN

Although Charles IX and Catherine de Medici recognized Elizabeth's good qualities and acknowledged her as an equal, they were not convinced by her repeated assurances of peaceful intent, and it is easy to discern a degree of mistrust in their correspondence with their ambassador. Moreover, this was exacerbated by her alleged assistance to the Huguenots in France's latest religious civil war. Susan Doran suggests that Elizabeth fully embraced the role of Protestant heroine by providing financial support to the rebels.[85] The correspondence between the French and English

[84] La Mothe Fénélon to the French king Charles IX, 68th Report, October 28, 1569, in *Correspondence diplomatique*, Tome II, 302, "l'ung d'eulx s'advança de. dire que selton les loix du pays ilz ne le trouvoient coulpable de rien « A liez, dict elle, ce que lesloix ne pourront sur sa teste, mon authorité le pourra. » [...] Ainsy fut le dict duc envoyé te lendemain à la Tour, et aussi tost ordonné de visiter ses maysons, ouvrir ses coures, saysir ses papiers, mandé tes gentishommes de Norfolcpour venir déposer et tesmoigner contre luy."

[85] Susan Doran, *England and Europe (1485–1603)* (London: Longman, 1986), 58–59.

courts reveals that the French royal family did not perceive her as a Protestant savior between 1568 and 1570; however, they did start to view her as a deceitful queen and a potential enemy.

In July 1569, Catherine explicitly expressed her concern over Elizabeth's policies toward the Huguenots and her increasingly belligerent attitude:

> Monsieur de la Mothe Fénélon, all we can learn from your last dispatches is that the Queen of England, my good sister, does not neglect any of the preparations that are necessary to go to war [...] [I believe] that the only thing that prevents her from declaring it openly is that she wants to see if we will first have some success over our enemies.[86]

The ambassador's letters fueled these concerns because he was duty bound to report any suspicious activities at court, particularly any hint that the queen might be on the verge of issuing a declaration of war. Although he continued to insist that Elizabeth was not actively seeking war with the French crown, the contents of his reports inevitably led to a different conclusion in Paris.

In December 1568, for example, La Mothe Fénélon informed Charles IX that William Winter, the Vice-Admiral of England, "went sailing and took with him the Queen's great ships."[87] This aroused suspicions that Winter was ferrying munitions to the Prince of Condé in La Rochelle for use against Charles's forces, even though the ambassador was unable to confirm the fleet's destination. Four months later, on April 6, 1569, La Mothe Fénélon reported that Elizabeth was endeavoring to preserve the peace between the two crowns in the face of concerted pressure from

---

[86] Catherine de Medici to La Mothe Fénélon, July 9, 1569, in *LCM*, Tome III, 260–1, "Monsieur de la Mothe-Fénélon, tout ce que nous pouvons recueillir de vos dernières dépescb.es, c'est. que la royne d'Angleterre, ma bonne soeur, n'oublie rien de tous les appretz qui sont nécessaires pour l'acheminement d'une guerre estimant bien que ce qui la peult retenir jusques icy de se déclarer ouvertement, c'est. qu'elle veult auparavant veoyr un peu clair à ce que auront d'heureux succez les affaires de nos ennemys."

[87] La Mothe Fénélon to the French king Charles IX, 6th Report, December 15, 1568, in *Correspondence diplomatique*, Tome I, 44, "M. Oynter visadmiral d'Angleterre, j'ay, depuis, envoyé sçavoir, au vray, s'il estoit encores party de la coste de deçà et m'a esté rapporté, Sire, que, pour certain, il a faict voile avec les ung grandz navires de ceste Royne, et disent aulcungs que c'est vers la Guyenne droict à la Rochelle, pour consigner au prince de Condé les canons, poudres et munitions."

some of her advisers to declare war.[88] Moreover, the following month he expressed concern that "people are demanding that the forces of the realm are mustered [...] [W]e fear that they are planning some enterprises outside the realm."[89]

French anxiety peaked in July 1569, when the ambassador informed the royal family that the English queen had "armed ships with men ready for an enterprise [...] [T]o me, she still seems inclined to maintain the peace [...] [but] the only way to make her preserve the peace will be to succeed in your affairs."[90] With the trust between the two crowns at an all-time low since Elizabeth's accession to the throne, Charles IX wrote to his ambassador in Spain. He was now convinced that he would have

> to prevent the Queen of England's and Duke of Casimir's invasion of my realm with the forces they have gathered for this. Thank God I feel sufficiently strong with the forces I have at my disposal to bring my enemies to reason, as long as they are not helped by outsiders. Some of them think that they can be saved by the Queen of England [...] [and] they will try to exploit this situation and use her bad intentions against me to ensure that many forces troops descend on my armies.[91]

[88] La Mothe Fénélon to the French king Charles IX, 28th Report, April 6, 1569, in *Correspondence diplomatique*, Tome I, 295, "je suis bien informé que la dicte Dame, encor que plusieurs la persuadent à la guerre et qu'elle veuille obtempérer, autant qu'il. possible, à ceulx de son conseil, si donne elle ordre qu' il y en ayt toutjours quelques ungs d'eulx qui luy conseillent la paix et l'espargne et elle trouve moyen de fère authoriser et approuver leurs oppinions."

[89] La Mothe Fénélon to the French king Charles IX, 37th Report, May 23, 1569, in *Correspondence diplomatique*, Tome I, 400, "est vray qu'on mande souvant à dresser l'ordre des forces de ce royaulme [...] qu'on y crainct, que pour fère quelque entreprinse hors du pays."

[90] La Mothe Fénélon to Catherine de Medici, July 5, 1569, in *Correspondence diplomatique*, Tome II, 77, "vaysseaulx armez et hommes prestz pour une occasion [...] qu'elle ne me semble de soy toutjour bien disposée à la paix [...] le seul bon succez de voz affaires la fera persévérér en la paix."

[91] Charles IX of France to Fourquevaux, July 5, 1569, BNF, MS Fr, n° 10,752, fol. 269, "pour empêcher que la royne d'Angleterre et le duc Casimir n'entrassent en mon royaume aveques les forces qu'ils assemblent pour cest effect. Dieu meicy, je me sents assez fort avec les forces que j'ay pour ranger mes ennemis à la raison, pourvru qu'ils ne soient secourus de dehors et tiens pour certain qu'ils doivent l'estre de la rovne d'Angleterre [...] de se servir de l'occasion el mettre à profit sa mauvaise volonté contre moy, de façon que considérant tant de forces me tomber sur les bras."

The French court was tense, and Elizabeth was viewed as a potential enemy who might declare war at any moment. Meanwhile, though, she had similar misgivings about the French royal family, whom she perceived as uncomfortably close to the Guises, one of several powerful Catholic families who sought her ruin.

Mary de Guise was Mary Stuart's mother, while her nephew, Henry I, Duke of Guise, was a fervent Catholic and staunch defender of both his religion and his family's interests at home and abroad. He became a leader of the Catholic factions during France's wars of religion and was renowned for his bravery and victories on the battlefield as well as his great hatred of Protestantism in general and the Huguenots in particular. When his cousin Mary fled to Protestant England, he was understandably concerned about the reception she would receive from Elizabeth.[92] Meanwhile, the queen was acutely aware of the threat that the Guises posed to her royal authority and her relations with the French royal family. Indeed, she informed the French ambassador that "she considered the members of the House of Guise to have declared themselves enemies of herself and her state, and she could not be reassured, given that they have great authority through both their armies and their counsel in France."[93]

This aversion to the Guise family had a significant impact on Elizabeth's relations with the French royal family. She feared that after resolving the civil war in France, Charles would decide to "do the same in England," and that was something she would rather "prevent than be warned." The French ambassador attempted to reassure her of France's good intentions by exhorting her to remember "the mutual friendship" between the two crowns and suggested that she should "not take into account the friendship or hatred that she might feel toward any of Charles IX's subjects."[94] Yet, Elizabeth found it increasingly difficult to trust the French royal

[92] Charles Cauvin, *Henry de Guise, Le Balafré: Histoire de France de 1563 à 1589* (Tours: Alfred Mame et Fils, 1881), 165.

[93] La Mothe Fénélon to the French king Charles IX, 7th Report, December 21, 1568, in *Correspondence diplomatique*, Tome I, 56, "qu'elle tenoit ceulx de la maison de Guise pour si declares ennemys d'elle et de-son estat, qu'elle ne se pouvoit assurer, voyant qu'ilz- avoient grand authorité tant aux armes que au conseil en France."

[94] La Mothe Fénélon to the French king Charles IX, 7th Report, December 21, 1568, 56, "mesmes qu'il estait eschappé à quelcung de votre conseil de dire, qu'après que vous auriez appaysé et remis les choses de!a relligion en votre- royauime, vous entendriez incontinent faire le mesmes en Angleterre, et qu'elle aymoit mieulx prévenir qu'estre prévenue. De quoy, Sire, je luy toucheray ung mot en ma première audiance, qu'elle m'a accordée à mercredy prochain, et luy remonstreray doulxemant que le debvoir de votre mutuelle amytié oblige de

family because she remained unsure of their intentions regarding her country, which in turn influenced the ways in which La Mothe Fénélon represented her in his reports. After one audience in April 1569, he informed Charles that "she will not go to war, unless she is greatly provoked."[95] Although such accounts were consistent with the ambassador's earlier depictions of a peace-loving queen, they also reminded the French royal family of the warnings he had issued regarding her temper, determination, and courage: she was a "lion" who would not hesitate to launch an attack if she felt threatened.

In April 1569, it emerged that her gravest fear was a Franco-Spanish alliance against England. La Mothe Fénélon reported that she despised "the Duke of Alva, whom she finds cruel, and the Spanish, who are intolerable." Moreover, "she has great suspicions regarding two enterprises that she has been assured will be launched soon against her and her state— one from France and the other from Flanders."[96] However, the following month, the queen's anxiety seemed to have eased slightly, as the French ambassador reported that "she remained satisfied" by his reassurances.[97]

Meanwhile, across the Channel, the French royal family's suspicions regarding Elizabeth's intentions were hardly assuaged when her thoughts turned Calais, which England had ceded to France in January 1558. For instance, in June 1569, she told La Mothe Fénélon that she "wanted to negotiate again about Calais, on which she had firm proposals."[98] Such declarations merely served to highlight the threat that England posed to France and invariably cranked up the tension between the two nations.

---

s'adjoind're à voz présentes intantions, sans mectre en aulcung compte ny l'amytié ny la ayne qu'elle pourroit avoir à aulcungs de voz subjectz."

[95] La Mothe Fénélon to the French king Charles IX, 28th Report, April 6, 1569, in *Correspondence diplomatique*, Tome I, 294, "qu'elle ne vous; commencera là guerre, si elle n'y est. bien fort provoquée."

[96] La Mothe Fénélon to the French king Charles IX, 28th Report, April 6, 1569, 294, "duc d'Alve et l'estime si cruel, et les Espaignolz si intollérables" and La Mothe Fénélon to the French king Charles IX, 37th Report, May 23, 1569, in *Correspondence diplomatique*, Tome I, 398, "Elle est. tumbée en grand souspeçon de deux entreprinses, qu'on l'eu asseurée se dresser et se debvoir bien prochainement exécuter contre elle et contre son estat, l'une, du costé de France, et l'aultre, du costé de Flandres."

[97] La Mothe Fénélon to the French king Charles IX, 37th Report, May 23, 1569, 398, "qu'elle en demeure satisfaicte."

[98] La Mothe Fénélon to the French king Charles IX, 41st Report, June 10, 1569, in *Correspondence diplomatique*, Tome II, 20, "la Royne d'Angleterre vouloit rentrer en demandes sur le faict de Callais, et en atacher bien ferme une pratique."

At times, Charles and Catherine were left incredulous by Elizabeth's repeated assurances of peaceful intent. Indeed, by now, Catherine was deeply suspicious of her "true sister." In July 1569, she ordered La Mothe Fénélon

> to visit the Queen of England, my good sister, as often as possible because I think that she is hiding important matters and knows how to disguise her real intentions, so, by meeting her often, it will be easier for you to discover the truth.[99]

The "truth" that Catherine sought was evidence that Elizabeth was helping her coreligionists, the Huguenots, in their rebellion against the French crown.

Seven months earlier, in his fourth report to the French king, La Mothe Fénélon had revealed that the English queen "has been pressured by those in favor of her religion, and they are ready to help the Huguenots with six cannons, powder, and munitions."[100] This reference to a queen under pressure offers an interesting contrast to the ambassador's usual depictions of Elizabeth as a powerful and self-assured ruler. However, he reverted to type in a supplementary letter to Catherine de Medici, written on the very same day, in which he presented Elizabeth's staunch assertion that the armaments would be used solely to protect English merchants from pirates during their voyages to and from Flanders.[101]

Her explanation fell on deaf ears, though, because the French rulers already viewed Elizabeth as a deceptive schemer. Despite all of her assertions

[99] Catherine de Medici to La Mothe Fénélon, July 18, 1569, in *LCM*, Tome III, 260–1, "de visiter la royne d'Angleterre, ma bonne soeur, le plus souvent qu'il vous est. possible; car, encore que j'estime qu'elle soit en ses propos bien fort réservé, et sache assez bien couvrir le font de ses intentions, sy esl-ce que, par cette fréquentation, il vous sera toujours aisé d'en découvrir quelque partie."

[100] La Mothe Fénélon to the French king Charles IX, 4th Report, December 5, 1568, in *Correspondence diplomatique*, Tome I, 24, "presses en faveur de ceulx de sa religion, et, possible, de leur prêter quelque secrèt secours, comme des six canons, pouldres et munitions."

[101] La Mothe Fénélon to Catherine de Medici, December 5, 1568, in *Correspondence diplomatique*, Tome I, 25, "Elle me respondit qu'elle ne faisoit doubte qu'on ne vous eust faict plusieurs rapportz là dessus, mais elle vous prioyt de croire que c'estoit seulement pour l'occasion des marchandises, que ses subjectz avoient à porter et rapporter de Flandres, et pour la flotte qu'ilz avoient envoyée pour les vins à Bourdeaux, qui estimoient le tout estre en danger à cause des pirates, et Portugals, et de tant de gens de guerre, qui passent et repassent maintenant en ceste mer." Robert Bruce Wernham discusses Elizabeth's foreign policy during these years in *The Making of Elizabethan Foreign Policy 1558–1603*, 38–41.

of peaceful intent, the French ambassador feared that "secretly and without declaring herself, she could be helping the Huguenots' enterprises."[102] In April 1569, again citing the need to defend English vessels from pirate attack, Elizabeth

> sent new ordinances and orders against them in each port [...] because they are stealing, at this time, as much from her subjects as from yours [Charles IX's] [...] [R]egarding the restitution of goods, she promised to me, with her Queen's words, to return everything that belonged to the French.[103]

Although Elizabeth repeatedly denied that England was providing any aid to the Huguenots, a letter from Jeanne d'Albret to the Tudor queen, which was sent a few days before La Mothe Fénélon's report, casts considerable doubt on her assertions: "If it pleases you, Madame, continue to display your good will by rescuing us with the means that God has given you, and do what will please Him and is worthy of your greatness and magnanimous heart."[104] Three months later, in July 1569, while the English queen still maintained that "she did not know that the fleet carried anything that could offend [the French king], and those in La Rochelle could not boast of receiving any money, munitions, or food from her,"[105] d'Albret wrote again from the port "humbly to thank you for the assistance that it has pleased you to give us and we humbly beg you to continue this favor."[106] These letters leave no doubt that the French royal

---

[102] La Mothe Fénélon to the French king Charles IX, 6th Report, December 15, 1568, in *Correspondence diplomatique*, Tome I, 47, "secrètement, et sans se déclairer, elle pourra aider leurs entreprinses."

[103] La Mothe Fénélon to the French king Charles IX, 30th Report, April 17, 1569, in *Correspondence diplomatique*, Tome I, 311, "elle avoit envoyé novelles ordonnances et provisions contre eulx par toutz ses portz, [...] car ilz pilloient, à ceste heure, aussi bien ses subjectz que les vôtres et quant à la restitution des prinses, qu'elle me prométoit, en parolle de Royne, de fère rendre tout ce qui apparoistroit appartenir aulx Françoys."

[104] Jeanne d'Albret to Elizabeth I of England, April 13, 1569, written in La Rochelle, TNA SP 70/106, fol. 110, "qu'il vous plaise, Madame, continuer ceste bonne volonté, nous secourant des moyens que Dieu vous a mis et, oullre ce que vous ferez une oeuvre qui lui sera agréable et digne de vostre grandeur et coeur magnanime."

[105] La Mothe Fénélon to the French king Charles IX, 47th Report, July 11, 1569, in *Correspondence diplomatique*, Tome II, 92, "qu'elle ne sçavoit qu'on eust aporté en la dicte flotte aulcune chose qui vous deût offancer, et que ceulx de la Rochelle ne se pouvoient vanter d'avoir eu de son argent, nyde ses munitions, ny de ses vivres."

[106] Jeanne d'Albret to Elizabeth I of England, July 19, 1569, written in La Rochelle, BL, Cottonian Library, E VI, 106, "vous remercier très humblement de l'assistance qu'il vous plaist nous faire, vous priant très humblement nous continuer cette faveur."

family's suspicions were entirely justified: Elizabeth was indeed helping the Huguenots. However, they were unable to prove it, despite Catherine's repeated instructions to La Mothe Fénélon to find some hard evidence of the queen's duplicity.[107]

In June 1569, Catherine told the French ambassador in Spain that she had "true and certain intelligence that for a few days the Queen of England has wanted to launch an attack in Picardy or Normandy."[108] Moreover, Charles started to express similar concerns in his letters. For instance, the following month, he ordered La Mothe Fénélon to demand the return of goods that English sailors had seized from French vessels,[109] and he raised the same issue in March 1570,[110] presumably because Elizabeth had ignored the first request. In addition, the French king often linked these piratical activities with his suspicions regarding the provision of English aid to the Huguenots.

In October 1569, the French ambassador complained bitterly to both Elizabeth and the French rulers that one of his packages had been stolen. In his letter to the French king, he stated that Elizabeth "begged me to believe that she was not involved in this, nor were the members of her Privy Council, and she was greatly displeased and would send a commissioner to investigate and give me good compensation that would please me."[111] However, he was much more candid in his letter Catherine, decrying the theft as "outrageous." He "begged [Catherine] to have a word with the English ambassador about it and insist that he must explain to

[107] Catherine de Medici to La Mothe Fénélon, July 9, 1569, and July 18, 1569, in *LCM*, Tome III, 260–2 and 263.

[108] Catherine de Medici to Monsieur de Fourquevaux, June 13, 1569, in *LCM*, Tome III, 249, "mais ayant un advis certain et véritable depuis peu de jours que la royne d'Angleterre voulloit faire faire une descente en Picardie et en Normandie."

[109] Charles IX to La Mothe Fénélon, July 8, 1569, in *Correspondence diplomatique*, Tome VII, 27, "desirant qu'il soit prins quelque fin et expédiant à la restitution des choses, qui ont été mal prises sur mes subjectz en Angleterre, et à celles qui ont esté mal prises aux Anglois de deçà, ainsy qu'il apartient à la commune amytié qui est. entre la Royne d'Angleterre, ma bonne soeur."

[110] Charles IX to La Mothe Fénélon, March 8, 1570, in *Correspondence diplomatique*, Tome VII, 98–99.

[111] La Mothe Fénélon to the French king Charles IX, 63rd Report, October 7, 1569, in *Correspondence diplomatique*, Tome II, 260, "elle me prioit de croyre que cella n'estoit aulcunement procédé d'elle, ny de son dict conseil, et qu'elle en estoit extrêmement déplaysante; dont envoyeroit ung commissaire sur le lieu pour en enquérir, et m'en feroit avoir si bonne réparation que j'en serois contant."

[Elizabeth] that your Majesties are greatly offended and demand that it is resolved."[112] The package had contained highly confidential letters in which Charles revealed that he was secretly involved in the planning for the marriage of Mary Stuart and the Duke of Norfolk.[113] A few weeks later, he was relieved to hear that the package had been restored to his ambassador.[114] Nevertheless, such incidents reinforced the perception of the English queen as a potential enemy in the minds of the French royal family and their ambassador.

This distrust was fueled by Elizabeth's steadfast defense of Protestantism. However, as we saw earlier, the French royal family's perception of Elizabeth was far more complex than contemporary English writers' depictions of her as a Protestant champion. Rather, they viewed her as a Protestant *trouble-maker*.[115] In the French ambassador's reports, Elizabeth's declarations regarding religion went beyond the usual "black-and-white" opinions that one might expect. More than merely defending her religion, she focused on protecting her realm, declaring that "she was ready to defend her religion and to prevent, by any means that God gave her, the danger that herself and her subjects might incur."[116] She feared that the civil strife in France would harm her own country's prosperity and encourage England's Catholics to rebel against her. As we have seen, this was a justified fear, as the earls of Westmorland and Northumberland did indeed rebel in 1569, followed two

---

[112] La Mothe Fénélon to Catherine de Medici, October 8, 1569, in *Correspondence diplomatique*, Tome II, 280, "encor que la Royne d'Angleterre ayt vollu faire quelque démonstration de me contanter sur l'oltrage qui m'a esté faict de la vollerie de mon paquet, je vous suplie néantmoins en parler si expressément à son ambassadeur qu'il ayt. occasion d'escripre à sa Mestresse que Voz Majestez en sentent une grande offance, et qu'elles veulent qu'elle soit réparée."

[113] Charles IX to La Mothe Fénélon, November 1, 1569, in *Supplément de la correspondence diplomatique de Bertrand de Salignac de la Mothe Fénélon, ambassadeur de France en Angleterre, de 1568 à 1575*, Tome VII (Paris et Londres: Archives du Royaume, 1840), 68–70.

[114] Charles IX to La Mothe Fénélon, November 19, 1569, in *Supplément de la correspondence diplomatique*, 74–75.

[115] As previously noted in 1569, John Day published *Christian Prayers and Meditations in English, French, Italian, Spanish, Greeke, and Latine* (London, 1569), STC 6428, in these prayers, a Protestant reputation of Elizabeth was fashioned, showing that at that time, English people were willing to perceive her as a Protestant champion.

[116] La Mothe Fénélon to the French king Charles IX, 8th Report, December 28, 1568, in *Correspondence diplomatique*, Tome I, 61 "la relligion de la quelle elle est., qu'elle estoit déjà prete pour la deffence d'icelle, et de prévenir, par toutz les moyens que Dieu luy avoit donnez, le danger, qu'elle et ses subjectz en pourroient encourir."

years later by the Ridolfi plot. Therefore, while the French royal family strongly suspected that Elizabeth was providing assistance to her coreligionists, the Huguenots, they neither perceived nor portrayed Protestantism as her primary motivation for doing so:

> [I]t is true that those of her religion are, at this time, pressurizing and persistent in obtaining some support and salvation from her and the members of her council, so I fear we will have to prevent their receipt of anything secretly.[117]

Ten months later, in February 1570, La Mothe Fénélon reported that Elizabeth was delighted that Charles was finally in the process of negotiating a peace agreement with the Huguenots:

> The said Lady, with a glad and joyful face, and after good, thankful words, asked me to tell you, having received such a positive communication regarding a peace agreement [*pourparlé*] with your subjects, that she is curious to read the articles of it, which I have endeavored to present as reasonable from your perspective, to show that those on the opposite side [the Huguenots] could not find any reason not to accept it.[118]

Throughout her audiences with La Mothe Fénélon, the Tudor queen seemed to display the belligerent aspect of her character as much as her determination to defend her religion, even though she never actually declared war on France. Nevertheless, as his reference to her "glad and joyful face" in this extract shows, the ambassador was also keen to report her goodwill toward her French counterparts.[119]

---

[117] La Mothe Fénélon to Catherine de Medici, April 12, 1569, in *Correspondence diplomatique*, Tome I, 307, "Il est. vray que ceulx de sa religion sont, à ceste heure, si pressans et si dilligens à procurer envers elle, et envers ceulx de son conseil, quelque remède et secours, que je crains qu'il y aura bien à fère d'empescher qu'ilz n'en obtiennent quelcun soubz mains."

[118] La Mothe Fénélon to the French king Charles IX, 90th Report, February 22, 1570, in *Correspondence diplomatique*, Tome III, 60, "La dicte Dame, d'ung visaige bien fort.joyeulx et contant, après plusieurs bien bonnes parolles du mercyement, qu'elle m'a prié de vous fère, pour une tant favorable communication du pourparté de paix avec vos subjectz, a curieusement vollu lire les articles d'icelluy et j'ay miz peyne de les lui fère trouver plus que raysonnables de vostre costé; et que, si ceulx de l'aultre part se monstrent tant sans rayson qu'ilz ne les acceptant."

[119] Matthieu Gellard analyses the French ambassador's interest in reporting Elizabeth's reactions. He also describes the differences of the protocols of the English and French courts

With respect to the peace negotiations, Elizabeth's primary concern was that "Charles IX had agreed to grant them [the Huguenots] the liberty of conscience."[120] In other words, she wanted to ensure that they would be free to practice their—and her—religion. La Mothe Fénélon did his best to reassure her by providing details of the terms of the draft peace treaty. Confirmation finally arrived in the summer of 1570 in the form of a memorandum from the Huguenot leaders, who took the opportunity to thank Elizabeth for her help during the rebellion:

> The princes of Navarre and Condé, the admiral and lords, gentlemen and others who followed them for the common defense of their religious cause now feel the fruits and effects of the favor and assistance received from the very great and powerful lady and princess the Queen of England because they have achieved peace, through the grace of God, and did not want to fail [...] to let her know and explain particularly how it happened.[121]

By depicting Elizabeth as the Protestant savior of the French Huguenots, La Mothe Fénélon undoubtedly cast a shadow over her reputation as a peacemaker and loyal "sister" to the royal family. On the other hand, his reports confirmed that she enjoyed significant royal authority and helped to create the image of monarch who was at least the equal of any king in Europe, which ultimately may have contributed to the preservation of peace with her French counterparts. Therefore, although Elizabeth's reputation was always intricately intertwined with her religion, it was multifaceted and evolved over time. The French rulers were not dupes—they had strong suspicions of the English queen's true intentions—but they also correctly perceived her as powerful potential enemy who could not be bullied.

---

and explained that the ambassador was at times received in a more personal chamber to discuss important matters, Gellard, *Une Reine Epistolaire*, 381–2.

[120] La Mothe Fénélon to the French king Charles IX, 78th Report, December 17, 1569, in *Correspondence diplomatique*, Tome II, 394, "qu'elle desiroit sçavoir si vous leur aviés concédé la liberté de leurs consciences."

[121] Mémoire adressé à la reine Elizabeth par les chefs protestants pour lui announcer la conclusion de la paix, August 1570, TNA SP 70/113, fol. 148, "Messieurs les princes de Navarre et de Condé, Monsieur l'admiral et les seigneurs, gentilshommes et autres qui les ont accompagnez en la commune défense de la cause de la religion, se ressentant maintenant du fruict et effect de la faveur et assistance qu'ilz ont reçue de très haulte et puissante dame et princesse la royne d'Angleterre par une paix qu'ilz onl, avec la grâce de Dieu, acquise, n'ont voulu faillir, incontinent après la publication d'icello, lui en donner advis et luy faire entendre particulièrement comme toutes choses se sont passes."

## CONCLUSION

As this chapter has demonstrated, the years 1568 to 1570 were pivotal for both the maintenance of good relations between England and France and the fashioning of Elizabeth's reputation outside her realm. The depictions of the queen in the correspondence between the French royal family and their ambassador are more complex, multi-layered, and variable than any of those that appear in contemporary English sources. Furthermore, they help to counterbalance the wholly negative portraits of the English queen that were so prevalent in Catholic circles at the time.[122] Of course, religious affiliation also played a role in the representations of the English queen that developed in the French diplomatic correspondence, but it was far from the paramount feature. By establishing herself as a "true sister" or even "second mother" to Charles IX, Elizabeth was able to assume the role of mediator between the French royal family and her cousin, Mary Stuart. Furthermore, through this virtual family bond and her constant references to peace and justice in her audiences with La Mothe Fénélon, she was able to offer advice to Charles and Catherine in the midst of the turmoil of France's third religious war. At the same time, by comparing her to "a rock" and "a lion," the French ambassador helped Elizabeth to enhance her reputation as a strong, powerful monarch. In particular, his reports of her demonstrations of strength and skillful use of princely rhetoric during the Northern Rebellion forced her French counterparts to perceive her as an equal.

The mistrust that is evident in the French royal correspondence is hardly surprising. After all, Elizabeth was a Protestant ruler who did, despite her protestations to the contrary, help the French Huguenots to defend their religion. But Charles and Catherine were sufficiently astute to view her as much more than a Protestant champion. It may even be argued that Elizabeth used the rebellion to demonstrate to the French royal family—and indeed herself—that she had the potential to become a powerful enemy and was more than capable of defending her country's interests. There can be little doubt that they got the message.

[122] For positive representations of Elizabeth, see the works of Susan Doran, *England and Europe (1485–1603)*; Linda Shenk, *Learned Queen*; Carole Levin, *The Heart and Stomach of a King*; and Mary Villeponteaux, *The Queen's Mercy*. Julia M. Walker (ed.), *Dissing Elizabeth: Negative Representations of Gloriana* (Durham, NC, and London: Duke University Press, 1998) explores the opposite side of the queen's reputation. See also discussion in the introduction.

Nevertheless, as the next chapter will show, the 1572 St. Bartholomew's Day massacre had consequences on Anglo-French relations as well as on how the Valois rulers perceived her—as they needed to preserve the alliance more than ever.

# "a germayne sister": The Impact of the St. Bartholomew's Day Massacre's on Representations of Queen Elizabeth—August 1572–June 1574

Francis Walsingham, the English ambassador at the French court and one of Elizabeth's closest advisers, related of the horrors of the St. Bartholomew's Day Massacre in an emotional account of the atrocity: "women, children, maids, young infants and sucking babes, were […] murthered, and cast into the river."[1] However, in a report to Lord Burghley, Sir Thomas Gargrave revealed that the reaction on the other side of the Channel was ambivalent, at best. He wrote that the people of the north of England "are, as I think, like others in other parts of the realm; one sort is pleased with the late affront in France; another sort lament, and are appalled at it; others would seem indifferent, and those be the greatest number."[2]

Four days earlier—two weeks after the massacre—Elizabeth had received the French ambassador in her private chamber, attended by her private councillors and some important gentlewomen of the court "in complete

---

[1] Dudley Digges, *The Compleat Ambassador: Or Two Treaties of the intended marriage of Qu. Elizabeth of Glorious Memory: Comprised in Letters of Negotiation of Sir Francis Walsingham, her Resident in France Together with the Answers of the Lord Burleigh, the Earl of Leicester, Sir Tho. Smith, and others Wherein, as in a dear Mirror, may be seen the Faces of the two Courts of England and France, as they then stood; with many remarkable passages of State, not at all mentioned in any History* (London: Thomas Newcomb, 1655), 298.

[2] Sir Thomas Gargrave to Lord Burghley, September 18, 1572, TNA, SP 15/21 fol. 175.

© The Author(s) 2019
E. Paranque, *Elizabeth I of England through Valois Eyes*, Queenship and Power, https://doi.org/10.1007/978-3-030-01529-9_4

silence."[3] Though it may be assumed that the entire court was "clothed fully in mourning attire," it is notable that La Mothe Fénélon, whose main aim when writing his report of the meeting was to reassure his masters that their relations with Elizabeth would survive the atrocity, made no reference to the queen's and her courtiers' dress.[4] This was an early example of the diplomatic dexterity he had to employ in the wake of the St. Bartholomew's Day Massacre in the interests of preserving the French crown's good relations with Elizabeth.[5]

One important aspect of the relationship between France and England continued after the massacre in the form of the marriage negotiations between Elizabeth and Francis, Duke of Alençon, the youngest son of Henry II and Catherine de Medici. As we have seen, Catherine had long been interested in marrying one of her sons to Elizabeth. However, the English queen repeatedly spurned Charles IX's advances, then showed even less interest in the idea of marrying Henry of Anjou, Charles's younger brother. All of the negotiations for the latter match went through ambassadors, with Elizabeth and Henry not even exchanging personal letters.[6] Ultimately, in January 1571, she confided to La Mothe Fénélon that "she would not want a husband who only honored her as queen if he did

[3] La Mothe Fénélon to the French king Charles IX, 274th Report, September 14, 1572, in *Correspondence diplomatique de Bertrand de Salignac de la Mothe Fénélon, ambassadeur de France en Angleterre, de 1568 à 1575*, Tome V, Années 1572 et 1573 (Paris et Londres: Archives du Royaume, 1840), 122, "elle m'a mandé venir; qui l'ay trouvée, accompaignée de pluseurs seigneurs de son conseil et des principalles dames de sa court, toutz en grand silence, dedans sa chambre privée."

[4] Nate Probasco, "Queen Elizabeth's reaction to the St. Bartholomew's Day Massacre," in *The Foreign Relation of Elizabeth I*, ed. Charles Beem (New York: Palgrave Macmillan, 2012), 78.

[5] A. G. Dickens discusses how the massacre shaped Anglo-French relations, see "The Elizabethans and St. Bartholomew," in *The Massacre of St. Bartholomew: Reappraisals and Documents*, ed. Alfred Soman (The Hague: Martinus Nijhoff, 1974), 52–70. Furthermore, David J.B. Trim argues that after the massacre, Elizabeth changed her foreign policies and became a defender of the Protestants, both in her realm and on the continent. See, "Seeking a Protestant Alliance and Liberty of Conscience on the Continent, 1558–85," in *Tudor England and its Neighbours*, eds. Susan Doran and Glenn Richardson (Houndmills: Palgrave Macmillan, 2005), 140–3.

[6] Matthieu Gellard, "Séduire par ambassadeur interposé. La négociation du mariage entre Élisabeth d'Angleterre et Henry d'Anjou en 1570–1571," in *La Communication en Europe de l'âge classique au siècle des Lumières*, ed. Pierre-Yves Beaurepaire (Paris: Belin, 2014), 298–303.

not love her as a woman."[7] A few months later, with the negotiations clearly going nowhere, Catherine played her final card and presented Francis, her youngest son, as a potential suitor. Although Francis was just sixteen and Elizabeth was in her late thirties, Catherine was optimistic. Indeed, by the following autumn, despite the negative impact of the massacre on Anglo-French relations, the French royal family remained more determined than ever to secure a match between the two crowns.[8] French diplomatic reports continued to portray the queen as a potential bride for the duke, and the marriage negotiations continued until 1574. However, the sudden death of Charles IX on May 30 of that year brought all of Catherine's plans to a shuddering halt.[9]

In the last two years of his life, Charles was embroiled in a fourth religious civil war, which erupted as a direct consequence of the massacre. Inevitably, this undermined France's alliance with England.[10] Fortunately for the French king, however, the situation in the Spanish Netherlands was equally complicated and fraught with tension, which meant Elizabeth had to exercise extreme caution in her foreign policy.[11] With instability rife

[7] La Mothe Fénélon to Catherine de Medici, January 18, 1571, in *Correspondence Diplomatique*, Tome III, 439, "elle ne vouldroit un mary qui ne l'honnorast seulement que pour Royne, s'il ne l'aymoit aussi pour femme."

[8] Susan Doran, Mark P. Holt, Guillaume Coatalen and Jonathan Gibson have argued that the prospects of any negotiations were ruined after Bartholomew's Day Massacre. See Mack P. Holt, *The Duke of Anjou and the Politique Struggle during the Wars of Religion* (Cambridge: Cambridge University Press, 1986), 21; Susan Doran, *Monarchy and Matrimony: The Courtships of Elizabeth I* (London & New York: Routledge, 1996), 137, and Guillaume Coatalan and Jonathan Gibson, "Six Holograph Letters in French from Queen Elizabeth I to the Duke of Anjou: Texts and Analysis," in *Elizabeth I's Foreign Correspondence*, 31. However, Wallace T. MacCaffrey has explained that the marriage negotiations were pursued but did not reveal the impact of such news on Elizabeth's representations. See Wallace T. MacCaffrey, *Queen Elizabeth and the Making of Policy 1572–1588*, 170.

[9] At first, although the French king had suffered serious health issues, he and his mother believed he would recover. For instance, on May 2, 1574, Charles informed La Mothe Fénélon that he "felt well enough to be hoping to be out in a few days," in *Correspondence diplomatique*, Tome VII, 468, "me trouver si bien, [...] que j'espère sortir dans peu de jours."

[10] The Treaty of Blois was signed between France and England to counter balance the power in Europe and to establish an alliance against Spain. See: Lynn A. Martin, "Papal Policy and the European Conflict, 1559–1572," in *Sixteenth Century Journal*, vol. 11, No. 2, Catholic Reformation (Summer, 1980): 35–48.

[11] Peter Limm, *The Dutch Revolt, 1559–1648* (London: Longman, 1989), 40.

across Northern Europe, every ruler appreciated the need to preserve alliances and maintain good relations with his or her neighbors.

In the previous chapter, we learned that some key events helped to shape the conflicting images of the Tudor queen that emerged in French royal correspondence and diplomatic dispatches. This chapter examines whether those images evolved, vanished, or persisted in the aftermath of the St. Bartholomew's Day Massacre. It explores the intentions of the French royal family and their expectations in terms of alliances and political strategies. In addition, it analyzes the shrewd tactics that they and their ambassador employed to safeguard their interests, notably when inviting the English queen to become the godmother of Charles and Elisabeth of Austria's baby daughter in October 1572. In doing so, it assesses the impact of the massacre on Elizabeth's representation as a good—if virtual—family member, tracing her evolution from "good sister" and "second mother" to "germayne sister" and prospective bride as the French crown strove to preserve the shaky alliance. Finally, it explores the paradoxical development of two contrasting representations of Elizabeth in the French diplomatic correspondence: powerful, solitary ruler in full control of England's destiny and malleable puppet of her own privy councillors.

## THE FRENCH ROYAL FAMILY'S PERCEPTION OF ELIZABETH'S REACTION TO THE MASSACRE

Almost a month after the massacre, Charles contacted La Mothe Fénélon to express his concerns regarding the preservation of the alliance with England: "as there is nothing else that I desire more in this world than continuing the perfect and sincere friendship between her and myself and our common subjects, as I hope, on her part, she will want as well."[12] The mass murder of French Protestants was a key event in Charles IX's reign and, specifically, in his efforts to assert his royal authority.[13] Yet, he knew that he could not allow the atrocity to destroy the Anglo-French alliance. Therefore, over subsequent months, the French ambassador had a crucial

---

[12] Charles IX to La Mothe Fénélon, September 22, 1572, in *Correspondence diplomatique*, Tome VII, 356, "comme je ne desire rien tant en ce monde que continuer en la parfaicte et sincère amytié d'entre elle et moy et nos commungs subjects, comme j'espère, de sa part, qu'elle voudra bien."

[13] Jean-Louis Bourgeon analyzes the effects of the St. Bartholomew's Day Massacre on the Valois king on different levels, political but also personal, in Jean-Louis Bourgeon, *Charles IX devant la Saint Barthélémy* (Geneva: Droz, 1995), 21–22.

dual role to play: he had to convince Elizabeth that Charles had played no part in the massacre; and he had to provide his master with detailed accounts of the queen's reaction to the events in Paris. Inevitably, then, La Mothe Fénélon's reports had unparalleled influence in shaping the king's perception of his English counterpart between 1572 and 1574.

Six days after the massacre, the ambassador informed Catherine, "You would not believe how much this news has greatly upset the whole kingdom."[14] A few days later, in one of his regular reports to Charles, he declared, "the whole kingdom is incredibly upset and every other matter is on hold—Monsieur the Duke, trade, the enterprises in Flanders, and everything else."[15] In his next report, he described widespread hostility to the French people throughout England,[16] while in another letter to Catherine, sent on the same day, he suggested, "never did an incident in any country have such an impact as the one that happened in Paris."[17] However, none of these letters contained any hint of enmity on the part of Elizabeth herself, so Charles and Catherine remained convinced that the alliance with England was safe.

Of course, after hearing of the massacre, Elizabeth was well aware that her reaction would be closely scrutinized not only by her French counterparts but also by the Huguenots who had long seen her as their savior.[18]

[14] La Mothe Fénélon to Catherine de Medici, August 30, 1572, in *Correspondence diplomatique*, Tome V, 115, "Il n'est pas à croyre combien ceste nouvelle esmeut grandement tout ce royaulme."
[15] La Mothe Fénélon to the French king Charles IX, 273rd Report, September 2, 1572, in *Correspondence diplomatique*, Tome V, 116, "tout ce royaulme en est merveitteusement esmeu, et qu'on met en suspens le propos de Monseigneur le Duc, cettuy du commerce, les entreprinses de Flandres et toutes aultres choses."
[16] La Mothe Fénélon to the French king Charles IX, 274th Report, September 14, 1572, in *Correspondence diplomatique*, Tome V, 121, "des choses advenues à Paris, avoit desjà immué le cueur des habitans; lesquelz ayant monstré auparavant d'avoir une fort grande affection à la France, ilz Font soubdein convertye en une extrême indignation et une merveilleuse hayne contre les Françoys."
[17] La Mothe Fénélon to Catherine de Medici, September 14, 1572, in *Correspondence diplomatique*, Tome V, 131, "jamais nul accidant ne se fit tant sentir, en nul pays, estrange comme celluy qui est advenu à Paris."
[18] We have seen this in the different letters sent to the English queen by Huguenots leaders and the Navaresse Queen Jeanne d'Albret in the first chapter. Furthermore in 1574, two years after the St. Bartholomew's Day Massacre, a book advocating Protestantism was printed in Edinburgh by Jacques James and written by Nicolas Barnaud (also known as Nicolas de Montand), a fervent and radical Huguenot who printed works under the pseudonym of Eusèbe Philadelphe Cosmopolite. The book was entitled *Réveille Matin des Français et de*

After a month of contemplation, La Mothe Fénélon was finally able to inform his master that the English queen had condemned "this extreme violence, which exceeded all humanity, against so many people who could not be plotters," and that she now had serious doubts about Charles's friendship and opinion of her, because she practiced the same religion as the victims of the massacre.[19] More importantly, during the same audience with the French ambassador, Elizabeth alluded to "the multiplication of tremendous excesses in your realm, about which she could not hear without tears, and which generated so much terror among her people that they now covered their ears."[20] In reporting these sentiments, La Mothe Fénélon issued a stark warning to his master. His reference to Elizabeth's "tears" must have left Charles in no doubt that she believed the Huguenots had suffered a great injustice and felt great sympathy for and kinship with

---

*leurs voisins* and was written "en forme de dialogues". James Emerson Phillips proposes that "to make it appear that his attack on the Queen of Scots originated in the British Isles, Barnaud issued his book with a false imprint of Edinburgh." Though it is unsure about where it was originally published, the book clearly aimed to promote Protestantism in Europe. While Phillips argues that Barnaud's work was pure propaganda against Mary Stuart, Alexander Wilkinson contends that the book did not focus entirely on Mary Stuart, and depicts *Réveille Matin* as also being "critical of Catherine de Medici." In *Catherine de Médicis and Others, Portraits of the Queen Mother: Polemics, Panegyrics, Letters*, the authors have translated some parts of *Réveille Matin*, including the area focusing on the similarities between Jézabel and Catherine, which supports the argument that this book not only defended Protestantism, but also attacked both the French queen and her former daughter-in-law. Both Phillips and Wilkinson mention that this book was dedicated to Queen Elizabeth I of England, however, they do not focus on the images of Elizabeth that the author chose to share. Barnaud portrayed the English queen as "the most excellent and most illustrious princess," and insisted on her "greatness," see the works of: James Emerson Phillips, *Images of a Queen: Mary Stuart in Sixteenth Century Literature* (Berkeley and Los Angeles: University of California Press, 1964), 71; Alexander Wilkinson, *Mary Queen of Scots and French Public Opinion, 1542–1600* (New York: Palgrave Macmillan, 2004), 94–95; and Leah L. Chang and Katherine Kong, *Catherine de Médicis and Others, Portraits of the Queen Mother: Polemics, Panegyrics, Letters* (Toronto: Centre for Reformation and Renaissance Studies, 2014), 231.

[19] La Mothe Fénélon to the French king Charles IX, 276th Report, September 29, 1572, in *Correspondence diplomatique*, Tome V, 142, "ceste extrême violence, qui excédoit toute humanité, contre ung si grand nombre d'aultres, qui ne pouvoient estre aulcunement conjurateurs, et jusques aux femmes et enfans, monstroit bien que Voz Majestez Très Chrestiennes, et toutz les vostres, aviez une extrême hayne contre ceulx de la mesmes religion, dont elle et les siens faysoient profession."

[20] La Mothe Fénélon to the French king Charles IX, 276th Report, September 29, 1572, 141, "m'a respondu que la multiplication des énormes excez de vostre royaulme, lesquelz elle ne pouvoit plus ouyr sans larmes, donnoient tant d'orreur a toutz tes siens qu'ilz bouchoient maintenant les oreilles."

the victims. Xavier Le Person explains that "tears were the sign of a profound humanity, of emotion and of virtue, the sign of a king who is inspired by Christ."[21] Therefore, in this context, they were not an emblem of Elizabeth's "feminine" weakness but rather of her "kingly" strength. Through this powerful emotional reaction, she revealed not only her humanity but also her divine right to rule over subjects who could not bear to hear of the massacre.

On the basis of a letter that Elizabeth sent to Walsingham in December 1572, Nate Probasco has rightly argued that "the killings had a profound effect on the queen."[22] Nevertheless, she maintained the alliance with France and her reputation among the French royal family continued to evolve. La Mothe Fénélon played a key role in this respect, as he increasingly portrayed her as a just monarch who defended innocent lives, with the implication being that this set her apart from other rulers, including the ambassador's own master, Charles IX.

For instance, in a letter to the king dated September 14, 1572, La Mothe Fénélon expressed Elizabeth's concerns regarding the massacre's negative impact on the ideal of justice in France. According to the ambassador, the queen was willing to accept that Charles was innocent of any involvement in the atrocity. However,

> what squeezed her heart was the fear she had for your reputation [...] [S]he is infinitely jealous of your honor and you may believe that she has defended your justification and innocence regarding the event [...] and has sworn on her life that, given your nature, your heart could not have intended all of these murders to occur, and they must have been due to some strange accident whose cause will be revealed over time.[23]

---

[21] Xavier Le Person, *"Practiques et Practiqueurs", La vie politique à la fin du règne de Henry III (1584–1589)* (Genève: Droz, 2002), 267, "Les larmes seraient le signe d'une humanité profonde, d'émotion et de vertu, le signe d'un roi habité par le Christ." Other works have focused on the link between the tears and the humanity aspect and even religious one, see Anne Vincent-Buffaut, *Histoire des larmes, XVIIIe-XIXe siècles* (Marseille: Rivages, 1986); Marc Angenot, "Les traités de l'éloquence du corps", *Semiotica*, vol. 8 (1) (1973); Piroska Nagy, *Le don des larmes au Moyen-Âge* (Paris: Albin Michel, 2000); and Sheila Page-Bayne, "Tears and Weeping: An Aspect of Emotional Climate reflected in Seventeenth Century French Literature," in *Etudes Littéraires Françaises*, vol. 16 (1981).

[22] Probasco, "Queen Elizabeth's reaction to the St. Bartholomew's Day Massacre," 94.

[23] La Mothe Fénélon to the French king Charles IX, 274th Report, September 14, 1572, in *Correspondence diplomatique*, Tome V, 125, "Mais ce qui luy pressait le cueur estoit la creinte qu'elle avoit de vostre reputation [...] elle estoit inffinyement jalouse de vostre honneur et

According to La Mothe Fénélon, Elizabeth "did not condemn the punishment that they [the Huguenot leaders] received, aside from the fact that she wished it had been ordered through justice."[24]

Two months later, however, the French ambassador reported a subtle change in Elizabeth's attitude toward both the massacre and Charles. With another reference to justice, she positioned herself definitively above the French king and not only offered advice but seemed to pass judgment on him. As La Mothe Fénélon reported:

> the death of the Admiral and his people touched her so little that she merely considered how it might impact your affairs and your reputation, although it is true that she fears that you provoked God's wrath by showing Him in your heart, and through your deeds, and in your style of ruling, that you wanted manslaughter not to be considered a sin in your realm [...] not recognizing that, even for princes, it is unlawful to kill or to order killings, aside from in just two cases—one in times of legitimate war and the other for the execution of justice to punish crimes—and that no one save for princes and sovereign magistrates can condemn anyone to death.[25]

Having mulled over the massacre for ten weeks, Elizabeth seemed most concerned that the victims had not been tried in a court of law and that no one seemed to know who had issued the order to kill them. The French ambassador attempted to defend his king's reputation by reminding Elizabeth that she might face a similar situation in the event of religious strife in her own realm, to which "she replied that she was willing to excuse

pouviez croire qu'elle avoit debbatu vostre justification et innocence [...]avoit assuré, sur sa vye, que, de vostre nature, ny d'aulcune intention qui fût procédée de vostre cueur, toutz ces meurtres n'estoient point advenus; et que c'estoit quelque accidant estrange duquel le temps esclarciroit les occasions."

[24] La Mothe Fénélon to the French king Charles IX, 274th Report, September 14, 1572, 125, "ny réprouvoit le chastiement qu'ilz en avoient reçeu, sinon seulement qu'elle heut bien voulu que ce heût esté par l'ordre de la justice."

[25] La Mothe Fénélon to the French king Charles IX, 282nd Report, November 2, 1572, in *Correspondence diplomatique*, Tome V, 186, "Que la mort de l'Amiral et des siens luy touch-oit si peu qu'elle n'y considéroit que le seul interest qui en pouvoit tomber sur voz affères et sur vostre reputation bien est vray qu'elle creignoit que provoquissiez l'yre de Dieu, en luy faysant voyr dans le cueur, et par voz oeuvres, et en vostre forme de régner, que vous voulez que l'ommicide en vostre royaulme ne soit point réputé péché [...] ne recognoissant que aulx mesmes princes il n'est licite de tuer ny faire tuer, sinon en deux cas seulement l'ung, de guerre légitime; et l'aultre, pour l'exécution de justice à punir les crimes, et. que nulz aultres, sinon les seutz princes et magistratz souverains ont authorité de mort."

what happened in Paris, but she could see no excuse for what followed in Rouen and other cities."[26] It is interesting that Elizabeth identified herself as someone who had the authority to excuse a massacre, because this reflects not only her stated intention to defend justice both inside and outside her realm but also her desire to be viewed as a prince who had the power to judge the actions of other—presumably lesser—princes.

Following this thinly veiled condemnation from his English counterpart, Charles sent La Mothe Fénélon

> a dozen books of an epistle written by Charpentier, which I wish to be secretly published and spread from hand to hand, without people knowing that it comes from either you or myself [...] [Instead, it should be] said and believed that it was published in Germany.[27]

Jacques Charpentier (1529–1574), a philosopher and Charles IX's personal physician, was the author of many essays and books, including the well-known *Orationes contra Ramum* in 1566.[28] The secret letter, which was probably written on the express order of Charles himself, presented a general defense of the king's authority, but first and foremost it claimed that he was innocent of any involvement in the massacre.[29] It was a typical example of the clandestine propaganda that the courts of Europe generated and distributed at the time.[30]

[26] La Mothe Fénélon to the French king Charles IX, 282nd Report, November 2, 1572, 187, "Je luy ay réplicqué plusieurs choses, et l'ay suplié de les vouloir bien examiner par la règle de ce qu'elle mesmes feroit contre ceulx de ses subjectz qui, au bout d'une, si horrible guerre, comme ceulx cy ont mené en vostre royaulme, l'espace de douze ans, se prépareroient de rechef contre la mésmes personne et la vye d'elle, et la subversion de son estat. Elle m'a respondu que, quand à ceulx de Paris, elle me vouloit le tout excuser; mais, quand à ce qui s'estoit depuis ensuivy à Roan et aurtres lieux lelle n'y voyoit autcun lieu d'excuse."

[27] Charles IX to La Mothe Fénélon, December 3, 1572, in *Correspondence diplomatique*, Tome VII, 402, "Monsieur de La Mothe, je vous envoyé une douzaine de livres d'une espistre faicte par Carpentier, que je desire qui soit secrètement publiée et faicte courir de main en main, sans que l'on saiche que cella vienne de vous ny de moy; mais que l'on dye et croye qu'elle a esté imprimée en Àllemaigne."

[28] See Philippe Renouard, *Imprimeurs et libraires parisiens du XVIe siècle* (Paris: Baquelier-Billon, 1979), 588.

[29] *Lettre de Pierre Charpentier addressée à Francis Portes, Candiois, par laquelle il monstre que les persécutions des Églises de France sont advenues non par la faulte de ceux qui faisoient profession de la religion, mais de ceux qui nourrissoient les factions et conspirations qu'on appelle la Cause* (Paris, 1572).

[30] Phillips explained that "Sir Henry Killegrew, then resident in France, sent to Cecil "a discourse in French" attacking the Queen of Scots "to be printed in England, and sent over

La Mothe Fénélon presumably followed his master's instructions and circulated the letter throughout the English court and beyond, but by depicting Elizabeth as a judge, he had already allowed her to assert her monarchical authority over her French counterpart. Furthermore, by focusing on the ideal of justice, he had highlighted her humanity. As a result, once again, he had helped the English queen to promote herself as at least the equal of—and probably superior to—any king.

Just four days after the massacre in Paris, before the news had reached England, La Mothe Fénélon described Elizabeth "riding a horse [...] returning from hunting."[31] It may be assumed that he included this seemingly inconsequential detail in his report in the hope of demonstrating that Charles and Elizabeth shared a common interest. Charles was renowned for his love of hunting and even wrote a book on the subject—*La Chasse Royale*.[32] Moreover, although earlier queens had hunted, it was viewed as a predominantly masculine activity, so the French ambassador was deliberately portraying Elizabeth as a *king*—and therefore Charles's true equal—rather than a queen.

La Mothe Fénélon's admiration for his host was even more apparent later in the same report:

> she has reigned for fourteen years in peace, and God has shown that in the midst of troubled, most dangerous times [a reference to the religious civil wars in France] he [God] knows how to rule and govern a monarchy under the authority of a princess, which is very rare, but this has made the said Lady the most famous princess who has ever ruled in the world a beautiful princess and full of majesty, whom they [her subjects] see filling this crown's throne with dignity, [so] they have willingly obeyed her until now.[33]

her secretly," in James Emerson Phillips, *Images of a Queen: Mary Stuart in Sixteenth Century Literature*, 252, also see: Elizabeth Evenden and Thomas S. Freeman, "Print, Profit and Propaganda: the Elizabethan Privy Council and the 1570 Edition of Foxe's 'Book of Martyrs'," *English Historical Review*, 119 (2004): 1288–307.

[31] La Mothe Fénélon to the French king Charles IX, 271st Report, August 28, 1572, in *Correspondence diplomatique*, Tome V, 99, "monstant à cheval [...] elle s'en retournoit en chassant."

[32] *La Chasse Royale* was posthumously published in 1625 and dedicated to Louis XIII of France. See a version of it printed during the nineteenth century: *La Chasse Royale Composée par le Roi Charles IX et dédiée au roi très-chrétien de France et de Navarre, Louis XIII*, Nouvelle édition précédée d'une introduction par Henry Chevreuil (Paris, 1807).

[33] La Mothe Fénélon to the French king Charles IX, 271st Report, August 28, 1572, 104, "voyantz qu'ette avoit régné quatorze ans en grande paix, et que Dieu avoit monstré qu'au

Almost all sixteenth-century monarchs asserted their divine right to rule, but here La Mothe Fénélon also echoed the self-representation that Elizabeth employed during her prayers, when she cast herself as God's handmaiden.[34] In addition, his report hinted that, rather than being disadvantaged by her lack of a husband, she had used her unique status as a single ruling "princess" to secure peace for her people and earn their obedience. This was highly significant because, in effect, Le Mothe Fénélon was suggesting not only that God had granted a woman the authority to rule a nation without any male assistance, but also that the woman in question had achieved something—domestic peace and the obedience of all her subjects—that his own master had singly failed to accomplish.

The French ambassador returned to this theme the following month, by which time the English court had heard about the atrocities in his homeland:

> regarding the greatness of the said Lady, and the dignified way she has reigned for fourteen years, with a reputation for great prudence, great honor, and great embellishment of all kinds of virtues, and regarding the other rare qualities that make her the most excellent among all the princesses of the world.[35]

Of course, Le Mothe Fénélon was duty bound to report the way in which Elizabeth presented herself to him. However, the way in which he chose to relate these representations both before and after news of the massacre reached England is telling. For instance, he would highlight her "princely" qualities whenever he felt that the French rulers needed to be reassured of

milieu des plus divers temps et plus dangereulx, il sçavoit régir et gouverner une monarquie soubz l'authorité d'une princesse, qui estoit ung fort rare exemple, mais qui rendoit la dite Dame la plus cellèbre princesse qui heust guière jamais régné au monde que toûtz ses subjectz recognoissoient estre fille et petite fille de leurs roys, belle princesse et pleyne de majesté, laquelle ilz vôyent remplir fort dignement le siège de ceste couronne, ilz luy avoient très volontiers obéy jusques icy."

[34] See: Private Prayers of Queen Elizabeth at Court, 1563, in *Elizabeth I: Collected works*, 136 and Queen Elizabeth's Prayers and Poems, 1569, *Christian Prayers and Meditations* and printed in *Elizabeth I: Collected works*, 147.

[35] La Mothe Fénélon to the French king Charles IX, 276th Report, September 29, 1572, in *Correspondence diplomatique*, Tome V, 141, "veu la grandeur de la dicte Dame et la digne façon de laquelle avoit régné quatorze ans, avec réputation de grande prudence de grand honneur et d'ung très grand ornement de toutes sortes de vertus et, veu les aultres rares qualités qui la rendoient excellante entre toutes les aultres princesses du monde."

Elizabeth's allegiance: for example, "knowing that she has a heart so royal and a conscience so good, and that her word, her honor, and her righteousness are held in great esteem."[36] In drawing a parallel between Elizabeth's royalty and her conscience, especially in times of crisis, he accorded her the stature of a great ruler.

The ambassador employed these representations of Elizabeth as a princess who could ride a horse, ruled with God's approval, and possessed "rare qualities" in the interests of preserving the Anglo-French alliance. When reporting his audiences with Elizabeth, he would frequently highlight her desire to see Charles maintain and even increase his authority over the French nation. For instance, in July 1573, he informed his master that Elizabeth had expressed concern over "the extent of your sovereign authority over your subjects as if she had wanted to proceed with it as her own cause, and that of her crown."[37] Then, shortly before the king's death in May 1574, he reported that she had "prayed to God that she desired the conservation of your state, your authority, and your greatness, as if it were her own."[38]

Clearly, the concept of monarchical authority remained paramount for Elizabeth, and she continued to defend every ruler's right to assert it, even after the killings in Paris. However, the massacre also allowed her to go further than ever before in promoting herself as at least the equal of any king—especially Charles—as well as a paragon of justice and mercy. Moreover, La Mothe Fénélon presented this image without a hint of cynicism in his reports. It was apparent that he felt she did indeed have the right to sit on judgment on her fellow monarchs, which forced Charles to declare his innocence and issue repeated reassurances to Elizabeth of the French royal family's goodwill toward England and herself.

---

[36] La Mothe Fénélon to the French king Charles IX, 377th Report, April 26, 1574, in *Correspondence diplomatique de Bertrand de Salignac de la Mothe Fénélon, ambassadeur de France en Angleterre, de 1568 à 1575*, Tome VI, Années 1574 et 1575 (Archives du Royaume: Paris et Londres, 1840), 87, "cognoissant qu'elle avoit le cueur si royal et la conscience si bonne, et avoit en si grande recommendation sa parolle, son honneur et la droicture."

[37] La Mothe Fénélon to the French king Charles IX, 329th Report, July 12, 1573, in *Correspondence diplomatique*, Tome V, 372, "les degrés de vostre souverayne authorité sur voz subjectz comme si elle eût voulu procéder en cella pour sa cause propre, et pour celle de sa couronne."

[38] La Mothe Fénélon to the French king Charles IX, 380th Report, May 10, 1574, in *Correspondence diplomatique*, Tome VI, 87, "juroit à Dieu qu'elle desiroit la conservation de vostre estât, de vostre authorité et de vostre grandeur, comme la sienne propre."

## Efforts to Include Elizabeth in the French Royal Family

Meanwhile, La Mothe Fénélon also reassured the French rulers that Elizabeth remained well disposed toward them and wished to preserve the alliance with France. In doing so, he continued to employ the familiar trope of one big happy family presiding over the two realms, and Catherine and Charles responded in kind. Moreover, in late 1572, Elisabeth of Austria's pregnancy gave the French royal family a golden opportunity to tighten the familial bonds with the Tudor queen by asking her to accept the role of godmother. They had also not quite given up on the idea of forging a marriage alliance, although by now there was no doubt that Elizabeth enjoyed the upper hand in the negotiations, which reflected the new balance of power in the alliance.

As we have seen, between 1568 and 1570, Elizabeth was routinely portrayed as a "true sister" to the French royal family. In the wake of the massacre, however, this representation underwent a subtle change as "true" was gradually dropped in favor of another adjective that suggested an even stronger bond with the French king: "germayne." This term denoted a particularly close sibling relationship, so when La Mothe Fénélon described Elizabeth as Charles's "germayne and natural sister," he accorded her the same status as Claude, Duchess of Lorraine, and Marguerite of Navarre, the king's biological sisters.[39] Interestingly, the French royal family first employed this adjective a year after the massacre, perhaps because they believed the alliance was unstable and needed to be reinforced. Alternative terms of address—such as "good sister"—persisted after the introduction of "germayne," but they were much less prominent than they had been prior to the massacre.[40] For example, in May 1574, La Mothe Fénélon insisted that Elizabeth had "all the great and excellent qualities of a good sister, she is germayne to Your Majesty."[41]

[39] La Mothe Fénélon to the French king Charles IX, 351st Report, November 18, 1573, in *Correspondence diplomatique*, Tome V, 448.

[40] Charles IX still referred to Elizabeth as his "good sister," in Charles IX to La Mothe Fénélon, September 22, 1572, Charles IX to La Mothe Fénélon, October 4, 1572, Charles IX to La Mothe Fénélon, October 27, 1572, in *Correspondence diplomatique*, Tome VII, 356, 369, and 378.

[41] La Mothe Fénélon to the French king Charles IX, 381st Report, May 16, 1574, in *Correspondence diplomatique*, Tome VI, 115, "toutes grandes et excellantes qualités de bonne seur, elle estoit germayne de Vostre Majesté."

Charles also referred to Mary Stuart as his sibling, but he rarely described her as "good" and never as "germayne."[42] While this may seem a minor idiomatic point, it is indicative of the fact that the French king came to realize that preserving the alliance with Elizabeth was much more important than defending Mary's interests. Prior to the massacre, the French rulers had consistently expressed great concern over the latter's predicament.[43] Thereafter, however, although they continued to raise the issue, it gradually dropped down the diplomatic agenda. Meanwhile, preserving and, if possible, improving Anglo-French relations became paramount.

On September 14, 1572, La Mothe Fénélon informed Catherine that the Scottish Queen was "in great danger."[44] Then, a few weeks later, he told the French king that some people "wanted her death." During an audience, the ambassador had explained to Elizabeth that

> people want to blame the Queen of Scotland for what happened in Paris, and I begged her to consider that the poor princess could not and never did know about it, so she should no longer be mistreated [...] to which she replied that the Queen of Scotland had enough sins of her own without attributing those of others to her.[45]

Although such exchanges revealed the French ambassador's ongoing anxiety about Mary Stuart's fate, he raised the matter less and less over

[42] Charles IX to La Mothe Fénélon, August 21, 1572, in *Correspondence diplomatique*, Tome VII, 319, "Je suis bien aise du retour de vostre secrétaire qu'aviez envoyé vers ma soeur, la Royne d'Escosse."

[43] In the months leading up to the massacre, La Mothe Fénélon reported the Queen of Scotland's situation and discussed with the French monarchs her situation in detail. He also raised the issue with Elizabeth herself. See: La Mothe Fénélon to the French king Charles IX, 254th Report, June 3, 1572, 3; 255th Report, June 5, 1572, 5; La Mothe Fénélon to Catherine, June 5, 1572, 8; La Mothe Fénélon to the French king Charles IX, 260th Report, July 1, 1572, 26, in *Correspondence diplomatique*, Tome V.

[44] La Mothe Fénélon to Catherine de Medici, September 14, 1572, in *Correspondence diplomatique*, Tome V, 133, "je vous puis assurer, Madame, qu'elle est en très grand danger."

[45] La Mothe Fénélon to the French king Charles IX, 277th Report, October 2, 1572, in *Correspondence diplomatique*, Tome V, 157, "qu'on a mis en dellihération icy comme l'on pourroit procéder contre la Royne d'Escoce pour la faire mourir, [...] j'ay bien voulu dire à!a Royne d'Angleterre qu'il sembloit qu'on se voulût prendre icy à la Royne d'Escoce de ce qui avoit esté faict à Paris, et que je la supliois de considérer que la pouvre princesse n'en pouvoit et n'en avoit jamais rien sceu, dont n'en debvoit estre plus mal trectée [...] A quoy elle m'a respondu que la dicte Royne d'Escoce avoit assez de ses propres péchés sans luy impétrer ceulx d'auttruy."

subsequent months. This reluctance to press the queen on the issue followed Charles's reference to "continuing always the good peace and amity between her and myself, which I want to preserve in full" in a letter of September 7, 1572. Indeed, the French king believed that remaining on good terms with Elizabeth would eventually give him "more means to help my said sister, the Queen of Scotland."[46] In practice, though, he provided little aid to the "said sister" as he had more pressing concerns, such as the eruption of yet another religious civil war as well as a potential conflict with Spain in the Netherlands, in which England's neutrality would be essential.[47] Consequently, La Mothe Fénélon was careful not to antagonize Elizabeth and did everything he could to maintain the alliance. He did, however, continue to report any news of Mary to his French masters.[48]

Although Charles seemed less interested in the travails of his erstwhile sister-in-law, the same could not be said of his subjects. In 1572, a notorious pamphlet first praised Mary's innocence and virtue, then described Elizabeth as a heretical, illegitimate queen and the cause of all of Mary's trouble.[49] The author, François de Belleforest, had spent some time at the court of Marguerite of Navarre.[50] Furthermore, the two printers—who were based in Reims and Lyon—had previously worked for the king, which many interpreted as confirmation of the French royal family's full support for Mary and disdain for her cousin. Fortunately for Charles, however, shortly after the pamphlet's publication, he was presented with a perfect opportunity to distance himself from de Belleforest's sentiments.

While the French royal family had utilized virtual family bonds to maintain a strong alliance with Elizabeth for more than a decade, in the autumn

---

[46] Charles IX to La Mothe Fénélon, September 7, 1572, in *Correspondence diplomatique*, Tome VII, 337, "de continuer tousjours la bonne paix et amitié d'entre elle et moy, que je veus entièrement conserver estimant que, quand je continueray en cela avec elle que j'auray plus de moyen d'ayder à ma dicte soeur, la Royne d'Escosse."

[47] Nicola-Mary Sutherland, *The Massacre of St Bartholomew and the European Conflict, 1559–1572* (London: Macmillan, 1973), 206 and Arlette Jouanna, *La France du XVIe siècle, 1483–1598*, 465.

[48] For examples, see: La Mothe Fénélon to the French king Charles IX, 365th Report, February 15, 1574, 367th Report, February 26, 1574, 374th Report, April 6, 1574, in *Correspondence diplomatique*, Tome VI, 34, 44, and 76.

[49] Francis de Belleforest, *L'Innocence de la trèsillustre, très-chaste, et débonnaire Princesse Madame Marie Royne d'Escosse. Où sont amplement refutés les calmonies faulces, & impositions iniques, publiées par un livre secrettement divulgué en France, l'an 1572* (Reims: Jean de Foigny, 1572 & Lyon: Jean de Tournes, 1572), 17.

[50] Michel Simonin, *Dictionnaire des lettres françaises. Le XVIème siècle* (Paris: Fayard, 2001).

of 1572 they attempted to establish a real one. On October 27, Charles's wife, Elisabeth of Austria, gave birth to the couple's first—and, as it transpired, only—child, Marie-Elisabeth.[51] Of course, the infant's safe arrival was a cause of great celebration in the French court.[52] More significantly, although MacCaffrey and Probasco have argued that the massacre soured Elizabeth's opinion of the French royal family,[53] La Mothe Fénélon reported her joy on hearing the news of the "beautiful little princess." Furthermore, when he asked if she "would agree to be the godmother," she proclaimed that she would "willingly accept [...] if we would do her the honor of asking."[54]

In response to this positive report, on November 19 Charles and his wife both sent formal requests to the queen.[55] Although Elisabeth of Austria is generally portrayed as playing no role in her husband's policy-making, it is notable that she not only beseeched the English queen "to be one of our daughter's godmothers and to send someone who is appropriate for this task," but also expressed the belief that her acceptance of the role would "strengthen the true and perfect friendship which is present, and let us hope to God that it will continue forever, between this crown and yours."[56] The French queen consort evidently appreciated the importance of the Anglo-French alliance to her adopted country, which prompted her to abandon her usual reticence and write directly to her

[51] The choice of the name "Marie-Elisabeth" was a tribute to both of her godmothers: her maternal grandmother Maria of Austria and Elizabeth I of England.

[52] *Hymne sur la naissance de Madame de France, fille du roy très-chrétien Charles IX*, dédié à Jacques Fouyn, prieur et seigneur d'Argenteuil, signé J. S. P. (Lyon: Benoist Rigaud, 1572 et Paris: Mathurin Martin, 1572).

[53] MacCaffrey, *Queen Elizabeth and the Making of Policy 1572–1588*, 173 and Probasco, "Queen Elizabeth's reaction to the St. Bartholomew's Day Massacre," 81.

[54] La Mothe Fénélon to the French king Charles IX, 283rd Report, November 4, 1572, in *Correspondence diplomatique*, Tome V, 195, "belle petite princesse [...] la Royne d'Angleterre vouldroit bien accepter d'en estre la marraine [...] qu'elle acceptera de bon cueur d'estre la marraine, si luy faictes l'honneur de l'en prier."

[55] Charles IX to Queen Elizabeth I of England, November 19, 1572 and Elisabeth of Austria, Queen of France to Queen Elizabeth of England, November 19,1572, in *Correspondence diplomatique*, Tome VII, 399 and 400.

[56] Elisabeth of Austria, Queen of France to Queen Elizabeth I of England, November 19, 1572, in *Correspondence diplomatique*, Tome VII, 400, "Nous vous prions donc que vous veuillés estre l'une des marraines de nostre dicte fille et envoyer de deçà personne convenable pour cest effect. [...] fortiffier ceste vraye et parfaicte amitié qui est de présent, et espérons en Dieu que continuera à tousjours, entre ceste couronne et la vostre."

namesake.[57] Interestingly, there was no letter from Catherine; this was one of the rare occasions when she was prepared to leave an important diplomatic matter entirely to others.

In response, Elizabeth not only agreed to become Marie-Elisabeth's godmother but sent her very best wishes to the princess. Following an audience with the queen, La Mothe Fénélon reported that, while she imagined that Charles had hoped for "a Dauphin," she assured him that "the little princess is welcome in this world and she prays that God will make her [Marie-Elisabeth] as happy as she [Elizabeth herself] is to be descended from a good lineage, and, like her [Elizabeth], she will be beautiful and virtuous."[58] According to the French ambassador, the English queen was also more than happy to serve as an example for the little princess to follow.

A few days later, La Mothe Fénélon informed Charles that Elizabeth fully appreciated the significance of her new role and knew that it had been offered in the hope of reinforcing the alliance between the two realms. Indeed, he was pleased that she understood "the offer that you made her to be a godmother to be one of the most certain demonstrations of true and perfect friendship that could be made not only between princes but also between any other intimate and united people."[59] Then, in his next report, he affirmed that Elizabeth "willingly accepted the honor that you did her to want her to be one of your elder daughter's godmothers, and took this as a strong, great, and singular reward."[60]

---

[57] For more information on Elisabeth of Austria, see Estelle Paranque, "Elisabeth of Austria and Marie-Elisabeth of France: Represented and remembered," in *Forgotten Queens in Medieval and Early Modern Europe: Political Agency, Myth-Making, and Patronage*, eds. Valerie Schutte and Estelle Paranque (London: Routledge, 2018), 114–28.

[58] La Mothe Fénélon to the French king Charles IX, 286th Report, November 23, 1572, in *Correspondence diplomatique*, Tome V, 205, "d'ung Dauphyn, et que néantmoins la petite princesse soit la bien venue au monde, et qu'elle prioit Dieu de t'y faire aultant heureuse comme elle y est de très grande extraction et comme elle s'assure qu'ette y sera belle et vertueuse."

[59] La Mothe Fénélon to the French king Charles IX, 288th Report, December 4, 1572, in *Correspondence diplomatique*, Tome V, 215, "qu'elle réputoit l'offre, que luy fesiez d'estre vostre commère, pour ung des plus certeins signes de vraye et parfaicte amityé qui se pouvoit uzer non seulement entre princes, mais entre toutes aultres plus inthimes et conjoinctes personnes."

[60] La Mothe Fénélon to the French king Charles IX, 289th Report, December 10, 1572, in *Correspondence diplomatique*, Tome V, 218, "Qu'elle accepte de bon cueur l'honneur que luy faictes de vouloir qu'elle soit l'une des marraines de vostre fille aynée, et prend cella pour

All of these accounts of the English queen's willingness—or even enthusiasm—to play the role of godmother reveal that La Mothe Fénélon was successful in his efforts to lubricate the diplomatic relations between the two courts. They also illustrate how little Marie-Elisabeth enabled the English queen and the French king to supplement their long-standing virtual family bonds with actual ones.[61] In a letter of February 1573, Catherine de Medici was at pains to stress the importance of these new bonds for the future of the Anglo-French alliance: "the good office that was made to hold in your name our granddaughter through the sacred font of baptism will confirm and assure even more the good friendship and relations between our two crowns of France and England."[62]

Elizabeth's new role also gave Charles an unprecedented opportunity to assess the sincerity of his counterpart's friendship. He asked the queen to send one of her most trusted privy councillors, the Earl of Leicester, as her representative at Marie-Elisabeth's christening, which was scheduled to take place on February 2, 1573.[63] Elizabeth ignored the request and sent "a lesser noble," William Somerset, the Earl of Worcester, instead.[64] The

une bien fort grande et singullière récompanse de la droicte affection dont elle s'est resjouye de sa nayssance."

[61] On how spiritual kingship bonds were created at baptisms, see the works of John Bossy, "Blood and Baptism: Kinship, Community and Christianity in Western Europe from the Fourteenth to the Seventeenth Centuries," in *Sanctity and Secularity: The Church and the World, papers read at the 11th summer and 12th winter meetings of the Ecclesiastical History Society*, ed. David Baker (Oxford: Basil Blackwell, 1973), 129–44; Mairi Cowan, "The Spiritual Ties of Kinship in Pre-Reformation Scotland," in *Finding the Family in Early Modern Scotland*, eds. Elizabeth Ewan and Janay Nugent (Aldershot: Ashgate, 2008) and Louis Haas, *The Renaissance Man and His Children: Childbirth and Early Childhood in Florence, 1300–1600* (Basingstoke: Macmillan, 1998).

[62] Catherine de Medici to Queen Elizabeth of England, February 9, 1573, in *Lettres de Catherine de Médicis* publiées par M. Le Cte Hector de la Ferrière, Tome IV, 1570–75 (Paris: Imprimerie Nationale, 1889), 165, "le bon office qu'il a faict de tenir en vostre nom nostre petite-fille sur les sainetz fonts de baptesme confirmera et asseurera d'aultant plus la bonne amytié et intelligence d'entre ces deux couronnes de France et d'Angleterre."

[63] Charles IX to La Mothe Fénélon, November 3, 1572, in *Correspondence diplomatique*, Tome VII, 383, "je vous en aye escript, si elle auroit agréable que je l'envoyasse prier d'envoyer tenir ma dicte fille sur les sainctz fonds de basteme par le Sr conte de Lecestre; car je pense que cella, ainsy que j'ay aussy veu par une de voz lettres, seroit bien à propos et ung vray moyen comme m'escripvés, de renouveller la vraye et entière amitié d'entre elle et moy et noz subjectz."

[64] Probasco, "Queen Elizabeth's reaction to the St. Bartholomew's Day Massacre," 81, and La Mothe Fénélon to the French king Charles IX, 298th Report, February 2, 1573, in *Correspondence diplomatique*, Tome V, 248, "La dicte Dame, d'une fort bonne et agréable

latter was a Catholic but Elizabeth trusted him implicitly. He undertook public duties, attended Parliament, and, crucially, had remained loyal to the queen during the Northern Rebellion.[65] Moreover, sending a Catholic envoy was a typically astute diplomatic move on Elizabeth's part. Even Charles had to acknowledge that Worcester was a more appropriate choice than the more senior—but Protestant—Leicester.[66]

Three weeks after the christening, La Mothe Fénélon reported that Elizabeth still felt

> honored to be named one of her godmothers and she prays God makes her as happy as she [Elizabeth] is great, and she is sure that she will be a virtuous princess and signal the start of a distinguished line of descendants for your Most Christian Majesties, and that she will soon be followed by many brothers.[67]

While the decision to ask Elizabeth to become Marie-Elisabeth's godmother was undeniably a deft political strategy that helped to reinforce the alliance, it also reflected the French rulers' anxiety that they might never persuade Elizabeth to marry into the family. In June 1572, two months before the massacre, Catherine had informed Elizabeth that Charles wished to make the alliance between the two nations "immortal." Of course, the king himself was no longer a marriage prospect, but his youngest brother Francis certainly was, as Catherine emphasized: "I love you as a mother does her daughter, and I hope for a happy day when I might name myself as such [...] I pray to God that you know the friendship and affection in which I hold you."[68] Three weeks later, she confided, "we

façon, m'a respondu qu'elle pensoit que le seul bonheur de l'occasion, pour laquelle elle vous dépeschoit le comte de Worcester, laquelle estoit saincte et privilégiée envers Dieu, et le debvoit estre envers les hommes, l'avoient ainsy préservé de ce grand dangier."

[65] Digges, *The Compleat Ambassador*, 314 and 328–9.

[66] Charles IX to M. de Saint-Gouard, February 8, 1573, BNF MS Fr 16,105, fol. 25.

[67] La Mothe Fénélon to the French king Charles IX, 303rd Report, February 27, 1573, in *Correspondence diplomatique*, Tome V, 264, "comme vous luy aviez faiet d'honneur de la convier d'en estre l'une des commères et qu'elle prioit Dieu de la rendre aussy heureuse comme elle estoit grande et comme elle s'assuroit qu'elle seroit vertueuse princesse, et de la fère ung commancement d'une si accomplie lignée à Voz Majestez Très Chrestiennes, que bientost elle eût une suyte d'aultant de frères."

[68] Catherine de Medici to Queen Elizabeth of England, 3 June 1572, in *LCM*, Tome IV, 104, "Roy mon fils, lequel l'embrasse de telle affection qu'il désire par tous moyens la faire immortelle [...] j 'ay toujours desire pouvoir avoir cet heur et honneur, que, ainsy que je vous

esteem you and have affection toward you [...] to tell you the truth, as much as toward my own daughter."[69] Finally, on August 21, just three days before the atrocity, she told La Mothe Fénélon that she had a strong desire for Elizabeth to become "my own daughter."[70]

The massacre brought Catherine's declarations of maternal affection to an abrupt end, for the time being at least, but the French royal family still clung to the hope that the marriage negotiations might eventually succeed. On August 28, La Mothe Fénélon sang the praises of the Duke of Alençon during an audience with Elizabeth, who instructed the ambassador to pass on her thanks to "the three of you, who have offered yourselves to her, one after another"—a reference to the earlier proposals of Charles and Henry.[71] Thereafter, she refused to entertain any questions or requests regarding a potential marriage to Francis, and the negotiations ground to a halt.[72] Catherine tried once again in the spring of 1573, when she told Elizabeth of her youngest son's desire "to serve you,"[73] but by then the queen had more pressing concerns because the massacre—as well as the fact that Mary Stuart was still in prison—had ratcheted up the religious tension in her own realm.[74]

Catherine and Charles were both determined to preserve the 1572 Treaty of Blois, which had established an alliance between France and England against Spain,[75] so their letters to the English court still abounded with expressions of goodwill toward the English queen, regardless of her

aime comme mère sa fille, que par une si heureuse occasion je me puisse nommer telle, [...] priant Dieu que puissiez congnoistre par effect l'amitié et affection que je vous porte."

[69] Catherine de Medici to Queen Elizabeth of England, June 21, 1572, in *LCM*, Tome IV, 105, "nous vous estimons et avons en affection et à vous dire vray autant que ma propre fille."

[70] Catherine de Medici to La Mothe Fénélon, August 21, 1572, in *LCM*, Tome IV, 111, "que si elle était ma propre fille."

[71] La Mothe Fénélon to the French king Charles IX, 271st Report, August 28, 1572, in *Correspondence diplomatique*, Tome V, 94 and 102, "remercyer de vous estre ainsy toutz troys, l'ung après l'aultre, offertz à elle."

[72] La Mothe Fénélon to the French king Charles IX, 282nd Report, November 2, 1572, in *Correspondence diplomatique*, Tome V, 194 "mais que de cella, ny du principal propos du mariage, elle ne m'y respondroit rien plus, pour ceste heure."

[73] Catherine de Medici to Queen Elizabeth of England, April 25, 1573, in *LCM*, Tome IV, 208, "que mon filzleDuc, qui continue de plus en plus en l'affection qu'il a de vous servir."

[74] Probasco, "Queen Elizabeth's reaction to the St. Bartholomew's Day Massacre," 89–91.

[75] Discussion of the treaty can be found in Lynn A. Martin, "Papal Policy and the European Conflict, 1559–1572," in *Sixteenth Century Journal*, 11:2 (1980): 35–48.

increasing indifference toward the marriage proposals. For instance, in October 1572, Charles informed La Mothe Fénélon that he was pleased

> to hear the assurance that my good said sister gives to me afresh and that she shows herself, in this instance, as affectionate toward me as I am toward her, which helps to confirm the good hope that I have had that no occasion will arise that might modify our said friendship, so I feel free to let her know more than ever that I am her true and sincere friend.[76]

In presenting himself as Elizabeth's "true and sincere friend," Charles expressed his strong desire to retain the queen as a firm ally. Catherine adopted a slightly different tactic, but her principal aim was the same: to safeguard the alliance between France and England. On September 13, 1572, she informed La Mothe Fénélon of a comment she had made to his counterpart in Paris, Sir Francis Walsingham:

> the deceased kings—Francis, my father-in-law, and King Henry of England, the queen's father—had different religions, but that did not prevent them from loving each other infinitely, and at that time we burned many people because of religion in France, but neither the said King Henry of England nor the other Protestant princes from Germany, with whom we were also friends at the time, were offended, and King Henry, my lord [Henry II of France, Catherine's husband], wanted to give my daughter [Elisabeth of Valois], who became Queen of Spain, to little King Edward, despite their different religions.[77]

By highlighting the long history of good relations between the two crowns, Catherine still hoped to convince the English queen to marry her

---

[76] Charles IX to La Mothe Fénélon, October 4, 1572, in *Correspondence diplomatique*, Tome VII, 369, "d'entandre t'asseurance que ma dicte bonne soeur m'en donnoit de nouveau, et de se montrer, en ce regard, autant aifectionnée à mon endroict que je montrois au sien qui me confirme de plus en plus en la bonne espérance, que j'ay ci devant eue, qu'il ne surviendra aucune ocasion qui puisse porter altération à nostre dicte amitié; car je suis délibéré de luy faire cognoistre, plus que jamais, que je luy suis vray et sincère amy."

[77] Catherine de Medici to La Mothe Fénélon, September 13, 1572, in *LCM*, Tome IV, 125, "A quoy je lui ay respondu que les feuz roys Francis mon beau-père et le roy Henry d'Angleterre père de la royne, sa maistresse, encore qu'ils feussent différents de la religion, ne laissoient pour cela de s'aymer infiniement, et que de ce temps-là l'on brusloit beaucoup de gens pour la religion en France, et que ledict roy Henry d'Angleterre, ny les autres princes de la Germanie protestans ausquels nous avions, dès lors, aussy amytié ne s'en altéroient point; que despuis, le Roy Henry, mon seigneur, avoit voulleu donner ma fille, qui feust depuis royne d'Espagne, au petit roy Edouard."

youngest son. Furthermore, she addressed the religious issue head on by explaining that it was not at all unusual for a potential royal couple to practice different faiths.

Catherine's obvious desperation to advance the marriage negotiations eventually gave Elizabeth the upper hand in her relations with the French royal family. Far from a feeble bride who needed the protection of a strong prince, she was able to adopt a traditionally male persona and appraise young Francis on the basis of his appearance. The French rulers had no option but to accept this presumably rather insulting role reversal because of their urgent need to safeguard the Anglo-French alliance. However, Elizabeth still needed an ally to project her preferred image to the French crown. She found one in the form of the French ambassador.

As we saw in Chap. 3, during the first few years of his tenure at the English court, La Mothe Fénélon was not averse to reporting Elizabeth's bad temper and angry outbursts, especially when he attempted to quiz her about Mary Stuart. However, his dispatches adopted a markedly different tone between 1572 and 1574. He started to highlight the queen's joyful mood and good humor in a bid to convince the French royal family that she would be receptive to all of their suggestions and proposals—up to and including marriage to the Duke of Alençon. It was through this tactic that he hoped to preserve good relations—and indeed the alliance—between the two sides. For instance, on August 28, 1572, before the awful news of the massacre had reached London, he noted that "the said lady, looking up, answered us with a better and more joyful face."[78] Anna Riehl Bertolet has argued that Elizabeth used her smile to give the impression that she had a "welcoming disposition,"[79] and she certainly seemed to have no trouble convincing La Mothe Fénélon of the fact. In his reports of their meetings in this period, he repeatedly informed his master of her contentment and good mood, and even went so far as to suggest that she remained enthusiastic regarding the potential union with Francis. For example, in May 1573, he reported that she had greeted him with "a happy face in a very modest manner."[80] Here, the term "modest" was a

[78] La Mothe Fénélon to the French king Charles IX, 271st Report, August 28, 1572, in *Correspondence diplomatique*, Tome V, 96, "La dicte Dame, réaulçant la teste, nous respondit, avec ung meilleur et plus joyeulx visage."

[79] Riehl Bertolet, *The Face of Queenship, Early modern representations of Elizabeth I*, 87.

[80] La Mothe Fénélon to the French king Charles IX, 316th Report, May 8, 1573, in *Correspondence diplomatique*, Tome V, 325, "La dicte Dame, d'ung visage contant et d'une façon bien modeste."

reference to Elizabeth's feminine attributes, so, yet again, La Mothe Fénélon was attempting to cast the queen in the traditional role of blushing bride.[81]

Later that summer, in order to highlight her receptivity, he twice reported the queen's "great happiness" on hearing the latest proposals from the French court.[82] Then, in October 1573, he hinted that some good news regarding the marriage negotiations might be forthcoming: "heartily she wanted you to be certain of what she had resolved to do [...] from her face and behavior, sir, it appeared that she felt greater satisfaction than I can possibly express."[83] According to the French ambassador, the queen's "satisfaction" and "happiness" were emblematic of her fervent desire to marry the Duke of Alençon. It is difficult to tell whether he genuinely believed that the main obstacle to the union—religion—had been overcome earlier in the year.

Elizabeth had expressed concerns over the two sides' religious differences since the very start of the marriage negotiations. However, by March 1573, she was more inclined to respond to the French ambassador's inquiries regarding the union, and La Mothe Fénélon was able to inform his master that she was willing to "allow him [Francis] and his servants, who are not subjects of this crown, the exercise of their religion in private."[84] This declaration echoed Francis Bacon's famous assertion: "Her majesty, not liking to make windows into men's hearts and secret thoughts except the abundance of them did overflow into overt and

---

[81] Modesty tropes were used by early modern women in order to write and have a voice in a male-dominated world, see Patricia Pender, *Early Modern Women's Writing and The Rhetoric of Modesty* (New York, NY: Palgrave Macmillan, 2012) but also how men expected women to behave, even the queen, and for instance how Aylmer "praises her learning, he couples his claims about her knowledge with parallel claims about her modesty." in Mary Villeponteaux, *The Queen's Mercy: Gender and Judgment in Representations of Elizabeth I*, 1.

[82] La Mothe Fénélon to the French king Charles IX, 329th Report, July 12, 1573, in *Correspondence diplomatique*, Tome V, 371, "Elle a monstré d'estre fort contante de la nouvelle" and 338th Report, August 31, 1573, 400, "A quoy elle, d'une démonstration pleyne de grand contantement."

[83] La Mothe Fénélon to the French king Charles IX, 344th Report, October 14, 1573, in *Correspondence diplomatique*, Tome V, 420, "de bon cueur qu'elle vous votût rendre maintenant certein de ce qu'elle avoit résolu d'en fère, il a apparu, Sire, en son visage et en ses contenances, une plus grande satisfaction que je ne la vous sçaurois exprimer."

[84] La Mothe Fénélon to the French king Charles IX, 306th Report, March 13, 1573, in *Correspondence diplomatique*, Tome V, 278, "elle ne le voulût tant contreindre en sa conscience que de ne luy laysser pour luy et ses domesticques, non subjectz de ceste couronne, l'exercice de sa religion en privée."

express acts and affirmations, tempered her law so as it restraineth only manifest disobedience."[85] In effect, according to La Mothe Fénélon, Elizabeth would permit the duke and his servants to practice their religion because they were not her subjects, so their adherence to Catholicism presented no challenge to her authority as a Protestant ruler. However, they must agree to celebrate their rites in private in order to preserve the peace of her realm. Elsewhere in the same report, the ambassador insisted that Elizabeth respected the duke "as a Catholic prince who cares with his heart for his God, his religion, and his conscience."[86] In short, he painted a picture of two people who were willing to respect each other's faith, with the implication being that the issue of religion no longer stood in the way of their happy union.

The Catholic La Mothe Fénélon never expressed any doubt about the Protestant queen's devotion to God. When Charles fell ill at the end of 1573, the French ambassador reported Elizabeth's concern: "God, who sees in her heart, knows that she has prayed for your convalescence, and she has truly prayed, and will not stop praying, with as much devotion as she can."[87] Two weeks later, La Mothe Fénélon insisted that the queen "will not reserve her best and most devoted prayers to God for herself."[88] The ambassador reported Elizabeth's religiosity in this way to convince his master of her piety, notwithstanding the two rulers' theological differences.

Prior to the massacre, La Mothe Fénélon had routinely portrayed the queen as "cautious and virtuous,"[89] two adjectives that highlighted her

---

[85] "A Discourse in Praise of Queen Elizabeth," *The Works of Francis Bacon: Baron of Verulam, Viscount St. Albans* ..., Ten Volumes, Volume 3 (London: W. Baynes and Son, 1824), 73. Also see: Kenneth L. Campbell, *Window's Into Men's Soul: Religious nonconformity in Tudor and Early Stuart England* (Plymouth: Lexington Books, 2012), 45 and Levin, *The Heart and Stomach of a King*, 18.

[86] La Mothe Fénélon to the French king Charles IX, 306th Report, March 13, 1573, in *Correspondence diplomatique*, Tome V, 277, "qu'elle jugeât ainsy de Monseigneur le Duc comme d'ung prince catholicque, qui avoit aultant à cueur ce qui estoit de son Dieu de sa religion et de sa conscience."

[87] La Mothe Fénélon to the French king Charles IX, 354th Report, December 5, 1573, in *Correspondence diplomatique*, Tome V, 457, "Dieu, qui voyoit son cueur, sçavoit qu'elle avoit pryé pour vostre convalescence, et que véritablement elle avoit pryé, et ne cesseroit de prier, avec le plus de dévotion qu'elle pourroit."

[88] La Mothe Fénélon to the French king Charles IX, 356th Report, December 17, 1573, in *Correspondence diplomatique*, Tome V, 464, "n'espargneroit elle non plus ses meilleures et plus devotes prières à Dieu qu'elle faysoit pour elle mesmes."

[89] La Mothe Fénélon to the French king Charles IX, 261st Report, July 5, 1572, in *Correspondence diplomatique*, Tome V, 32, "estoit si prudente et vertueuse."

unique status as a powerful, single, female monarch.[90] In the sixteenth century, few men would describe any woman as "cautious." On the contrary, John Knox's argument that women's counsel was "foolishness" was much more prevalent.[91] Furthermore, by combining an adjective that was usually reserved for men (cautious) with one that was commonly applied to women (virtuous), La Mothe Fénélon represented the English queen as a male as well as a female ruler. In another dispatch, the French ambassador described one of Elizabeth's speeches in typically glowing terms: "such a beautiful order of words, uttered with affection and with so much grace, and with so much embellishment, that the two of us [the ambassador and his secretary] and her people were deeply amazed."[92] Here, once again, La Mothe Fénélon combined his admiration for a supposedly masculine quality—erudition—with praise for the traditionally feminine attributes of "affection" and "grace." Such references to Elizabeth's virtue and grace helped the ambassador to fashion a portrait of a chaste, unblemished queen who possessed all of the qualities that the French royal family expected of a potential bride for Francis. Indeed, in July 1573, he reported that Elizabeth was eager for Charles to "know that she is pure."[93] Purity was another essential feminine quality at the time, and asserting it counterbalanced Elizabeth's more "masculine" behavior, such as her assessments of the Duke of Alençon's beauty, or otherwise.

In the early phase of the marriage negotiations, as we have seen, Elizabeth's principal concerns had been the religious issue and the age difference between herself and the Duke.[94] However, after the massacre, much of her attention turned to Francis's appearance. He had caught smallpox at just eight years of age, and his face was badly scarred as a

---

[90] Kevin Sharpe explains that "her sex enabled Elizabeth herself to represent both vulnerability and strength," in Sharpe, *Selling the Tudor Monarchy*, 323.

[91] Knox, *The first blast of the trumpet against the monstruous regiment of women*, 10.

[92] La Mothe Fénélon to the French king Charles IX, 271st Report, August 28, 1572, in *Correspondence diplomatique*, Tome V, 102–103, "Et exprima la dicte Dame toutes ces choses beaucoup plus amplement, et avec ung si bel ordre de parolles, prononcées d'affection et avec tant de grâce, et encores avec tant d'ornement, que nous deux, et les siens mesmes en restâmes bien fort esmerveillés."

[93] La Mothe Fénélon to the French king Charles IX, 329th Report, July 12, 1573, in *Correspondence diplomatique*, Tome V, 371, "eussiez cognu qu'elle estoit pure."

[94] La Mothe Fénélon to the French king Charles IX, 271st Report, August 28, 1572, in *Correspondence diplomatique*, Tome V, 102, "voyr'si les difficultez de l'eage et aultres qui se trouvoient entre elle et luy."

result.[95] This allowed the English queen to adopt the traditional male role of suitor and insist that the duke's physical appearance was an important issue, which in turn enabled her to establish that her future husband would never be her master. La Mothe Fénélon reported that "she wants him to be entirely hers and to come into her possession."[96] This notion that Francis would be "hers"—that is, Elizabeth's chattel—rather than vice versa, highlighted that the queen expected to enjoy the dominant—masculine—role in the marriage.

It was not unusual for Elizabeth to insist on seeing her suitors in the flesh. For instance, in one of his dispatches, the Spanish ambassador Diego Guzman de Silva reported that "she cannot accord to take any person to her husband whom she shall not first see."[97] She made a similar demand with respect to Francis in April 1573, which reinforced her image as the dominant party in the marriage negotiations.[98] Interestingly, in July 1571, Catherine had asked La Mothe Fénélon for a better miniature of Elizabeth, because the one she had was quite banal.[99] Immediately after the massacre, however, there was a significant shift in the balance of power, as the French ambassador repeatedly reported the queen's concerns over the duke's scars. For example, in light of "what she has been told regarding the face," this "will be such an intense issue that she will never be pleased with it."[100] The "hindrance of the face" was still an "intense issue" almost a year

[95] Jacqueline Boucher, "Autour de Francis, duc d'Alençon et d'Anjou, un parti d'opposition à Charles IX et Henry III," in *Henry III et son temps: actes du Colloque international du Centre de la Renaissance de Tours, octobre 1989* (Paris: Librairie philosophique J. Vrin, 1992), 121–31, also Elizabeth I of England caught smallpox in 1562 so it was a disease that she knew would impact physical appearance.

[96] La Mothe Fénélon to Catherine de Medici, April 13, 1573, in *Correspondence diplomatique*, Tome V, 298, "qu'elle le voulût accepter comme entièrement sien, et qu'il se viendroit mettre en sa possession."

[97] *Calendar of the Letters and State Papers to English Affairs Preserved in, originally Belonging to, the Archives of Simancas*, ed. Martin Hume, vol. 1 (London: HMSO, 1892), 70.

[98] Doran, *Monarchy and Matrimony* and La Mothe Fénélon to Catherine, April 13, 1573, in *Correspondence diplomatique*, Tome V, 300, "de ne s'obliger jamays à aulcun mariage qu'elle n'eût veu celluy qu'elle espouseroit."

[99] Catherine de Mecidi to La Mothe Fénélon, July 3, 1571, in *LCM*, Tome IV, 53.

[100] La Mothe Fénélon to the French king Charles IX, 271st Report, August 28, 1572, in *Correspondence diplomatique*, Tome V, 94, "luy avoit rapporté du visage seroient objetz si véhémentz qu'elle ne s'en peut jamais contanter."

later,[101] and the French ambassador reiterated Elizabeth's concerns in February 1574, writing that she "wanted to be assured that the smallpox had not left him with any deformities on any aspect of his face that she could never be pleased with."[102] Even more significant than the comments themselves, however, was the fact that the French rulers deigned to defend Francis's appearance and therefore implicitly recognized Elizabeth's right to question his attractiveness. Once again, this reinforced her image as the masculine suitor and the dominant party in the negotiations.[103] For example, in a letter of March 1573, Catherine informed La Mothe Fénélon:

> [Francis] has no deformity [...] on the contrary, he is of a good, dignified height, from the same house and issue as his own father and mother, has a very good heart and hearing too, and there is nothing to say about his face aside from that it happened by accident [i.e., the scars were due to smallpox, not hereditary] [...] [Otherwise,] he is like my son the Duke of Anjou, whom she loved so much.[104]

This reference to the marriage negotiations between Elizabeth and Henry, Duke of Anjou, which had broken down in 1571, indicates that Catherine was fully aware of Elizabeth's predilection for attractive suitors. Her intention was to remind La Mothe Fénélon that the English queen had been more than pleased with Henry's physical appearance, so she would not be disappointed by his brother, notwithstanding Francis's scars.

Six months later, Charles offered further reassurance in a personal letter to Elizabeth:

---

[101] La Mothe Fénélon to the French king Charles IX, 331st Report, 26 July 1573, in *Correspondence diplomatique*, Tome V, 383, "l'empeschement du visage."

[102] La Mothe Fénélon to the French king Charles IX, 363rd Report, February 9, 1574, in *Correspondence diplomatique*, Tome VI, 22, "voulu assurer que la petite vérolle luy avoit layssé je ne sçay quy de difformité en quelque endroit du vysage, qu'elle ne s'en pourroit jamays contanter."

[103] Furthermore, this issue of attractiveness seems to be reminiscent among the Tudors as Henry VIII (Elizabeth's father) was deeply concerned with his fourth wife Anne of Cleves' appearance and was disappointed when he finally met her. See Levin, *The Heart and Stomach of a King*, 50.

[104] Catherine de Medici to La Mothe Fénélon, March 30, 1573, in *LCM*, Tome IV, 190, "il n'a voit rien de difforme, et au contraire qu'il estoit de fort belle taille, de la mesme maison et sorty des propre père et mère, ayant le coeur très bon et l'entendement de mesme et qu'il n'y avoit rien à dire sinon le visage; encore c'estoit par accident, qu'il ne fust tout tel. que mon filz le duc d'Anjou qu'elle a tant aymé."

my said brother Alençon [...] contrary to what has been published, has recovered from the disease that latterly purged him, removing many of the red spots that the smallpox had left on his face [...] Now, with the beard that is growing, he is more agreeable than has been said [...] he is a strong and vigorous prince and as great a height as may be found in Christendom.[105]

These somewhat desperate efforts to portray Francis as a handsome, energetic prince reveal the extent to which Elizabeth had claimed the upper hand in the marriage negotiations by 1573.

The images of the "germayne" sister, the godmother, the perfect ally, and the "male" suitor were all consistent with the development of an overall representation of Elizabeth as a full—as opposed to virtual—member of the French royal family, regardless of the fact that she had not yet married into it. Nevertheless, although Charles and Catherine were desperate to maintain the alliance and hoped to strengthen it by persuading Elizabeth to marry Francis, their suspicions remained. Moreover, some of her decisions—and especially her indecision—often left them mystified.

## IN CONTROL OR UNDER CONTROL: ELIZABETH'S INDECISION AND POLITICAL SKILLS

As we have seen, many scholars have studied the balance of power within the Elizabethan government.[106] However, few, if any, of these authors have consulted the French diplomatic correspondence of the time. These fascinating documents reveal that the question of who was in control of England's affairs evolved significantly after the St. Bartholomew's Day Massacre as a more complex image of Elizabeth started to emerge. Scholars such as Carolly Erikson and Christopher Haigh have claimed that

[105] Charles IX to La Mothe Fénélon, September 26, 1573, in *Correspondence diplomatique*, Tome VII, 446, "mon dict frère d'Alençon; lequel, au contraire de ce qu'on a publié, est beaucoup amandé de ceste maladie dernière qui l'a purgé, luy ayant osté beaucoup de rougeurs que la petite vérolle luy av.oit laissées au visage estant maintenant, avec la barbe qui luy vient fort, beaucoup plus agréable qu'ilz n'ont dict.de delà [...] il est aussy droict et gaillard prince et d'aùssy belle taille qu'il y en ait en la Chrestienté."
[106] See discussion in the introduction. Also see Michael Barraclough Pullman, *The Elizabethan privy council in the fifteen-seventies* (Berkeley and Los Angeles: CA, 1971); John Guy, "The Rhetoric of Counsel in early modern England," in *Tudor political culture*, ed. Dale Hoak (Cambridge: Cambridge University Press, 1995), 292–310.

Elizabeth's councillors and ambassadors viewed her as indecisive,[107] but their studies lack a foreign perspective on her personality and capacity to rule—an oversight I aim to address here.

La Mothe Fénélon counterbalanced his conventional praise for Elizabeth with occasional complaints about postponed or canceled audiences and barbed comments about the excessive influence of her privy councillors. For instance, in August 1572, the French ambassador reported that Elizabeth "begged us to give her the leisure to have one entire day to deliberate,"[108] and following month he wrote that "she begged me to give her two days to think about it and then give an answer."[109] La Mothe Fénélon frequently interpreted this procrastination as indicative of the fact that the queen was overly reliant on her councillors' opinions, which left her unable to reach a firm decision quickly. For example, in August 1573, he wrote, "to satisfy those of her council, she beseeched me to give her time,"[110] and there are countless other references to the Privy Council's influence throughout his dispatches.[111] Indeed, in January 1574, Elizabeth bluntly informed the ambassador that some members of the council were absent from the court while others were ill, which left her unable to reach

---

[107] Christopher Haigh, *Elizabeth I* (Harlow: Pearson Education Limited, Second Edition, 1998), 176 and 183 and Carolly Erickson, *The First Elizabeth*, (New York: Macmillan, 1983), 350.

[108] La Mothe Fénélon to the French king Charles IX, 271st Report, August 28, 1572, in *Correspondence diplomatique*, Tome V, 97, "Elle nous pria de luy donner encores le loysir d'ung jour entier pour dellibérer."

[109] La Mothe Fénélon to the French king Charles IX, 276th Report, September 29, 1572, in *Correspondence diplomatique*, Tome V, 147, "elle m'a prié de luy donner deux jours pour y penser, et qu'eue me feroit avoir responce."

[110] La Mothe Fénélon to the French king Charles IX, 334th Report, August 9, 1573, in *Correspondence diplomatique*, Tome V, 390, "pour satisfère à ceulx de son conseil, elle me prioit de [uy donner temps."

[111] La Mothe Fénélon to the French king Charles IX, 358th Report, December 31, 1573, in *Correspondence diplomatique*, Tome V, 475, "elle m'a néantmoins fort conjure de ne me douloyr de ce petit dellay, qui luy faysoit encores besoing, car m'assuroit qu'il ne seroit long."; La Mothe Fénélon to the French king Charles IX, 362nd Report, January 26, 1574, in *Correspondence diplomatique*, Tome VI, 16, "pour presser ceste princesse de me vouloir fère sa response sur le propos de Monseigneur le Duc, et elle a monster qu'elle estoit preste dele fère, et que nulle dimcutté, ny argument du passé, y donuoit plus d'empéschement, s'en estant elle, avec ceulx de son conseil, entièrement bien résolue mais de nouveau, aulcuns escrupules, autxquels elle pensoit'que Vostre Majesté pourroit facittement satisfère" and La Mothe Fénélon to the French king Charles IX, 369th Report, March 7, 1574, in *Correspondence diplomatique*, Tome VI, 49, "Sire, parce que la Royne d'Angleterre veult prendre ung peu de temps à dettibérer de ce qu'elle aura à respondre."

any decisions on important matters or even discuss them with him.[112] These reports of postponed audiences and delayed responses to the French rulers' requests conveyed an image of a queen who was not only indecisive but also susceptible to manipulation and unable to assert complete control over England's policy-making.

In September 1572, La Mothe Fénélon reported: "All the most important members of the council of England went to find this Queen and draft new legislation for the realm."[113] The following month, his criticism of the councillors was even more explicit: "they are determined to make this princess doubtful and mistrustful."[114] Moreover, by January 1573, he was accusing some councillors of arranging clandestine meetings with Huguenot leaders with a view to providing support for their fellow Protestants in the fourth religious civil war: "though those of La Rochelle were not openly heard by the Queen and those of her council, regarding their requests, they are however secretly received."[115]

Charles echoed his ambassador's concerns over what seemed to be the increasing influence of Elizabeth's council, especially in the aftermath of the St. Bartholomew's Day Massacre. For instance, in September 1572, he urged La Mothe Fénélon to keep a close eye on "the queen of England and the said lords of her council, all of whom I am sure are arming themselves on sea and on land to launch an attack against me."[116]

[112] La Mothe Fénélon to the French king Charles IX, 359th Report, January 5, 1574, in *Correspondence diplomatique*, Tome VI, 2, "qu'il estoit très raysonnable qu'elle vous lit bientost sçavoir la response qu'attandiés maintenant d'elle, laquelle elle ne vous voutoit nullement diuérer, et me prioit seulement de luy donner deux ou troys jours de terme pour en dellibérer avec ses conseillers, desquelz l'absence des ungs, et la maladye des aultres, estoit cause qu'elle n'y avoit peu vacquer, durant ces festes, ainsy qu'elle me l'avoit promis."

[113] La Mothe Fénélon to the French king Charles IX, 275th Report, September 18, 1572, in *Correspondence diplomatique*, Tome V, 136, "Toutz les principaulx du conseil d'Angleterre sont allez trouver ceste Royne, et ont mis quelques nouveaulx ordres par le royaulme."

[114] La Mothe Fénélon to the French king Charles IX, 280th Report, October 18, 1572, in *Correspondence diplomatique*, Tome V, 173, "mot à mot, comme ilz le luy ont dict, qui monstre bien, Sire, qu'itz mettent grand peyne de faire devenir ceste princesse fort ombrageuse et deffiante."

[115] La Mothe Fénélon to the French king Charles IX, 296th Report, January 22, 1573, in *Correspondence diplomatique*, Tome V, 242, "et nonobstant que ceulx de la Rochelle ne soient ouvertement ouyz par la Royne ny de ceulx de son conseil, en leurs instances, elles sont toutesfoys secrettement reçues" also see: La Mothe Fénélon to the French king Charles IX, 297th Report, January 25, 1573, 245.

[116] Charles IX to La Mothe Fénélon, September 22, 1572, in *Correspondence diplomatique*, Tome VII, 356, "la Royne d'Angleterre et les dicts'seigneurs de son conseil, que, tout ainsy

Clearly, then, the French rulers and their ambassador had little doubt that the queen's councillors exercised significant influence over her decision-making. Therefore, it is hardly surprising that they attempted to recruit them as potential allies in their efforts to convince Elizabeth to marry the Duke of Alençon. In February 1573, their lobbying seemed to have paid dividends, as La Mothe Fénélon reported that the councillors were on the verge of approving the terms of the marriage and "saw it as a necessity for their queen and her realm."[117] The negotiations dragged on, but the following April La Mothe Fénélon informed the French king that one of Elizabeth's principal councillors had assured him that the queen and her council still believed that the marriage was essential.[118] Consequently, the French royal family remained optimistic that an agreement would be reached, not least because the ambassador reported that some of the councillors shared their frustration over the pace of the negotiations. For example, in July 1573, La Mothe Fénélon had a meeting with William Cecil, Lord Burghley, during which the latter confided that he was "very puzzled [...] [H]e knew his Mistress was willing to marry, and did not think she had changed her mind again, and, for his part, he desired it more than anything else in the world."[119]

However, while both the ambassador and his masters in Paris surely welcomed the news that one of Elizabeth's most senior and trusted advisers was in favor of the marriage, such reports simultaneously challenged the received wisdom regarding England's governance. Specifically, if La Mothe Fénélon and Charles were correct and the Privy Council did indeed

que je tiens pour certain que ce qu'ettc arme maintenant par mer et par terre n'est pour entreprendre contre moy."

[117] La Mothe Fénélon to the French king Charles IX, 300th Report, February 13, 1573, in *Correspondence diplomatique*, Tome V, 257, "le propos du mariage ne tarderoit après d'estre approuvé par toutz ceulx de ce conseil, comme chose qu'ilz voyent bien qui est plus nécessayre à teur Mestresse et à son royaulme."

[118] La Mothe Fénélon to the French king Charles IX, 375th Report, April 15, 1574, in *Correspondence diplomatique*, Tome VI, 78–79, "Ung de ses principaulx conseillers, sur une nostre privée communicquation, m'a faict sçavoyr que la dicte Dame et ceulx de son conseil ne-furent oncques mieulx disposés qu'à présent au propos du mariage, parce qu'ilz prévoyent, plus que jamays, par une occulte nécessité qui est dans cest estat, qu'elle et toutz eulx sont ruynés, si elle ne se marye."

[119] La Mothe Fénélon to the French king Charles IX, 331th Report, July 26, 1573, in *Correspondence diplomatique*, Tome V, 382, "Le dict milord s'est trouvé fort perplex, [...] il.m'a dict que, devant Dieu et en sa conscience, il avoit cognu sa Mestresse en intention de se marier, et ne voyoit pas qu'elle eûtencores changé, et que, de sa part, il le desiroit.ptus que chose du monde."

exert considerable—and possibly excessive—influence over Elizabeth's decision-making, why had her councillors not yet managed to convince her to marry Francis? The only conclusion was that she had rather more control over her own—and England's—destiny than the ambassador's reports often implied. Indeed, on one occasion, La Mothe Fénélon admitted that, while most of the councillors supported the union, the marriage would go ahead only if "the person of my said Lord could please their Mistress."[120] This was just one of several occasions when the ambassador used the term "Mistress" when reporting the opinions of privy councillors, a term of address that implied the queen was in full control of the marriage negotiations.[121] Moreover, if that were the case, then La Mothe Fénélon and the French royal family had to consider the possibility that, far from being a puppet of her councillors, Elizabeth was actually a puppet master who used the Privy Council as a shield to conceal her own policies and actions, and to buy herself more time when contemplating difficult political decisions.

After the massacre and the eruption of the fourth religious civil war, many Huguenots, including their leader Gabriel de Montgomery, sought refuge in England.[122] Previously, Montgomery had been an important figure at the French court. It was he who had mortally wounded Henry II during a jousting tournament, and he was almost killed himself during the massacre in Paris. Once in England, he orchestrated a number of plots against Catholics in France, and the French royal family suspected that Elizabeth was already supporting him and might soon help him to besiege the crucial port of La Rochelle.[123] Therefore, Charles instructed La Mothe Fénélon to make some "discreet" inquiries.[124] In January 1573, the

---

[120] La Mothe Fénélon to the French king Charles IX, 340th Report, September 20, 1573, in *Correspondence diplomatique*, Tome V, 408, "pourveu que la personne de Mon dict Seigneur puisse comptère à leur Mestresse."

[121] See: La Mothe Fénélon to Catherine de Medici, February 20, 1574, *Correspondence diplomatique*, Tome VI, 37; La Mothe Fénélon to the French king Charles IX, 367th Report, February 26, 1574, in *Correspondence diplomatique*, Tome VI, 40 and La Mothe Fénélon to the French king Charles IX, 347th Report, October 26, 1573, in *Correspondence diplomatique*, Tome V, 430.

[122] Arlette Jouanna, *La France du XVIe siècle, 1483–1598*, 500; also see the works of Diefendorf, *Beneath the Cross*, and Robin Briggs, *Early Modern France 1560–1715*, (Oxford, London, and New York: Oxford University Press, 1977).

[123] MacCaffrey, *Queen Elizabeth and the Making of Policy*, 180.

[124] Charles IX to La Mothe Fénélon, August 27, 1572, in *Correspondence diplomatique*, Tome VII, 330, "vous priant aussy de vous enquérir doucement quels de mes subjects de la religion se sont retires en Angleterre, et principalement Montgomery."

ambassador sent his report: "the queen of England gave as a gift a vessel with six hundred barrels, and two others of five hundred barrels each, to her admiral," while, "to rescue La Rochelle, I have to tell you that they are now in a rush to execute their enterprises promptly."[125]

This dispatch meant that the French royal family faced a dilemma. As this chapter has repeatedly demonstrated, they were desperate to preserve the alliance with England, so they could not afford to accuse the English queen of supporting the Protestant insurgency or being an enemy of France. As for Elizabeth, she had no desire to breach the Treaty of Blois, particularly as the situation in the Netherlands was deteriorating and she needed Charles's help to counteract the growing power of Philip II of Spain.

Ironically, the cause of much of the suspicion—La Mothe Fénélon—played a crucial role in maintaining good relations between the two sides over the ensuing months. In late February 1573, he assured Charles that Elizabeth "had ordered all English captains who were about to go to La Rochelle not to go, on pain of death."[126] A few weeks later, the ambassador reported that members of the nobility and the clergy had criticized this decision on the grounds that,

> more than hurting herself, her crown and her subjects, she had abandoned the defense of their religion [...] [S]he could not have offended God and her own conscience any more than by forbidding the said Montgomery to support his country, through whatever means he could, and his religion's cause.[127]

[125] La Mothe Fénélon to the French king Charles IX, 396th Report, January 22, 1573, in *Correspondence diplomatique*, Tome V, 243, "la Royne d'Angleterre a faict présant d'ung navyre de six centz tonneaulx, et de deux aultres de cent cinquante tonneaulx chacun, à son admiral" and La Mothe Fénélon to the French king Charles IX, 297th Report, January 25, 1573, 245, "de secourir la Rochelle, j'ay à vous dire maintenant qu'ilz préparent à furie d'en exécuter promptement leurs entreprinses."

[126] La Mothe Fénélon to the French king Charles IX, 303rd Report, February 27, 1573, in *Correspondence diplomatique*, Tome V, 263, "elle a faict deffendre à aulcuns cappitaines anglois, lesquelles s'apprestoient d'aller en cours, que, sur peyne de vye, ilz n'aillent poinct à la Rochelle."

[127] La Mothe Fénélon to the French king Charles IX, 303rd Report, March 19, 1573, in *Correspondence diplomatique*, Tome V, 282, "que les évesques et plusieurs principaux personnages de ce royaulme luy estoient venus remonstrer que, oultre le tort qu'elle faysoit à elle mesmes, à sa couronne et à ses subjectz, d'abandonner la deffance de leur religion, elle ne pourroit plus griefvement otfaneer Dieu et à sa conscience que d'empescher que le dict de

The question of religion remained intricately intertwined with politics in both countries. Elizabeth's defense of the Protestant cause, which had helped her to preserve unity and peace both inside and outside her borders, was at stake. In June 1573, La Mothe Fénélon revealed the English queen's desire for greater religious tolerance towards Protestants in France: "she answered me freely that she wanted you to grant your subjects moderate exercise of their religion, which would be neither insulting nor insolent against your other subjects of the Catholic religion."[128] In another dispatch, Elizabeth displayed not only a talent for arguing her case but also her knowledge of recent Anglo-French history:

> she could swear, in truth, that she did not know [...] that the Count of Montgomery was in her realm, and that if he did come, she would answer to you in the same way as the late King, your father, did to the late Queen Mary, her sister, that "he did not want to be the executioner of the Queen of England" [...] [T]herefore, if your Majesty will excuse her, she does not want to be the executioner of [followers of] her religion, just as he had not wanted to be the one of those who were not of his own.[129]

By presenting this parallel between Elizabeth and Henry II without comment, La Mothe Fénélon helped the queen to deflect any criticism regarding her political decision-making. Furthermore, he allowed her to remind Charles of the massacre and the fourth religious civil war while presenting herself as a model of benevolent, principled rule. It was a typically deft and subtle political maneuver by Elizabeth, and the French ambassador acted as her willing mouthpiece.

---

Montgommery n'allât soubstenir en son pays, par les moyens qu'il pourroit, la cause de sa religion."

[128] La Mothe Fénélon to the French king Charles IX, 325th Report, June 22, 1573, in *Correspondence diplomatique*, Tome V, 359, "Elle m'a respondu fort librement qu'.elle voudroit qu'octroyssiez à voz subjectz leur retigion, avec quelque exercice modéré, qui ne fût ny injurieutx, ny insolant, contre voz aultres subjectz de la religion catholicque."

[129] La Mothe Fénélon to the French king Charles IX, 320th Report, June 3, 1573, in *Correspondence diplomatique*, Tome V, 339, "qu'elle me pouvoit jurer, avec vérité, qu'elle ne sçavoit, en façon du monde, que le comte de Montgommery fût en ce royaulme, et, quand il y viendroit, elle vous respondroit de mesmes que feist le feu Roy, vostre père à la feu Royne Marie, sa soeur, "Qu'il ne vouloit estre le bourreau de la Royne d'Angleterre;" Et ainsy, que Vostre Majesté l'excusât, si elle ne-vouloit être le bourreau de ceulx de sa religion, non plus qu'il ne l'avoit voulu estre de ceulx qui n'estoient pas de la sienne."

Overall, then, while the French ambassador's reports often portrayed the English queen as an indecisive woman who was easily manipulated by her advisers, on other occasions he depicted her as a skillful politician who knew how to defend her interests in difficult circumstances and therefore retained complete control over the decision-making process in her realm.

## CONCLUSION

After the St Bartholomew's Day Massacre, recalibrating the image of Elizabeth as a good family member became paramount for the French rulers. Having been a "good sister," Elizabeth became a "germayne" one; Charles and his wife also made her the godmother of their only child. Furthermore, she was not only perceived but consistently presented as a potential bride for the Duke of Alençon, partly to highlight the fact that she was a true ally of the French royal family. Yet, because the French court and their ambassador went to such great lengths to assuage Elizabeth's doubts about the duke's physical appearance, they allowed her to assume the role of male suitor in the marriage negotiations, and therefore gain the upper hand in the alliance between the two crowns.

This was just one example of the political skills that Elizabeth exhibited in her dealings with the French ambassador and his masters in Paris. I believe that La Mothe Fénélon himself was sufficiently astute to realize that he was at the court of an accomplished politician, and he attempted to convey as much to Charles and Catherine, rather than present the queen as nothing more than a potential champion of Europe's Protestants— the simplistic role that many of Elizabeth's own councillors ascribed to her. Far from being one-dimensional, his representations of her remained ambivalent and multifaceted long after the massacre. In that respect, they provide an accurate reflection of the woman herself.

The next chapter will explore how Elizabeth's reputation continued to evolve among her French counterparts during the ongoing marriage negotiations and in the midst of a number of important events that occurred between 1579 and 1581.

# "he will have the honor to marry her this time": Last Chance to Marry the "Frog," 1579–1581

I grieve and dare not show my discontent;
I love, and yet am forced to seem to hate;
I do, yet dare not say I ever meant;
I seem stark mute, but inwardly do prate.[1]

This poem, written after the Duke of Anjou (formerly the Duke of Alençon) left England for good in 1581, is widely attributed to Elizabeth.[2] It not only marked the end of ten years of intense negotiations to unite the crowns of England and France but also expressed the queen's melancholy as her last chance of marriage slipped away.[3] Three years later, she sent it to Catherine de Medici to express her profound grief on hearing the news of the duke's premature death.[4]

---

[1] "On Monsieur's Departure" circa 1582, in *Elizabeth I: Collected Works*, 302.

[2] The author of the poem remains a matter of debate, although both Bell, *The Voice of a Monarch*, 145 and Steven May, *Queen Elizabeth: Selected Works* (New York: Washington Square Press, 2004), 13, insist that it was written by Elizabeth herself.

[3] For Ilona Bell, "'On Monsieur's Departure,' is intensely personal," in *The Voice of a Monarch*, 145. Furthermore, Bell gives a thorough analysis of the poem within its political context, 153–71.

[4] Elizabeth I of England to Catherine de Medici, Queen Mother of France, on Monsieur's death, circa July 1584, in *Elizabeth I: Collected Works*, 260 and also see Levin, *The Heart and Stomach of a King*, 64.

© The Author(s) 2019
E. Paranque, *Elizabeth I of England through Valois Eyes*, Queenship and Power, https://doi.org/10.1007/978-3-030-01529-9_5

Francis was the first of Elizabeth's three French suitors to visit her in England—he did so twice, in 1579 and 1581—which demonstrated that the marriage negotiations between the two crowns reached a more advanced stage than they ever had before.[5] Inevitably, then, this phase of the negotiations had a profound impact on both the Anglo-French alliance and the French rulers' perception of their English counterpart. Meanwhile, relations with Spain became more strained due to the unstable situation in the Netherlands.[6] William "the Silent" of Orange hoped that the Anglo-French alliance would protect the Low Countries from Spanish domination,[7] but the alliance itself was far from secure. France was embroiled in year-long religious civil war from November 1579 (its seventh in less than twenty years), and then the marriage negotiations collapsed with potentially dire consequences for Anglo-French relations.[8]

Scholars who have studied the marriage negotiations between Elizabeth and Anjou—such as Patrick Collinson, Natalie Mears, Jonathan Gibson, and Debra Barrett-Grave—have tended to focus on the political agendas of their two countries and the consequences of the process with respect to the stability of the English government, or its impact on a more personal level.[9] Such works provide insightful, important explanations of how marriage negotiations may influence political and religious as well as personal rela-

[5] Levin, *The Heart and Stomach of a King*, 61–63 and Holt, *The Duke of Anjou and the Politique Struggle during the Wars of Religion*, 161.

[6] Jouanna, *La France du XVIe siècle*, 570–1.

[7] Jouanna, *La France du XVIe siècle*, 571.

[8] Robert Knecht, *Hero or Tyrant? Henry III, King of France, 1574–89* (Farnham: Ashgate, 2014), 175.

[9] As noted in the introduction, historians have been fascinated with the ways the English government ruled under Elizabeth and how it influenced the Elizabethan public sphere and Elizabeth's own royal authority, see the works of Patrick Collinson, *Elizabethan Essays* (London and Rio Grande: The Hambledon Press, 1994) and the works of Natalie Mears such as *Queenship and Political Discourse in the Elizabethan realms* (Cambridge: Cambridge University Press, 2005) particularly chapter "Elizabeth I and the politics of intimacy," 33 and Mears, "Counsel, Public Debate and Queenship: John Stubbs's The discoverie of a gaping gulf," *The Historical Journal*, 44 (2001): 629–50. As for the works focusing on a more private level, see Jonathan Gibson, "'Dedans la plié de mon fidelle affection': Familiarity and Materiality in Elizabeth's Letters to Anjou," in *Elizabeth I's Foreign Correspondence: Letters, Rhetoric, and Politics*, 63–89 and Debra Barrett-Graves, "'Highly touched in honour': Elizabeth I and the Alençon Controversy," in *Elizabeth I: Always her own free woman*, eds. Carole Levin, Jo Eldridge Carney and Debra Barrett-Graves (Aldershot: Ashgate, 2003), 43–62.

tions. Furthermore, in her work on the Tudor queen's diplomacy, Rayne Allinson has looked at their impact on Elizabeth's and Catherine's relationship (but not the former's relationships with Henry III and Anjou).[10] By contrast, this chapter will explore how the final attempts of the French royal family to marry the heir to the throne to the English queen precipitated a shift in the representations of Elizabeth in their correspondence.

Between 1579 and 1581, although Elizabeth was still depicted as a potential bride with many admirable qualities who usually greeted the French ambassador with a joyful demeanor, this representation was increasingly supplemented with alternative—frequently rather negative—images of the English queen. Furthermore, while English authors would heap praise on Elizabeth for her virtue and virginity in the 1580s, the French royal correspondence at the start of the decade scarcely mentioned these qualities, even though they were usually considered essential attributes in a potential bride.[11] Indeed, Michel de Castelnau, Seigneur de Mauvissière, who had succeeded La Mothe Fénélon as French ambassador to the English court in 1575, alluded to Elizabeth's virginity only once, when assuring Henry III that the English queen "promised on her honor that she had never known nor courted a man" in September 1579.[12] Susan Doran explains that the image of the Virgin Queen was developed between 1579 and 1583, and that "the patrons of these early representations of the Virgin Queen were some of her subjects who opposed the French match."[13] Therefore, rather than being a token of Elizabeth's suitability as a bride, her virginity served as an emblem of her celibacy. This could explain why both it and her good character were seldom mentioned in the French royal correspondence during these years.

By focusing on the last two years of the marriage negotiations, this chapter examines the complexities of Anglo-French diplomatic relations during a very volatile period, as well as their impact on representations of

---

[10] Rayne Allinson, *A Monarchy in Letter*, 94–109.
[11] Susan Doran, "Why Did Elizabeth Not Marry?," in *Dissing Elizabeth: Negative Representations of Gloriana*, ed. Julia M. Walker (Durham and London: Duke University Press, 1998), 30 and John Cooper, *The Queen's Agent*, 123.
[12] Mauvissière to Henry III of France, 262nd Report, September 2, 1579, BNF MS. Fr. 15973, fol. 176v°, "a promis sur son honneur la dite royne quelle na jamais connu ni frequente homme."
[13] Doran, "Why Did Elizabeth Not Marry?," 37; Also see Strong, *The Cult of Elizabeth: Elizabethan Portraiture and Pageantry* (London: Pimlico, 1999).

the English queen among her French counterparts. Specifically, it highlights a shift in representations of Elizabeth in the correspondence of the Valois family and their ambassadors. As earlier chapters have emphasized, it was crucial for France and England to remain allies because of their mutual interest in countering Spain's power, and this continued into the 1579–1581 period. However, the Portuguese succession crisis, the Dutch revolt, the start of the seventh religious civil war in France, and disputes over the regency in Scotland all strained the alliance between the two nations, with the effect that it proved ever more difficult to maintain.[14]

While Chaps. 3 and 4 have focused on the impact of specific events—such as Mary Stuart's arrival in England and the St. Bartholomew's Day Massacre—on depictions of Elizabeth in the French diplomatic correspondence, this chapter explores how an ongoing process—namely, the final years of marriage negotiations—had significant consequences for the English queen's reputation abroad. From the final obstacles in the marriage negotiations to the political context in which France persistently endeavored to preserve the alliance with England, it provides a thorough analysis of the evolution of Anglo-French royal relations in the late 1570s and early 1580s.

## THE FINAL OBSTACLES IN THE MARRIAGE NEGOTIATIONS

In August 1579, the Puritan lawyer John Stubbs published a pamphlet entitled *The Discoverie of a Galping Gulf whereinto England is liked to be swallowed* that openly criticized the English queen's intention to marry the Duke of Anjou.[15] Elizabeth's reaction was fierce: she ordered the removal of the right hands of both Stubbs and his publisher.[16] In the pamphlet, Stubbs referred to Elizabeth as "a natural mother" and "the

---

[14] Jean Delumeau (ed.), *Une Histoire du Monde aux Temps Modernes* (Lavis: Bibliothèque Historique Larousse, 2013), 107–9.

[15] Ilona Bell, "'Soueraigne Lord of lordly Lady of this land': Elizabeth, Stubbs, and the Gaping Gvlf," in *Dissing Elizabeth*, 99–100.

[16] See Barrett-Graves, "'Highly touched in honour': Elizabeth I and the Alençon Controversy," 49–50; Mears, "Counsel, Public Debate and Queenship: John Stubbs's The discoverie of a gaping gulf," 649; Doran, "Why Did Elizabeth Not Marry?," 49; and Helen Hackett, "The rhetoric of (in)fertility, Shifting responses to Elizabeth I's childlessness," in *Rhetoric, Women and Politics in Early Modern England*, eds. Jennifer Richards and Alison Thorne (London and New York: Routledge, 2007), 155–6.

honorable Dame and (as in humbleness I may say) the Goodwife of England," and suggested that she was being "led blindfold as a poor lamb to the slaughter."[17] The French diplomatic correspondence of the time presented a rather different image—or rather images—of the English queen.

Natalie Mears has examined "the relationship between court politics and public debate" during this difficult period, while Debra Barrett-Graves has analyzed Elizabeth's extreme reaction to Stubbs's pamphlet.[18] This chapter supplements their excellent studies by exploring how the French rulers' and ambassador's perception of obstacles to the favorable conclusion of the marriage negotiations eventually generated distrust, defiance, and negative images of the English queen. One particularly interesting representation of Elizabeth emerged in their correspondence during the final phase of negotiations—that of a ruler who needed constant counsel and approval from her country—which was a marked contrast to the image of a powerful, self-assured, if occasionally temperamental and procrastinatory, queen that previous ambassadors had cultivated. Furthermore, the religious issue had yet to be resolved to both sides' satisfaction.

At the beginning of 1579, the French ambassador had reported that "the disorders in her realm are linked to the marriage"—an indication that the English people were already demonstrating their disapproval of the union between their queen and the Duke of Anjou.[19] Although none of Mauvissière's August and September dispatches referred directly to Stubbs's pamphlet, on September 1 he reported that the queen "denounced the malice and the treacherous intentions of those who have wanted to offend and ruin your goals."[20] This reference to "your goals" may be interpreted in one of two ways: either Mauvissière was referring to the

[17] John Stubbs, *The discoverie of a galping gulf whereinto England is like to be swallowed by another French marriage, if the Lord forbid not the banes, by letting her maiestie see the sin and punishment thereof* (London: H. Singleton for W. Page), 3, 7 and 24.

[18] Mears, "Counsel, Public Debate and Queenship: John Stubbs's The discoverie of a gaping gulf," 630 and Barrett-Graves, "'Highly touched in honour': Elizabeth I and the Alençon Controversy," 49–50.

[19] Mauvissière to Henry III of France, 233rd Report, January 20, 1579, BNF MS. Fr. 15973, fol. 94r°, "les troubles de son royaume son liés au mariage."

[20] Mauvissière to Henry III of France, 261st Report, September 1, 1579, BNF MS. Fr. 15973, fol. 173v°, "elle denonce la méchanceté et tromperies intentions de ceulx qui ont voullu obsensive et nuire a vos finalités."

king's own aims, or he meant the aspiration that Henry shared with Elizabeth—a successful outcome to the marriage negotiations. Given the political context, the second interpretation is more feasible, as many English pamphlets were expressing discontent over the Anjou match. The following month, Mauvissière reassured Catherine that those who objected to the match were focusing most of their criticism on Elizabeth, rather than the queen mother's youngest son: "the enemies of this marriage [...] have attacked her to start a rebellion in her realm rather than him."[21] Again, there was no explicit reference to Stubbs's pamphlet, but it was certainly a flagrant attack on Elizabeth's royal authority.[22]

In itself, it seems that the Stubbs episode did not unduly alarm the French royal family, presumably because they were not the main targets of his opprobrium.[23] Nevertheless, they were extremely concerned about the incessant demands for an end to the negotiations from some sectors of the English population. A few months later, Mauvissière informed the French king of "the discontent, which shows that some people in this realm, such as Puritans and Protestants, do not wish for the marriage nor for the alliance with France."[24] Henry was already well aware of the threat posed by the Protestants' opposition to the Anglo-French alliance. On the very same day, he wrote: "it should not be doubted that such things are done precisely by the Puritans and other enemies of the said marriage, not only to delay it but also to destroy it if they can."[25]

[21] Mauvissière to Catherine de Medici, October 16, 1579, BNF MS. Fr. 15973, fol. 194v°, "les ennemis de ce marriage ... ce sont plustot attaqué à elle pour faire une rebellion en son estat que non a luy."

[22] See Barrett-Graves, "'Highly touched in honour': Elizabeth I and the Alençon Controversy," 43–62 and Bell, "'Soueraigne Lord of lordly Lady of this land': Elizabeth, Stubbs, and the Gaping Gvlf," 99–117.

[23] Helen Hackett explains that "many of her subjects were now hostile towards the prospect of her marriage to a French Catholic prince. Popular ballads and Latin verses appeared expressing this antipathy, including two pasquins which were posted on the Lord Mayor of London's door." In Hackett, "The rhetoric of (in)fertility, Shifting responses to Elizabeth I's childlessness," 155.

[24] Mauvissière to Henry III of France, 278th Report, February 8, 1580, BNF MS. Fr. 15973, fol. 231v°, "des mecontentements qui font que le royaume avec les uns et les autres comme les puritains et les protestants ne demandent ny le mariage ny l'alliance de France."

[25] Henry III of France to Mauvissière, February 8, 1580, BNF MS. Fr. 3307, fol. 5, "il ne fault pas doubter que telles choses se facent expressement par les puritins et aultres ennemis dudict mariage, non seullement pour le retarder d'icelluy mais aussy pour le rompre du tout s'ilz peuvent."

Even before the publication of Stubbs's pamphlet, in April 1579, Mauvissière had reported that the queen "had consulted [her council] and for advice [...] she summoned her parliament."[26] The following month, "the queen admitted to having gathered the great lords of her realm and lawyers [...] to have their opinion."[27] Such reports portray a queen who had lost much of her royal authority and was increasingly reliant on the advice of her "great lords." As such, they are consistent with Stubbs's representation of Elizabeth three months later. As Bell suggests, "Elizabeth may be the king, but when it comes to choosing a husband, Stubbs argues, she is like any other helpless daughter—sorely in need of patriarchal guidance."[28]

In December 1580, Henry III informed Mauvissière that his English counterpart at the French court, Sir Henry Cobham, had advised him to negotiate his own trade agreement with Portugal without seeking Elizabeth's assistance, because "the said lady queen is only a woman."[29] At first sight, this seems to be an obvious, gender-based slight against Elizabeth and her royal authority from one of her most senior diplomats. However, it should be pointed out that Cobham did not trust Henry or Catherine, whom he regarded as "removing princes" and suspected of "some cloaked ente[r]prises."[30] Therefore, his comment may have been a cunning ploy to stoke the French king's ego in the hope of learning more about his true intentions toward England. Interestingly, Henry claimed that he did not respond to the jibe, but the fact that he reported it to Mauvissière suggests that he concurred with the misogynistic sentiment.[31]

Regardless of Cobham's true opinion of his mistress, though, perceptions of Elizabeth had certainly changed on both sides of the Channel, with her enemies in England and the French court both now viewing her

[26] Mauvissière to Henry III of France, 245th Report, April 29, 1579, BNF MS. Fr. 15973, fol. 131v°, "après les avoir consulté et délibéré ... elle fit assemble son parlement."
[27] Mauvissière to Henry III of France, 246th Report, May 9, 1579, BNF MS. Fr. 15973, fol. 134v°, "la royne a admis d'assembler les plus grans suffisants de son royaume et les hommes de loix ... pour prendre leur opinion."
[28] Bell, "'Soueraigne Lord of lordly Lady of this land': Elizabeth, Stubbs, and the Gaping Gvlf," 110.
[29] Henry III of France to Mauvissière, December 12, 1580, BNF MS. Fr. 3307, fol. 28r°, "que la dicte dame royne n'étoist juste une femme."
[30] Henry Cobham to Francis Walsingham, May 27, 1581, SP 78/5 fol. 80.
[31] Furthermore, in a letter sent to his primary adviser in 1586, Henry III named Elizabeth "this woman from England" ("cette fame d'Angleterre") revealing his own views on Elizabeth's gender, in Henry III of France to Villeroy, August 7, 1586, BNF Nouv. Acq., Fr. 1244, fol. 165 v°.

as a feeble woman who needed men's help to maintain her royal authority. Moreover, she was reportedly torn between a desire to reinforce the Anglo-French alliance by marrying the Duke of Anjou and the need to appease her own subjects, whose protests about the match were becoming increasingly vociferous. This dilemma ultimately resulted in more negative portraits of the queen in France and England, as well as mounting suspicion between the two crowns. Furthermore, the issue of religion remained a significant obstacle in the marriage negotiations, with the French court insisting on guarantees that the duke would be allowed to remain a practicing Catholic once he became king consort of England. In February 1580, Catherine expressed her concerns to the English queen directly:

> when [Francis] told me that you wished to discuss some points regarding his religion, it worried me deeply, for I feared that it was an excuse to break off this good and useful achievement for these two realms, which makes me beg you not to renege on what has already been agreed and to understand that nothing touches more than the conscience and religion that we hold on to [...] I beg you to let him have that which has already been agreed by you and which is [necessary] for his salvation.[32]

Ensuring that Francis would be able to practice his religion without hindrance was extremely important to Catherine. Two months later, she wrote to her elder son, the French king, to insist that

> the said queen will have to agree with you on the matter of the practice of our Catholic religion for your brother and for his fellowmen, not with a promise on the side that will not be in the treaty, but written and signed in the hand of the said lady queen.[33]

---

[32] Catherine de Medici to Elizabeth I of England, February 8, 1580, in *Lettres de Catherine de Médicis* publiées par M. Le Cte Baguenault de Puchesse, Tome VII, 1579–81 (Paris: Imprimerie Nationale, 1899), 225, "quand il m'a dict que désiriez de retrancher quelque poinct de sa relligion, cella m'a cuidé fayre ung grand ennuy, de peur que ce soit une excuse de rompre ung si bon oeuvre et tant utille pour ces deulx royaulmes: qui me faict vous supplier ne vous retirer de ce qui desjà est accordé et penser que rien ne touché tant que ce qui est de la conscience et religion que l'on tient ... je vous suppllie luy laisser ce qui est par vous desjà accordé et qui est de son salut."

[33] Catherine de Medici to Henry III of France, April 16, 1580, in *LCM*, Tome VII, 245, "de ce que icelle dame royne vous accordoit pour le faict de l'exercice de nostre relligion catholique pour vostre frère et pour les siens; niais que par une promesse à part, qui ne sera pas dans le traité, ains seulement escript et signé de la main d'icelle dame royne...".

Meanwhile, broader concerns, similarly rooted in religion, also divided the rulers of the two nations. In an important dispatch of February 1580, Mauvissière raised another potential stumbling block with Henry. During an audience, Elizabeth had reminded the ambassador of her personal issues with Catholicism in general and the Pope in particular. She referred specifically to her father's break with Rome, the Catholic Church's declaration that his marriage to Anne Boleyn was illegitimate, and her own consequent bastardization. Elizabeth assured the ambassador that she was still willing to marry Francis, but expressed the concern that the union would give England's Catholic community a perfect opportunity to overthrow her, as the Church's stance meant they had never recognized her legitimacy. Mauvissière reported the queen's suspicion that "the Pope would not only agree to a divorce or repudiation but would also give the realm to Monsieur as an opportunity to reestablish the Catholic religion, which would deprive her of her royal authority."[34] The ambassador attempted to placate her by declaring that she was "their great queen, daughter of a great king [...] the legitimate daughter [...] who has ruled for twenty years with good authority, great honor, and in peace with her subjects."[35] However, despite his protestations, Elizabeth remained unconvinced and continued to fear that Catholicism would be reinstated as England's state religion, with Francis as the nation's ruler. As a result, there was no further progress in the marriage negotiations.

[34] Mauvissière to Henry III of France, 279th Report, February 18, 1580, BNF MS. Fr. 15973, fol. 235v°–236r°, "la royne me raconta que encore que le mariage fut de grande honneur et commodité et lalliance de France ... le feu roy son père ne se trouvait pas loppinion du catolicisme cy ce temps le subject a leglise romaine avoir legitimement espouser la royne sa mere n'avoi este dispense du pappe et par consequent elle avoit issue de ce mariage declaree batarde ... le pappe l'avoir excommunié defaut quelle regnoit illegitimeent et plusieurs des catholiques de ce royaume qui estoyent en grand nombre et assez promt a la faction disoyant le semblable.... Monseigneur estoit un jeune prince garillaird et ambitieux de religion fort catholique et confiant en icelle don't elle legitimement advantage que venant a respondu il lui ferait famille en peu de temps ... quelle feroit bastarde heretique aurait regné illegitimement comme excommunié en eligse romaine que le pappe constendroit non seulement au divorce ou repudation mays remettre le royaume d'Angleterre à Monseigneur sous un pretexted y remettre la religion catholique la deposeroit de ceste authorité royalle."
[35] Mauvissière to Henry III of France, 279th Report, February 18, 1580, 236v°, "leur grande royne, fille d'un grand roy ... la fille legitime ... qui a regne vingt ans avec une bonne possession, beaucoup d'honneur et de repos a ses subjects."

Interestingly, while many English Protestants were predictably delighted by the stalemate, the same could be said of a significant proportion of the nation's Catholics. According to Mauvissière, the Protestants were worried that the marriage would "diminish their religion," while the Catholics "fear that this marriage will be the complete ruin of Spain."[36] The two courts' inability to reach a religious compromise between Elizabeth's subjects, the queen herself, and Francis, as well as the virulent English propaganda against the union, ultimately caused the marriage negotiations to grind to a complete halt.

Meanwhile, the volatility of the European political scene increased the tension between the two crowns and exacerbated the atmosphere of defiance and distrust within the Anglo-French alliance. This mood was reflected in the letters of the French royal family and the reports of their ambassador at the English court, most notably in their representations of Elizabeth.

In 1578, the death of Sebastian, King of Portugal, triggered a succession crisis. His uncle Henry succeeded to the throne, but he had no descendants and when he died two years later three of King Manuel I of Portugal's grandchildren—including Philip II of Spain—all claimed the throne.[37] France and England feared that Philip's accession would hand even more power to Spain, but both were eager to preserve their valuable trade agreements with Portugal, so they had no option but to deal with him when he seized the crown in 1581. The French king asked Mauvissière to ascertain "the queen of England's intentions regarding this issue,"[38] and the protracted trade negotiations that followed contributed to increasingly negative representations of Elizabeth in the French diplomatic correspondence.

As noted earlier, Elizabeth cast herself as a "second mother" to King Charles IX, and her counsel was often forthright. For example, she issued a stern lecture on how he should deal with the Huguenots. However, Charles's younger brother Henry was much less inclined (at least at that

---

[36] Mauvissière to Henry III of France, 257th Report, July 24, 1579, BNF MS. Fr. 15973, fol. 164v°, "pour la crainte quils ont du future mariage affirmant de la pourrait faire la diminution en leur religion … les catholiques qui craignoyent que ce mariage ne fult la totale ruine de lespagne."

[37] *Une Histoire du Monde aux Temps Modernes*, 107–9.

[38] Henry III of France to Mauvissière, August 1, 1581, BNF MS. Fr. 3307, fol. 37r°, "que je sache premièrement les intentions de la royne d'Angleterre."

time) to entertain the English queen's advice. In July 1580, he told Mauvissière, "it should be that she no longer meddles in my affairs with my subjects, [and] nor will I with hers."[39] This declaration was linked to the seventh religious civil war, because, like his brother before him, Henry suspected that Elizabeth might be providing aid to the Huguenots. Even more importantly, though, he had no desire to be lectured on how to deal with the problems in his realm. Catherine's distrust of Elizabeth was equally apparent, as that February she had urged the French ambassador to ensure that "the queen of England will not allow, secretly nor otherwise, any one of her subjects to give favor or help to people so disloyal."[40] Moreover, a year later, in reference to the becalmed marriage negotiations, she advised the king that Elizabeth "will not want to put herself at risk of going to war out of love for him [Francis]."[41] Her youngest son was embroiled in the fight against Spain in the Low Countries at the time.[42]

Meanwhile, on the other side of the Channel, Elizabeth was worried that French Catholics were arriving in her realm to plot against her.[43] In July 1580, Henry replied to one of Mauvissière's dispatches, in which the ambassador had reported Elizabeth's complaints about these activities:

> And as for what she told you about the seminary in Reims, from which she said that more than five hundred priests left to sing the Mass in her realm, during which they foment prejudice against her laws and ordinances and wish to disturb the peace, she can be assured that this is something that does

---

[39] Henry III of France to Mauvissière, July 10, 1580, BNF MS. Fr. 3307, fol. 13, "n'est il pas a propos qu'elle se mesle plus avant des affaires d'entre moy et mes subjectz non plus que moi des siens."

[40] Catherine de Medici to Mauvissière, February 8, 1580, in *LCM*, Tome VII, 223, "que la royne d'Angleterre ne permettra que, soubs main ny aultrement, pas ung de ses subjects ne donnera faveur ny assistance à telles gens si desloyaux."

[41] Catherine de Medici to Henry III of France, February 1581, in *LCM*, Tome VII, 333, "qu'elle ne l'espousant, ne se vouldra mettre en danger d'une guerre sur les bras pour l'amour de luy."

[42] Catherine de Medici to Henry III of France, February 1581, 332–4.

[43] Cardinal William Allen left England in 1567 and endeavoured to form English Catholic priests on the continent. In 1568, he created the English College in Douai. In March 1578, he moved the college from Douai to Reims and continued his activities. He represented a real threat for the English crown as he did not recognise Elizabeth's legitimacy. In 1580, Jesuits Edmund Campion and Robert Persons joined Cardinal Allen's mission to send Catholic priests to England to challenge the English government. See, Cooper, *The Queen's Agent*, 137.

not at all come from me, nor from any of my subjects, and if there are any English priests in this realm, she has to ascribe that to religious freedom.[44]

Here, Henry's implication seems to be that Elizabeth's policy of allowing her subjects religious freedom was the cause of the unrest she was facing, so she had no reason to blame him.

Alongside the turmoil on the European mainland and increasing religious tension in England, the situation in Scotland remained a thorn in Anglo-French relations. The envoy of a French lord, Esmé Stewart, Sieur d'Aubigné (a first cousin of James VI of Scotland's father Henry Stuart), was in the process of challenging the regency of James Douglas, the Earl of Morton.[45] Mauvissière reported that "a lot is happening in the said Scotland that does not please the queen of England much,"[46] but assured Henry that "I will try to ensure that you do not enter any dispute with this princess over the affairs of the said Scotland."[47]

In marked contrast to his predecessor La Mothe Fénélon, Mauvissière had little respect for Elizabeth. In one letter to the French king, he frankly observed, "I do not trust her, I will keep an eye on things."[48] A month later, "regarding the affairs in Scotland," Henry instructed his ambassador "to keep an eye open and prevent with all the diplomacy at your disposal my said good sister doing anything or pursuing anything that might be detrimental to the peace of the realm and the alliance between the said

---

[44] Henry III of France to Mauvissière, July 10, 1580, BNF MS. Fr. 3307, fol. 14, "Et quant à ce qu'elle vous a dict du seminaire qu'elle dict qui st a Reims d'ou elle vous a dict aussy qu'il est party plus de cinq cens prestres qui chantent la messe en son royaulme et qui y font des menées au prejudice de ses loix et ordonnances et pour y troubler le repoz, c'est chose qu'elle se peult asseurer ne venir aulcunement de moy ny de qui que ce soit de mes subjectz et s'il n'est faict aulcun prestre angloix en ce royaulme, elle doibt attribuer cella a la liberté que la religion permect."

[45] Roger Lockyer, *James VI and I* (London: Longman, 1998), 11–12 and Alan Stewart, *The Cradle King: A Life of James VI & I* (London: Chatto and Windus, 2003), 51–63.

[46] Mauvissière to Henry III of France, December 20, 1579, Biblothèque Imperiale, Fonds de Saint Germain, n°223, fol. 119, "il se faict beaucoup de choses au dict Ecosse, qui ne plaisent pas trop à la royne d'Angleterre."

[47] Mauvissière to Henry III of France, April 15, 1581, Biblothèque Imperiale, Fonds de Saint Germain, n°223, fol. 208, J'essayerai de vous garantir entrer en aucune alteration avec cette princesse pour les affaires du dict Ecosse."

[48] Mauvissière to Henry III of France, July 29, 1579, Biblothèque Imperiale, Fonds de Saint Germain, n°223, fol. 88, "pour ne m'en fier du tout en elle, j'y aurai l'oeil."

realm and mine."[49] Meanwhile, the English government clearly entertained identical suspicions regarding the intentions of the French crown, as Mauvissière reported that "her council is in great defiance."[50]

In June 1580, during an extraordinary audience with the queen, the French ambassador finally gave vent to all of his private concerns, as he explained in a report to Henry:

> I replied that I was afraid that she was no longer a mistress of good intent, something she was not pleased about, being told that she was not the mistress [...] I had to annoy her that day [...] and to tell you the truth, she is naturally tormented by the various resolutions.[51]

Elizabeth then canceled the meeting that had been scheduled for the following day: "the queen of England remained sick in bed [...] I have not seen her since and she has had two bouts of fever."[52] Earlier, we saw that Elizabeth sometimes feigned illness to give herself more time to deliberate over important policy issues. In this instance, however, she seemed to avoid Mauvissière simply because the ambassador had upset her.

To some extent, this report suggests that Elizabeth had lost the dominant position in Anglo-French relations that she had acquired in the wake of the St. Bartholomew Massacre's Day. Moreover, Mauvissière's references to a "tormented" queen who was unable to discuss important matters of state because she was "sick in bed" imply that Elizabeth's royal authority had significantly diminished over the preceding eight years.

---

[49] Henry III of France to Mauvissière, August 15, 1579, BNF V° Colbert, n° 471, fol. 233, "Quant a ce qui concerne les affaires d'Escosse, je vous prie d'avoir tousjours l'oeil ouvert, et empescher par toute la dexterité qu'il vous sera possible que madicte bonne soeur n'y face ou prousuivre aucune chose au prejudice du repoz du pays et aux alliance qui sont entre ledict royaume et le mien."

[50] Mauvissière to Henry III of France, 242nd Report, April 25, 1579, BNF MS. Fr. 15973, fol. 127v°, "son conseil est en grande defiance."

[51] Mauvissière to Henry III of France, 292nd Report, June 29, 1580, BNF MS. Fr. 15973, fol. 296v°, "je luy ai répliqué sir que j'avais bien peur qu'elle lust pas maistresse de la bonne intention qui estoit chose qui ne luy plaise pas que l'on luy dise qu'elle ne soit la maistresse ... Il a bien fut ce jour la contrarier autant ... et pour dire vray elle est naturellement tourmentee de diverses resolutions."

[52] Mauvissière to Henry III of France, 292nd Report, June 29, 1580, fol. 303r°, "le lendemayn de mon audience la royne d'angleterre demeura mallade au lit, je ne lay pu voir depuis et a eu deux acces de fievre."

These representations of a once great mistress who had lost her way are fairly consistent with contemporaneous English depictions of the queen, but they contrast sharply with those of previous French ambassadors, who had tended to highlight Elizabeth's positive attributes.

Another representation of the queen, which was similarly linked to the growing distrust between the two realms, emerged around the same time: that of a queen who promoted piracy and reckless expeditions. In 1579, Henry complained to his ambassador about "the pillages that customarily are perpetrated at sea by so many English on my subjects."[53] The following year, he instructed Mauvissière to intervene in the case of "Jacques Labbé and Jean de Bruis, Breton merchants whose ship *La Julienne* has been seized with the merchandise that it was carrying to Ireland by two pirate boats from Westford and Rochester."[54] Then, in April 1580, Henry wrote directly to Elizabeth to request justice for "André Jessé, heir of the late Jean Delpuech, Guillaume Brye, and Guillaume Bohier, merchants from Toulouse," who had been remanded in custody in London for four years, awaiting trial over a dispute with some of the city's merchants who had refused to pay for their products.[55] Mauvissière raised the same issue with Walsingham a month later: "I beg you to get the Lords to write to the Judge of the Admiralty that he may hear the arguments on both sides and give his decision."[56] It is not known whether these interventions had any effect, but they reveal that the French court had no confidence in Elizabeth's ability—or indeed inclination—to stop English pirates attacking French vessels.[57]

Although Henry complained about the absence of justice for French mariners and merchants, he had grudging respect for Elizabeth's sailors, and especially Francis Drake, "who has discovered so many beautiful and

[53] Henry III of France to Mauvissière, August 15, 1579, BNF V° Colbert, n°471, fol. 233, "pilleryes qui se font ordinairement sur mer tant par les Angloix sur mes subjectz."
[54] Henry III of France to Mauvissière, February 5, 1580, BNF MS. Fr. 3307, fol. 3v°, "justice soyt rendue à Jacques Labbe et Jean de Bruis, marchants Bretons dont le navire La Julienne a ete saisy, avec les marchandises qu'il transportait en Irlande, par deux navires pirate de Ouastefort et Rochester."
[55] Henry III of France to Elizabeth I of England, April 1, 1580, TNA, SP 78/4, fol. 41.
[56] Mauvissière to Walsingham, May 19, 1580, SP 78/4A.
[57] A number of scholars have analysed Elizabeth's encouragement of her merchants and sailors to be merciless at sea. See the works of Susan Ronald, *The Pirate Queen: Queen Elizabeth I, Her Pirate Adventurers, and the Dawn of Empire* (New York: HarperCollins Publishers, 2007) and Harry Kelsey, *Sir John Hawkins, Queen Elizabeth's Slave Trader* (New York: Yale University Press, 2003).

excellent things, in addition to the rewards that he has brought back to the queen, my said good sister, who is right to praise and greatly esteem the said voyage."[58] Later, when the French king learned that Elizabeth was sending Drake and other armed vessels to intervene against Philip II of Spain's attempt to seize the crown of Portugal, he asked Mauvissière to express his approval to the queen.[59]

However, in the main, this period was characterized by suspicion of and opposition to Elizabeth, whose royal authority was frequently undermined both at home and abroad. She was also increasingly perceived and represented as an unjust ruler and an apologist for piracy. As a result, between 1579 and 1581, the correspondence between the French royal family and their ambassador exhibited a loss of patience in the English queen and increasingly insistent demands for a resolution of the decade-long marriage negotiations.

## The French Royal Family's Growing Irritation

Francis, Duke of Anjou, visited Elizabeth twice in the space of two years in the hope of resolving the remaining obstacles to their union and establishing himself as King of England.[60] However, he failed, which left the French royal family even more frustrated and irritated over Elizabeth's indecision. Of course, their impatience at the endless rounds of negotiations had a significant impact on their perceptions and representations of Elizabeth. Close analysis of the diplomatic correspondence among Mauvissière, Henry III, and Catherine reveals all three individuals'

[58] Henry III of France to Mauvissière, November 14, 1580, BNF MS. Fr. 3307, fol. 23v°, "Drace, qui a le mérite d'avoir descouvert tant de belles et excellentes choses, oultre le proffict qu'il en a rapporté à la Royne ma dicte bonne seur qui a grandement raison de louer et estimer beaucoup le dict voyage."
[59] Henry III of France to Mauvissière, July 14, 1581, BNF MS. Fr. 3307, fol. 36r°, "Duc Antonio de Portugal m'a faict entendre que la royne d'Angleterre madame ma bonne seur et cousine pense d'envoyer par Drake mestre Hacquin et aultres quinze ou seize vaisseaux armés en guerres et des soldats pour assister le duc Antonio en asseurant d'un costé de Porgutal dont je suis bien aise comme vous pouvez faire entendre de ma part à la dicte dame royne."
[60] Robert Knecht explains that Anjou had demands regarding his marriage with Elizabeth and two of them were "to be crowned king of England rather than just be a consort" and "to have joint authority with Elizabeth over the royal estate," in Robert Knecht, *Hero or Tyrant?*, 169.

attempts to manage and control their irritation as well as their use of a variety of rhetorical devices to express it.

Francis's second visit to the English court in late 1581 was widely viewed as the last chance to resolve the outstanding issues that were blocking his union with Elizabeth. However, yet again, little progress was made, and the French ambassador's accounts of the couple's meetings, as well as Henry's and Catherine's responses, give a sense of the mounting frustration that the French royal family now felt toward Elizabeth.[61] Moreover, their correspondence reveals the full complexity of the Anglo-French alliance at the time.

In his dispatches, the French ambassador repeatedly insisted that he was working diligently to broker an agreement on the marriage issue. For instance, in June 1579, he informed Henry that he had "again talked to the queen of England, your good sister, at great length."[62] Four months later, he was bold enough to suggest that they were nearing "the end of this long marriage negotiation between the queen of England, your good sister, and Monsieur, your brother."[63] This somewhat exasperated reference to the length of the negotiations highlights the frustration that both Mauvissière and his master must have felt. The former's irritation is particularly understandable, because it was incumbent on him to resolve all of the issues that had hamstrung the negotiations for almost a decade, which meant he had to endure hours of tortuous discussions with the consistently indecisive Elizabeth. However, Henry was becoming equally irascible. A month after receiving the aforementioned report, he replied, "I hope that these things will be successful and will soon have a good and happy ending."[64] In February 1580, he informed Mauvissière that he was "impatient to know what will be the queen of England's response."[65]

---

[61] See Debra Barrett-Graves, "'Highly touched in honour': Elizabeth I and the Alençon Controversy," 45.

[62] Mauvissière to Henry III of France, 254th Report, June 20, 1579, BNF MS. Fr. 15973, fol. 155v°, "j'ay encore aujourdhui fort longuement parlé à la royne d'Angleterre vostre bonne seur."

[63] Mauvissière to Henry III of France, 272nd Report, November 22, 1579, BNF MS. Fr. 15973, fol. 205r°, "la fin de ceste longue negotiation de mariage entre la royne d'Angleterre vostre bonne suer et Monseigneur vostre frère."

[64] Henry III of France to Mauvissière, December 27, 1579, BNF MS. Fr. 3330, fol. 61, "j'espère que les choses seront pour reussir et prendre bientost une bonne et heureuse fin."

[65] Henry to Mauvissière, February 27, 1580, BNF MS. Fr. 3307, fol. 7v°, "on est impatient de savoir quelle reponse fera la reine d'Angleterre."

Then, two months later, he wrote directly to William Cecil to thank him for his work during the marriage negotiations and the warm welcome he had extended to Francis the previous August. However, he added that he needed "to know if the said things will result in the good outcome that we desire for the wellbeing of these two realms as the time that has been lost infinitely displeases us."[66] This explicit declaration of annoyance reveals that Henry had lost all patience with the queen by the spring of 1580, even though he still hoped that a union might be negotiated.

Although Catherine was possibly even more desperate to see her youngest son marry Elizabeth, the tone of her letters tended to be more measured and generally more optimistic. Nevertheless, she, too, was not averse to expressing her impatience at the pace of the negotiations. For instance, in August 1580, she wrote to Elizabeth: "I do not know how to begin to tell you the pleasure I felt when I heard from Sir Stafford, the envoy, your good resolution and that it was no longer just words or delays."[67] The final remark was a cutting reminder that Elizabeth had been promising to marry the Duke of Anjou for *nine years*; however, it was at least counterbalanced by Catherine's delight at the English queen's "good resolution."

Similarly, Catherine adopted a rather more nuanced approach than her son in her confidential letters to the French ambassador. In November 1581, she first informed Mauvissière of "the great danger that my son the Duke of Anjou experienced at sea when traveling to England [...] I praise God heartily for the grace that he bestowed on us and him that meant he survived the journey," then expressed the "hope that God will make my son so happy that he will have the honor to marry her this time."[68] By

---

[66] Henry III of France to William Cecil, Lord Burghley, April 6, 1580, BNF Collection Moreau, n° 720, fol. 112, "Monsieur de Bourgley, au retour du voyage que mon frère le duc d'Anjou a faict en Angleterre, il m'a particulierement dict les bons offices que vous luy avez faictz pour le regard d'advancer son mariage avec la royne d'Angleterre ma bonne soeur, et je sçay que vous continuez encores tous les jours en ceste bonne intention qui nous oblige grandement a le recognoistre si lesdictes choses prennent la bonne yssue que nous desirons pour le bien de ces deux royaulmes ou le temps perdu nous desplaist infiniment."

[67] Catherine de Medici to Elizabeth I of England, August 15, 1580, in *LCM*, Tome VII, 277, "Madame ma bonne seur, je ne se coment comenser à vous dire l'ayse que jé reseu quant, par le sieur de Stafort présant porteur, j'é entendu vostre résolution et que ce n'étoyt plus paroles ne delay."

[68] Catherine de Medici to Mauvissière, November 14, 1581, in *LCM*, Tome VII, 416, "du grand danger qu'a couru sur la mer mon filz le duc d'Anjou en son passaige d'Angleterre, louant Dieu de bon coeur de la grace qu'il nous a faicte et à luy que enfin il est venuà bon

drawing attention to Francis's perilous voyage, Catherine highlighted the fact that he was taking significant risks to woo the queen and finally conclude the marriage negotiations. Meanwhile, her use of the expression "this time"—an obvious reference to all of the previous failures to finalize a deal—was a subtle indication that even her patience was wearing thin. Similarly, the previous August, in a personal letter to Elizabeth in which she had attempted to retain an air of optimism, Catherine had emphasized that "this negotiation has lasted so long that I am greatly afraid that I will not have the time to see the end of it."[69]

All of the French royal family's frustration and irritation stemmed from Elizabeth's inability or unwillingness to reach a firm decision about the marriage. Moreover, their correspondence is littered with suspicions about her ultimate intentions. For instance, a month before his younger brother was due to visit England for the first time, Henry informed Mauvissière:

> [S]he answered the issues that you put to her [by saying] that if she were not resolved to marry my said brother, there would be no need for him to come to England [...] [But then s]he ordered her ambassador Sir Polet [Sir Amias Paulet], who is staying with me, to tell me the contents of her letter [...] From this letter, I have inferred two things: first, that my said good sister is not that resolved to conclude the marriage with my said brother ... and [second,] that she has no willingness to see the said meeting take place [...] I hereby instruct you to determine the intentions of my said good sister and also to learn if there has been some cooling in the resolution that she demonstrated when agreeing to marry my said brother.[70]

port ... espérant que Dieu fera mon filz sy heureux qu'il aura cest honneur ceste fois de l'épouzer."

[69] Catherine de Medici to Elizabeth I of England, August 15, 1580, in *LCM*, Tome VII, 277, "cete négotiation, qui a tent duré que je avoys grent peur n'avoyr l'heur d'en voyr la fin."

[70] Henry III of France to Mauvissière, July 6, 1579, BNF V° Colbert, n°337, fol. 745, "respondu sur le propos que luy avez tenu, que si elle n'estoit bien resolue d'espouser mondict frère, il ne seroit poinct besoing de le faire passer en Angleterre ... qu'elle a donné charge au sʳ Polet, son ambassadeur resident pres de moy, de me dire le contnu en la coppie de lettre ... par laquelle lettre je faict jugement de deux choses, l'une que madicte bonne soeur n'est pas si résolue a parachever le mariage avec mondict frère ... l'aultre, qu'elle n'a aussy du tout telle volunté à l'execution de ladicte entrevue [...]affin qu'il vous serve d'esclercissement pour mieulx juger de l'intention de madicte bonne soeur et aussy par ce que vous en pourrez apprendre ailleurs s'il n'y aura poinct quelque refroidissement en la resolution que cy devant elle monstroit avoir prise d'espouser mondict frère."

This lengthy letter reveals that the English queen informed Mauvissière that she still intended to marry Francis, and presented the invitation that she had extended to the duke as proof of her sincerity. On the other hand, she then instructed her ambassador to share the contents of a letter that seemed to suggest that she had had second thoughts about both the duke's visit and the marriage itself. These conflicting messages mystified Henry, who reached the only logical conclusion: the queen was as undecided as ever. Ultimately, the visit went ahead as planned—presumably after Henry had received the requested reassurance from Mauvissière—but a year after Francis and Elizabeth had met face to face her persistent vacillation remained one of the principal topics in the French royal correspondence.

In November 1580, a jaded Henry wrote, "we will see this time what she wants it to be."[71] Evidently, the king was no closer to determining his English counterpart's true intentions, so his exasperation at Elizabeth's perpetual capriciousness is entirely understandable. In addition, though, this brief comment reveals that the King of France felt utterly powerless when it came to persuading a ruler who had supposedly lost most of her royal authority to reach a decision.

Catherine also continued to express concern over Elizabeth's uncertainty and ambivalence with respect to the union with her youngest son. In April 1580, she informed Henry that Francis had assured her that "things are on better terms than ever on the said queen's part."[72] The next day, she added, "my son has shown me letters written in her own hand [...] in which she shows she still desires the marriage and has great affection for your brother."[73] Clearly, then, Catherine was still deeply involved in her children's lives, to such an extent that she had access to Elizabeth's private correspondence with Francis. In yet another letter to the king, written the following day, she explained that she was interested in what Elizabeth had to say "in order to know the truth from the mouth of the queen herself when she would like to receive the envoys that we need to

---

[71] Henry III of France to Mauvissière, October 25, 1580, BNF MS. Fr. 3307, fol. 22r° "Nous verrons cestefois ce qu'elle desire qu'il en soit."

[72] Catherine de Medici to Henry III of France, April 15, 1580, in *LCM*, Tome VII, 241, "les choses du costé de ladite royne soient en meilleurs termes que jamais."

[73] Catherine de Medici to Henry III of France, April 16, 1580, in *LCM*, Tome VII, 244, "mon fils m'a faict veoir plusieurs lettres de la main de la royne, une entre autres, par laquelle elle monstre tousjours désirer le mariage et porter très grande affection à vostre frère."

send for the marriage treaty."[74] Later that year, Henry justified Catherine's involvement in their personal affairs by explaining to his younger brother, "our said good mother [...] has no other care in this world than for our own wellbeing, greatness, progression, and satisfaction."[75]

Although she remained more optimistic than either Henry or Mauvissière, by the summer of 1580 even Catherine had to acknowledge, "I very much regret to see, as is easy to judge from your last letter, that the queen of England has cooled about the marriage between her and my son the Duke of Anjou."[76] She found some comfort in the fact that Elizabeth continued to display considerable affection in her personal letters to Francis, yet, to some extent, the queen's terms of endearment merely intensified the royal family's puzzlement, given the usual tenor of the reports that Mauvissière was sending from the English court.

This is not to say that the French ambassador's accounts were entirely negative. Rather, they were a fair—if understandably tetchy—reflection of the queen's own inconsistency. For instance, in June 1579, Mauvissière sent an upbeat message about Elizabeth's excitement over Francis's first visit to England and assured the French king that "lots of preparations have been decided as it should be."[77] The previous month, he had attested to "the final resolution of the queen your good sister for the marriage with my Lord your brother"[78] and a few days later had even insisted that "the queen has never been more willing to conclude [the negotiations]."[79] In February 1580, the French ambassador disclosed that "the said queen is

---

[74] Catherine de Medici to Henry III of France, April 17, 1580, *LCM*, Tome VII, 247, "affin de sçavoir au vray de la bousche mesme de la royne quand elle aura agréable que les commissaires, que nous debvons envoyer pour le traicté de mariaige."

[75] Henry III of France to Francis, Duke of Anjou, October 28, 1580, BNF Nouv. Acq. Fr. 6003, fol. 101, "nostre dite bonne mere qui n'a d'aultre soing en ce monde que pour nostre bien, grandeur, advancement et contantement."

[76] Catherine de Medici to Mauvissière, July 10, 1580, in *LCM*, Tome VII, 272, "j'ay très grand regrect de voir, comme il se peut aisément juger par vostre dernière lettre, que la royne d'Angleterre est refroidie du mariaige entre elle et mon fils le duc d'Anjou."

[77] Mauvissière to Henry III of France, 253rd Report, June 18, 1579, BNF MS. Fr. 15973, fol. 134r°, "la finalle resollution de la royne vostre tres bonne seur pour le mariage de Monseigneur vostre frere."

[78] Mauvissière to Henry III of France, 246th Report, May 9, 1579, BNF MS. Fr. 15973, fol. 135r°, "beaucoup de preparatif estan resollu comme il se doist."

[79] Mauvissière to Henry III of France, 248th Report, May 14, 1579, BNF MS. Fr. 15973, fol. 139v°, "la royne ne fut jamais en meilleur volonté de conclure."

so greatly resolved not to wait any longer to accomplish her marriage that she no longer sleeps either during the day or at night" and confided that "she shows such joy."[80] Such reports seemed to confirm Elizabeth's sincerity, although the phrase "not wait any longer" must have reminded Henry of her infuriating procrastination over the course of many years. Nevertheless, Mauvissière ended his report on a positive note with his reference to Elizabeth's "joy," and similar optimism was evident in two dispatches from later the same year. In March, the ambassador assured Henry that "it is not possible to see her in better disposition" regarding the marriage,[81] while in May he asserted, "she wants to finalize the marriage so she can no longer delay nor prolong as she has."[82]

Interestingly, then, although Mauvissière was well aware of Elizabeth's habit of delaying the marriage negotiations, he was still prepared to predict a satisfactory conclusion. Moreover, as we have seen, he was more willing than any previous ambassador to take the queen to task about her behavior. For instance, in one report of March 1580, he informed Henry:

> [S]he wanted to ride a horse to talk to me more freely [...] regarding the marriage with my Lord [...] [S]he has shown for some time to be as resolved as ever and has begged me to tell you, your majesties, that the delays were due to a great reason for her. I replied that they seemed to be her fault because it was her intention to procrastinate and delay things in order that she would never have to deal with the marriage issues, and that the time she has wasted will never be recovered.[83]

---

[80] Mauvissière to Henry III of France, 278th Report, February 8, 1580, BNF MS. Fr. 15973, fol. 230v°, "ceste grande resolution qu'avait prise la dite royne de ne voulloir plus perdre de temps a effectuer son mariage quelle ne dormait ny jour ny nuit. [...] elle temoigne une telle allegresse."

[81] Mauvissière to Henry III of France, 281st Report, March 21, 1580, BNF MS. Fr. 15973, fol. 245v°, "quil nestoit possible de la voir en meilleur disposition."

[82] Mauvissière to Henry III of France, 288th Report, May 27, 1580, BNF MS. Fr. 15973, fol. 278r°, "elle veult parachever le mariage aussy ni le peult elle plut differer ni prolonger comme elle a faict."

[83] Mauvissière to Henry III of France, 281st Report, March 21, 1580, Bnf MS. Fr. 15973, fol. 244v°, "elle avoit foulu monter a cheval pour me parler plus librement [...] pour le regard du mariage avec Monseigneur elle a monstrer depuis quelque temps estre plus resolue que jamais me priant de faire entendre a vos majestez que les retardements estoient fondez sur la grande raison pour elle. Je luy ay repondu quil semblait que sa faulte son intention de temporiser et de mettre les choses en longueur pour jamais venir aux effects du mariage que cependant elle perdoit le temps qui luy estoit."

This report contains a faint echo of earlier representations of Elizabeth in the form of Mauvissière's reference to the queen's wish to ride a horse. As we saw in previous chapters, this may have reflected her desire to assert her authority and present herself as the equal of any king by engaging in a traditionally male activity. Moreover, by stressing that the unconventional audience would give her an opportunity to speak "more freely," she highlighted the fact that she could still insist on meeting ambassadors on her own terms, without any interference from her councillors. On the other hand, she then immediately undermined the authority she had endeavored to establish by seeking the French king's indulgence for the unspecified "great reason" that had supposedly caused her to drag her feet in the marriage negotiations. But the ambassador was having none of it and placed the blame for the delays squarely on Elizabeth herself, before concluding, "I also told her that she had been very dilatory in changing her colors, and that it seems that [Francis] now believes that the marriage is broken […] [She replied] that she did not know on what he based that opinion."[84]

The laborious marriage negotiations gradually eroded the dominant position that Elizabeth had enjoyed in her dealings with the French royal family and their diplomats in the wake of the St. Bartholomew's Day Massacre. In May 1580, Mauvissière depicted her as a feeble, troubled monarch who "has not slept well and has eaten only a little for eight days" due to her inability to reach a decision over the marriage and a raft of domestic issues.[85] A few months later, he again had no hesitation in informing the queen that "it was her fault that the marriage [negotiations] had dragged on so long."[86]

This was just one of countless references to Elizabeth's dilatoriness in the correspondence between the French rulers and Mauvissière. The overriding impression is of a queen who ran hot and cold and found it impos-

---

[84] Mauvissière to Henry III of France, 281ˢᵗ Report, March 21, 1580, 245v°, "je luy monstre aussi comme a pouvoir voir quelle fut fort dilatoire en changeant de coulleur et quil sembloit quil tint le mariage pour rompu et quele ne scavait par ou il fondait ceste opinion."

[85] Mauvissière to Catherine de Medici, May 27, 1580, BNF MS. Fr. 15973, fol. 281v°, "quil y avoit huit jours qu'elle navoyt dormi ni bien et mange que bien peu de choses", see Patrick Collinson, *Elizabethan Essays*, 74–77 in which the opposition to the Anjou match is clearly analysed.

[86] Mauvissière to Henry III of France, 306ᵗʰ Report, October 20, 1580, BNF MS. Fr. 15973, fol. 355r°, "je luy ay replique quelle y estoit cause pour avoir laisser et longuement trainer le mariage."

sible to reach a firm decision on anything, and especially whether she wanted to marry Francis. Yet, it must be emphasized that, while the queen's reputation was seriously undermined by the way she dealt with the marriage negotiations, the French royal family's perseverance indicates that they remained desperate to maintain the alliance with England. Moreover, notwithstanding all of the annoyance she caused them, they continued to refer to Elizabeth as a member of the family.

## Ongoing Efforts to Preserve the Anglo-French Alliance

While it is widely known that Elizabeth "often assumes a pseudo-familial role in [her] letters, becoming, for example, James VI's mother, Catherine de Medici's daughter and Henry III's sister,"[87] far less attention has been paid to the more important fact that her French counterparts acknowledged and accepted these self-representations in their own correspondence by addressing the English queen as "true sister" and even "germayne sister." However, this "pseudo-familial role" was highly complex and continued to evolve as the politico-religious situation progressed.

Elizabeth's varying status as a virtual member of the French royal family parallels England's diplomatic relations with France through the course of her reign—from relative closeness in the late 1560s to the ingrained mutual suspicion of the early 1580s. The years 1579–1581 were especially significant in this respect as it was in this period that the French royal family and their ambassador abandoned the affectionate, respectful "germayne sister" in favor of the rather formal "good sister and cousin."[88] Moreover,

---

[87] Jonathan Gibson, "'Dedans la plié de mon fidelle affection': Familiarity and Materiality in Elizabeth's Letters to Anjou," in *Elizabeth I's Foreign Correspondence: Letters, Rhetoric, and Politics*, 42; see also Orlin "The Fictional Families of Elizabeth I," which was previously discussed in Chap. 2.

[88] See Henry III of France to Mauvissière, July 6, 1579, BNF V° Colvert, n°337, fol. 745, "la royne d'Angleterre, ma bonne seur;" Henry III of France to Mauvissière, December 8, 1580, BNF MS. Fr. 3307, fol. 23v°, "la bonne amitié de la royne d'Angleterre ma bonne seur" and 24r° "la dame royne ma bonne seur;" Henry III of France to Mauvissière, December 12, 1580, BNF MS. Fr. 3307, fol. 27r°, "la Royne d'Angleterre ma bonne seur et cousine;" Henry III of France to Mauvissière, January 20, 1581, BNF MS. Fr. 3307, fol. 29v°, "la Royne d'Angleterre, ma bonne seur et cousine;" Henry III of France to Mauvissière, February 18, 1581, BNF MS. Fr. 3307, fol. 31r° "la dicte dame yoryne ma dicte bonne seur et cousine."

Henry III even started to employ the latter form of address in his private letters to the queen: "very high, very excellent and very powerful princess, our very dear and much beloved good sister and cousin."[89] Although "our very dear and much beloved" may be construed as a term of affection, in reality this was simply the routine idiom of formal diplomacy. In addition, it should be noted that there was no evidence of fondness when Henry discussed Elizabeth with others, including Catherine de Medici and Mauvissière, aside from a single instance in December 1580 when he called her "true sister of mine."[90] Indeed, he did not use the expression "germayne sister" once in all his correspondence with the ambassador. By 1580, even Catherine was calling Elizabeth "the queen of England, my good sister and cousin" rather than "my own daughter," although she did continue to use somewhat warmer language when writing to the queen directly. Nevertheless, overall, there was an undeniable cooling in the French court's attitude toward the English monarch, which reflected the fact that the Anglo-French alliance was much more brittle than it had been in the aftermath of the St. Bartholomew's Day Massacre.[91]

Elizabeth was in her mid-forties by 1579, so the possibility of producing an heir was disappearing fast. Furthermore, this was as much a concern for the French court as it was for the English, as it was not just the House of Tudor that was under threat. Henry's marriage to Louise of Lorraine had failed to produce any offspring in four years of trying, so most of the hope for continuation of the Valois line now rested firmly with his younger brother Francis and his prospective bride. But everyone was well aware that they now had to act fast. Indeed, the sense of urgency to conclude the union became increasingly palpable in the French diplomatic correspondence. For instance, in October 1581, Catherine instructed Mauvissière:

[89] See for examples of this greeting: Henry III of France to Elizabeth I of England, February 28, 1581, BNF MS. Fr. 3308, fol. 5 and Henry III of France to Elizabeth I of England, March 5, 1581, BNF MS. Fr. 3308, fol. 6, "Tres haulte, tres excellente et tres puissante princesse, nostre tres chere et tres amee bonne seur et cousine."

[90] Henry III of France to Mauvissière, December 8, 1580, BNF MS. Fr. 3307, fol. 24r°, "la vraye seur de moy."

[91] For the importance of demonstrating affection between rulers, see Gary Schneider, *The Culture of Espitolarity: Vernacular Letters and Letter Writing in Early Modern England, 1500–1700* (Newark, Delaware: University of Delaware Press, 2005), 42.

Tell them, from me, both that I desire [the marriage] and that, if it should happen, it must be today rather than tomorrow, so as not to lose any days and so that God can give them the grace to see their children soon.[92]

She was even more blunt in a letter to her elder son: "Time is pressing upon us—on the queen of England's part, who hopes to have children, and on my part, given my age."[93] However, as hopes for the marriage—and especially producing an heir—started to fade, so did the political capital that Elizabeth had accumulated in 1572.

Just as La Mothe Fénélon had echoed Charles IX's affectionate term of address—"germayne sister"—to strengthen the ties between the two courts, his successor Mauvissière took his cue from Henry and referred to Elizabeth simply, formally, as "the queen of England, your good sister."[94] Later, he dropped the pseudo-familial language altogether and described her as "the best friend of your majesty and of your house."[95] She was back to being "a good sister and friend"[96] by the summer of 1580 and "the best sister and friend that you could have"[97] near the end of the marriage negotiations in June 1581. However, while Mauvissière's repeated use of the term "best" could be seen as relatively positive, in the diplomatic idiom of the day "best friend" was a significantly cooler form of address than "germayne sister" or even "true sister." While La Mothe Fénélon's reports had also contained countless references to the "friendship" that existed between England and France, he had never used the term in isolation, and

[92] Catherine de Medici to Mauvissière, October 31, 1581, in *LCM*, Tome VII, 411, "dites leur, de ma part, à tous deux que je desire et qu'il faut, si se doibt faire, que ce soit plustost aujourdhuy que demain, afin que les jours ne se perdent et que Dieu leur puisse faire la grâce de leur veoir bientostdes enfans."

[93] Catherine de Medici to Henry of France, April 14, 1580, in *LCM*, Tome VII, 238, "le temps pressoil du costé de la dame royne d'Angleterre qui en vouldroit espérer des enfans, et que de mon costé aussi, considérant mon age."

[94] Mauvissière to Henry III of France, 235th Report, February 13, 1579, BNF MS. Fr. 15973, fol. 100r°, "la royne d'Angleterre vostre bonne seur."

[95] Mauvissière to Henry III of France, 269th Report, October 29, 1579, BNF MS. Fr. 15973, fol. 197v°, "la dite royne assure estre la meilleure amye de vostre majesté et de vostre mayson."

[96] Mauvissière to Henry III of France, 297th Report, August 8, 1580, BNF MS. Fr. 15973, fol. 320r°, "qu'elle vous est une bonne soeur et amye."

[97] Mauvissière to Henry III of France, 324th Report, June 20, 1581, BNF MS. Fr. 15973, fol. 337r°, "la meilleure soeur et amye que vous pourriez avoir."

his primary metaphors had always been familial in order to highlight the two monarchs' personal affection for each other. Hence, by downgrading Elizabeth to the status of a "friend"—and/or a "good" rather than a "true" or "germayne" sister"—Mauvissière signaled the French court's increasing exasperation with Elizabeth's procrastination in the marriage negotiations: "germayne" sisters had to be trustworthy, and the king's trust was ebbing away.

Of course, La Mothe Fénélon enjoyed a much closer personal relationship with Elizabeth than Mauvissière ever did, and this should be taken into consideration when exploring the language they used in reference to the queen, but the political and religious contexts in which they wrote their reports were critical, too. In marked contrast to the former ambassador's dispatches of 1572, Mauvissière never referred to Elizabeth as a potential daughter in his letters to Catherine; instead, in January 1579, he used the formal appellation *"belle fille"* (daughter-in-law).[98] Similarly, three months later, he informed Catherine of "the good resolution of the queen of England as regards the offer to become [your] daughter-in-law."[99] Interestingly, then, Mauvissière shifted the focus from Elizabeth becoming Francis's wife to her becoming Catherine's daughter-in-law. Therefore, the issue was no longer whether she would marry Francis but whether she would become part of the French royal family at all. In June 1579, once again, the ambassador reported on "the resolution of the queen of England, whom I cannot help but call your daughter-in-law, to marry my Lord, your son."[100] While such statements revealed Mauvissière's inclination to portray Elizabeth as a daughter-in-law, they also reassured Catherine that Elizabeth herself was happy to be viewed as such. Indeed, later that year, the ambassador declared: "I have always heard your good sister saying that she wants to be your daughter-in-law and that it is her inclination and desire to marry and form an alliance with the house of France."[101] Even these letters were far less confident than the earlier cor-

[98] Mauvissière to Catherine de Medici, January 15, 1579, BNF MS. Fr. 15973, fol. 88v°.
[99] Mauvissière to Catherine de Medici, April 29, 1579, BNF MS. Fr. 15973, fol. 132v°, "la bonne resolution de la royne d'Angleterre pour offre de devenir belle fille."
[100] Mauvissière to Catherine de Medici, June 16, 1579, BNF MS. Fr. 15973, fol. 153r°, "la resolution prise de la Royne d'Angleterre que je ne puis me garder d'appeller vostre belle fille despouser Monseigneur vostre fils."
[101] Mauvissière to Catherine de Medici, November 22, 1579, BNF MS. Fr. 15973, fol. 206v°, "vostre bonne seur que j'ay tousjours ecouté dire voulloir estre votre belle fille et que

respondence, however. Mauvissière's tone reflected the fact that not only the marriage negotiations but the Anglo-French alliance itself seemed to be on the brink of collapse.

Whereas Henry and Mauvissière reacted to the deteriorating political situation by adopting more formal terms than their two predecessors, Catherine's response was less consistent. Although she told the ambassador that she hoped "to see her [Elizabeth] as my daughter-in-law in order to love her,"[102] she started to use the much more formal "madam my good sister" not only in letters to Mauvissière but even when writing to Elizabeth herself.[103] Similarly, in May 1581, she adopted Henry's eulogistic formula at the end of a personal letter to the queen by begging "the Creator, very high, to hold you, very excellent and very powerful princess, very dear and much beloved good sister and cousin, in his safe and admirable keeping."[104] The language was affectionate, but there was no evidence of heartfelt kinship.

Nevertheless, Catherine still saw Elizabeth as a potential member of the French royal family, so she continued to employ familial terms right to the very end of the marriage negotiations, often in combination with hints that she was clinging to the hope that an agreement might finally be reached: "your good sister and cousin, awaiting the time when I will be able to say what I desire so much and yet do not dare"; "your good and affectionate sister and cousin, who continues to desire"; and even "your good sister and cousin, who begs God to have the honor to say mother

c'était son inclination et vollonté de vouloir se marier et prendre alliance en la maison de France en elle."

[102] Catherine de Medici to Mauvissiere, February 28, 1580, in *LCM*, Tome VII, 227, "d'estre si heureuse de la veoir ma bellefille pour l'aymer."

[103] See Catherine de Medici to Mauvissière, January 12, 1580, in *LCM*, Tome VII, 220, "la royne d'Angleterre, madame ma bonne seur;" Catherine de Medici to Elizabeth I of England, August 15, 1580, in *LCM*, Tome VII, 277, "Madame ma bonne seur;" Catherine de Medici to Mauvissiere, December 8, 1580, in *LCM*, Tome VII, 298, "la royne d'Angleterre, ma bonne seur;" Catherine de Medici to Elizabeth I of England, December 11, 1580, in *LCM*, Tome VII, 299, "Madame ma bonne seur;" Catherine de Medici to Elizabeth I of England, September 1581, in *LCM*, Tome VII, 397, "Madame ma bonne seur;" Catherine de Medici to Mauvissiere, October 31, 1581, in *LCM*, Tome VII, 411, "madame ma bonne seur et cousine."

[104] See Catherine de Medici to Elizabeth I of England, May 5, 1581, in *LCM*, Tome VII, 375, "suppliant le Créateur, très haulte, très excellente et très puissante princesse, très chère et très amée bonne soeur et cousine, qu'il vous ayt en sa saincle et digne garde."

soon."[105] In weaving these hints into otherwise formal diplomatic correspondence, Catherine shrewdly signaled her desire to see the marriage take place without imposing too much pressure on Elizabeth to reach a decision.

As we saw in Chap. 1, the mother tends to have authority over the daughter in any mother–daughter relationship.[106] However, by begging God to give her "the honor" to identify herself as Elizabeth's mother, Catherine cleverly reversed the traditional hierarchy and gifted the power to her nominal daughter. She had used this strategy once before, in August 1580, when declaring her "wish to see myself honored with such a daughter."[107] It was clearly designed to leave Elizabeth in no doubt about how much Catherine valued their relationship.

Although "good sister" was Catherine's preferred form of address in her letters to Elizabeth, she continued to stress that she would be "so happy to be able to name you, instead of sister, daughter."[108] Two months later, in early 1581, she reiterated her "satisfaction to see my good sister and cousin the queen of England becoming my daughter."[109] Interestingly, while Rayne Allinson has argued that "Catherine's prolonged status as a potential mother-in-law to Elizabeth also effected an important shift in the tenor of Anglo-French relations," Catherine never referred to herself as Elizabeth's "*belle-mère*." Instead, she presented herself as a potential *mother* to the English queen, which implied a much stronger bond between the two women.[110]

---

[105] Catherine de Medici to Elizabeth I of England, August 15, 1580, in *LCM*, Tome VII, 277, "Vostre bonne seur et cousine, en atendent l'heur de povoyr dire cet que je tent desire que je n'ause encore;" Catherine de Medici to Elizabeth I of England, December 11, 1580, in *LCM*, Tome VII, 299, "Vostre bonne et affectionnée soeur et cousine, qui continue en son désir" and Catherine de Medici to Elizabeth I of England, February 18, 1581, in *LCM*, Tome VII, 358, "Vostre bonne soeur et cousine, qui supplie Dieu bientost avoir l'honneur de dire mère."

[106] Kruse, "The Virgin and the Widow," 129.

[107] Catherine de Medici to Elizabeth I of England, August 15, 1580, in *LCM*, Tome VII, 277, "ayent en mon suhayt de me voyr honnorée d'une tele fille."

[108] Catherine de Medici to Elizabeth I of England, December 11, 1580, in *LCM*, Tome VII, 299, "si heureuse de vous povoir nommer, en lieu de soeur, fille."

[109] Catherine de Medici to Mauvissiere, February 15, 1581, in *LCM*, Tome VII, 356, "contentement de veoir ma bonne seur et cousine la royne d'Angleterre estre ma fille."

[110] Allinson, *A Monarchy in Letters*, 94.

Susan Doran rightly asserts that Elizabeth's advisers were in favor of the marriage for purely political reasons. However, Catherine's letters reveal that, for her at least, there was also a deeply personal motivation: she wanted to become a grandmother again.[111] As the matriarch of the House of Valois, she was determined to see the continuation of her royal line, which was why she assumed the traditionally male role of leading the marriage negotiations herself.[112] Indeed, in a personal letter to Elizabeth in August 1580, she abandoned her normal prudence and blurted out her desire for "a good line, which I hope to see from you two."[113] A month later, she expressed the same sentiment to Mauvissière:

hoping that God will make my son happy, that he will have the honor to marry her this time, and that we will soon have the pleasure to see them having children, which is what I desire in this world as one of the greatest pleasures.[114]

[111] Doran, "Why Did Elizabeth Not Marry?," 31.

[112] This is not meant to imply that no other queens interfered in their children's lives or played no role in negotiating dynastic marriages. See the works of Lois L. Huneycutt, "Public Lives, Private Ties: Royal Mothers in England and Scotland, 1070–1204," in *Medieval Mothering*, eds. John Carmi Parson and Bonnie Wheeler (New York and London: Garland Publishing Inc., 1996), 295–312; Fatima Rhorchi, "Consorts of Moroccan Sultans: Lalla Khnata Bint Bakkar 'A Woman With Three Kings'," in *Queenship in the Mediterranean: Negotiating the Role of the Queen in the Medieval and Early Modern Eras*, ed. Elena Woodacre (New York: Palgrave Macmillan, 2013), 229–45; Joseph F. O'Callaghan, "The Many Roles of the Medieval Queen: Some Examples from Castile," in *Queenship and Political Power in Medieval and Early Modern Spain*, ed. Theresa Earenfeight (Aldershot: Ashgate, 2005), 21–32 and Sharon L. Jansen, *The Monstrous Regiment of Women: Female Rulers in Early Modern Europe* (New York: Palgrave Macmillan, 2002). On Catherine playing both maternal and paternal roles to her children, see Estelle Paranque, "Catherine of Medici: Henry III's Inspiration to be a Father to his People," in *Royal Mothers and their Ruling Children: Wielding Political Authority from Antiquity to the Early Modern Era*, eds. Elena Woodacre and Carey Fleiner (New York: Palgrave Macmillan, 2015), 226.

[113] Catherine de Medici to Elizabeth I of England, August 15, 1580, in *LCM*, Tome VII, 277, "d'une belle lignée que j'espère voyr de vous deus."

[114] Catherine de Medici to Mauvissière, November 14, 1581, in *LCM*, Tome VII, 416, "espérant que Dieu fera mon filz sy heureux qu'il aura cest honneur ceste fois de l'épouzer, et que bien tost nous aurons ce contentement de leur veoir des enffens, qui est ce que je désire en ce monde pour ung des plus grandz contentemens."

This eagerness to see her youngest son procreate is evident in many of Catherine's other letters, too.[115] Therefore, in addition to casting Elizabeth as a potential daughter or daughter-in-law, Catherine represented her as a potential mother. Maybe she felt that constant reminders of the prospect of motherhood would encourage Elizabeth to stop deliberating and finally conclude the marriage negotiations; if so, the strategy backfired badly. For instance, in August 1580, Catherine wrote, "I pray to God that I will see the day when you become a mother,' before hastily adding, "I beg your pardon for my eagerness, which makes me say more than I should."[116] By apologizing for her candor, Catherine once again surrendered some of her natural authority in the mother–daughter relationship to Elizabeth. Furthermore, her comment suggests that she suspected Elizabeth was already rather irritated by her frequent references to motherhood.

Four months later, Mauvissière delivered the news that Catherine must have been dreading: it seemed that Elizabeth no longer expected to have children. The bewilderment is palpable in Catherine's reply:

> She told you that, if the marriage took place and she could not have children, she would consent to and even facilitate my son the Duke of Anjou finding another wife [...] That is not normal, [but] I hope that if the marriage happens, God will have the good grace to give them children.[117]

Therefore, Elizabeth must have told the ambassador that she now doubted that she would ever conceive, but she was willing to agree to an amicable divorce from Francis if that proved to be the case. Three days later, Catherine still seemed unable to believe what she had just read, as she wrote to Elizabeth, "before I die, I will see you as a mother of a beautiful

---

[115] Catherine already had twelve grandchildren. The author is currently working on a project that focuses on her grandmotherhood.

[116] Catherine de Medici to Elizabeth I of England, August 15, 1580, in *LCM*, Tome VII, 277, "que je prie a Dieu m'achever cet heur de vous voyr byentost mère. Je vous suplie m'escuser cet l'ayse que je ay me trensporte de dire' plus que ne devrès."

[117] Catherine de Medici to Mauvissiere, December 8, 1580, in *LCM*, Tome VII, 298, "je vous diray sur ce qu'elle vous a premièrement declare que, se faisant le mariage et qu'elle vit ne pouvoir avoir enfans, qu'elle consentiroit, et elle-mesme pourchasseroit de donner à mon fils le duc d'Anjou une aultre femme, que c'est chose qui n'est pas usitée, aussy que j'ay bonne espérance que si le mariaige estoit faict, Dieu nous feroit la grace de leur donner des enfans."

son."[118] The strong implication was that it was Elizabeth's duty as a queen *and a woman* to marry Francis and give birth to his "beautiful son." However, as Carole Levin explains, Elizabeth had good reason to be less than enthusiastic about the prospect of motherhood, which carried significant risks for a woman of her age at the time.[119] More to the point, she had never exhibited any great desire to become a mother, even in her youth. Rather, her motives for the union echoed those of her Privy Council, because they were overwhelmingly political rather than personal, in marked contrast to Catherine's, which were a combination of the two.

These contrasting motivations only increased the tension between Elizabeth and the French court. Nevertheless, despite Henry's, Mauvissière's, and even Catherine's growing suspicion and irritation, all three still wanted to see a marriage between Elizabeth and Francis. Furthermore, for Catherine, the union was important not only for international political reasons but also to help her maintain her domestic status within the French royal family. It was, in a sense, her last chance to preserve and maybe even augment her matriarchal authority. In a letter sent to Mauvissière, Catherine ordered him

> to assure the queen of England, madam my good sister and cousin, that she will always find in my children and myself true and perfect friendship and that there is nothing that we esteem more than hers [...] [As for] the marriage between her and my son the Duke of Anjou, I hope [this] will happen soon, with God's help.[120]

The word "children"—a reference to Henry and Francis—diminished both the former's rank as king and the latter's role as groom, placing Catherine at the apex of the royal family. Twenty days later, she again insisted:

---

[118] Catherine de Medici to Elizabeth I of England, December 11, 1580, in *LCM*, Tome VII, 299, "avant que ne meure, je vous voye mère d'ung beau fils."

[119] Levin, *The Heart and Stomach of a King*, 65.

[120] Catherine de Medici to Mauvissière, February 8, 1580, in *LCM*, Tome VII, 224, "d'asseurer la royne d'Angleterre, madame ma bonne seur et cousine, qu'elle trouvera tousjours en mes enffans et en moy toute vraye et parfaicte amityé et qu'il n'y a rien que nous estimions plus que la sienne, avec le mariage d'elle et de mon filz le duc d'Anjou, que j'espère qui se parachèvera bien tost de l'ayde de Dieu."

> I will only tell you that there is nothing in this world that I have desired—
> and continue to desire—more than the marriage of the queen of England,
> madam my good sister and cousin, and my son the Duke of Anjou.[121]

Catherine must have felt that the constant reiteration of these sentiments might yet convince the English queen to overcome her qualms about the union and finally conclude the negotiations, despite all evidence to the contrary. Such letters tended to be direct responses to the increasingly exasperated Mauvissière's reports, in which he depicted an ambivalent queen who veered between eagerness and deep reluctance to marry Francis, seemingly on an almost daily basis. For instance, at one stage, the couple exchanged rings as proof of their commitment to each other, only for Elizabeth later to dismiss hers as nothing more than "a pledge of perpetual friendship."[122]

In marked contrast to his predecessor La Mothe Fénélon, Mauvissière did not laud the queen's estimable qualities in an effort to lubricate the marriage negotiations, although he did rather grudgingly acknowledge that "she has been a great queen for a long time."[123] He also shrewdly referred to the coats of arms of both realms when writing to Francis: "the divine fleur-de-lis and the lion, which are two great houses."[124] This comment underlined the importance of the union for two powerful—but precarious—dynasties. Moreover, Henry acknowledged as much when he expressed his hope "that this common friendship and good relationship will be further confirmed and corroborated by the marriage with my said brother."[125]

Two days later, in another letter to Mauvissière, the French king described his brother as the "second person of the first king of Christendom and until now his heir."[126] The following month, shortly before Francis's

---

[121] Catherine de Medici to Mauvissière, February 28, 1580, in *LCM*, Tome VII, 227, "je vous diray seullement qu'il n'y a rien en ce monde que j'aye tant désiré et désire encores que le mariage de la royne d'Angleterre."

[122] See Levin, *The Heart and Stomach of a King*, 63.

[123] Mauvissière to Catherine de Medici, September 1, 1579, BNF MS. Fr. 15973, fol. 175r°, "il y a longtemps qu'elle est une grande royne."

[124] Mauvissière to Francis, Duke of Anjou, January 15, 1579, BNF MS. Fr. 15973, fol. 91v°, "la divine fleure de lye et le lyon a qui reste de deux maysons grandeur."

[125] Henry III of France to Mauvissière, July 6, 1579, BNF, V° Colbert, n°337, fol. 745, "j'esperois que ceste commune amitié et bonne intelligence seroit daventaige confirmee et corroboree par le mariage de mondict frère."

[126] Henry III of France to Mauvissière, July 8, 1579, BNF V° Colbert, n° 337, fol. 753, "la seconde personne du premier roy de la chrétienté et jusques icy son heritier." Henry was still hoping at that time to have a son.

first visit to England, Henry wrote to Elizabeth to express his pleasure that the meeting had finally been arranged, and took the opportunity to remind her of his closeness to the prince—"my brother who is my second self."[127] By the following February, Francis was Henry's "very dear and much beloved, unique brother, the Duke of Anjou," notwithstanding the fact that the king had always had a rather difficult relationship with his younger brother.[128] All of these insincere declarations of fraternal affection were issued with the same aim: to convince Elizabeth to marry the "much beloved" Francis and thereby secure the Anglo-French alliance against the threat posed by Spain. And if the couple also managed to produce an heir for both realms, so much the better.

However, after a decade of negotiations and two face-to-face meetings between Elizabeth and Francis, the French court finally had to face the reality of the situation: the marriage might never happen. Ilona Bell has argued that Henry was prepared to dissolve the political alliance if—or, as seemed increasingly likely, when—the marriage negotiations broke down irrevocably, but his letters to his ambassador suggest otherwise.[129] For example, on July 12, 1581, he instructed Mauvissière: "if the said marriage cannot be concluded […] I do not want to lose the good friendship between myself and the said lady queen."[130] For Henry, the coalition with England had always been paramount, and Catherine eventually reached a similar conclusion. In June 1580, she ordered Mauvissière to propose a treaty that would assure peace between the two realms "whether it [the marriage] happens or not."[131]

---

[127] Henry III of France to Elizabeth I of England, August 3, 1580, TNA SP 78/4, fol. 128, "Madame, est-il possible que bouche ny papier puisse exprimer l'extremité de l'ayse que mes sens qui en sont avec toute extremité ravis […] je la diray en ceste lettre l'heur que je veois si bien preparé a mon frère qui est ung second moy-mesmes."

[128] Henry III of France to Elizabeth I of England, February 28, 1581, BNF MS. Fr. 3307, fol. 5r°, "nostre tres cher et tres ame fere unicque le duc d'Anjou et d'Allençon." On the tumultuous relationship between the French princes, see Knecht, *Hero or Tyrant*, 163–83. Also a letter of Catherine de Medici to Anjou clearly reveals the tensions between her two sons, Catherine de Medici to Anjou, December 23, 1580, in *LCM*, Tome VII, 304–9.

[129] Ilona Bell, *Elizabeth I: The Voice of a Monarch*, 151.

[130] Henry III of France to Mauvissière, July 12, 1581, BNF MS. Fr. 3307, fol. 33v°, "si le dict mariage ne se pouvoit parchever […], je ne veux pourtant me départir de la bonne amityé entre moy & la dicte dame royne."

[131] Catherine de Medici to Mauvissière, February 8, 1580, in *LCM*, Tome VII, 264, "Mais, soit qu'il se fasse ou non, il faut, comme vous nous avez escript, qu'elle se laisse entendre qu'elle désire que nous estreignions par la confirmation de nostre traicté, si fort nostre amitié et bonne intelligence."

As we have seen throughout this chapter, Henry had serious doubts about Elizabeth's commitment to the marriage negotiations. Interestingly, though, he found her much more trustworthy in their diplomatic and political engagements: "I always see a clear demonstration of her friendship and benevolence, which I discern emanating from true honesty and sincerity."[132] Later, in February 1580, he referred to Elizabeth's "honest words" and her pledge "to prevent, as much as she will be able to, those who will want to come again to this realm," while offering an assurance that, "reciprocally, I will do likewise against those who would want to trouble hers as well."[133] Henry also alluded to Elizabeth's "honesty" when asking her to refrain from intervening in France's seventh religious civil war. More importantly, although the marriage negotiations certainly had a detrimental effect on Anglo-French relations, the king insisted on "the continuity of our friendship,"[134] and continued to describe the accord between the two nations as "perfect," "indissoluble," and "true."[135] He reiterated his desire to maintain "between the queen, myself, and our common subjects a perpetual and indissoluble friendship"[136] on several occasions, and often alluded to "the persistence of this perfect friendship [...] not only between us but also between our common subjects."[137]

[132] Henry III of France to Mauvissière, July 6, 1579, BNF V° Colbert, n° 337, fol. 745, "je comprens toujours une plus claire demonstration de son amitié et bienveillance, laquelle comme jestime procesder d'une vraye franchise et sincerite."

[133] Henry III of France to Mauvissière, February 8, 1580, BNF MS. Fr. 3307, fol. 5v°, "remerciant cependant icelle dame royne des honnestes propos qu'elle vous a tenuz de vouloir empescher, aultant qu'elle pourra, ceult qui auroient envie de retrouver encores ce royaulme; vous priant l'assurer qu'aussy reciproquement en feray je contre ceult qui vouldroient brouiller le sien."

[134] Henry III of France to Mauvissière, December 8, 1580, BNF MS. Fr. 3307, fol. 24r°, "la continuité de notre amityé."

[135] See for example, Henry III of France to Elizabeth I of England, September 13, 1581, BNF MS. Fr. 3307, fol. 44v°, "vous prier de vous asseurer tousjours de nostre vraye et parfaicte amytié en vostre endroict et laquelle nous desirons encores esteindre en toute perfection d'un lien indissoluble" and Henry III of France to Mauvissière, July 12, 1581, BNF MS. Fr. 3307, fol. 32r°, "de la bonne vraye amityé que je luy porte."

[136] Henry III of France to Mauvissière, August 23, 1580, BNF MS. Fr. 3307, fol. 24r°, "entre la royne, moy et nos communs subjectz d'une amitié perdurable et indissoluble."

[137] Henry III of France to Mauvissière, January 20, 1581, BNF MS. Fr. 3307, fol. 24r°, "continue d'une si parfaicte amityé [...] non seullement entre nous mais aussy entre nos communs subjectz."

According to Mauvissière, Elizabeth held identical views on the importance of maintaining the friendship between the two royal houses.[138] For
instance, in October 1579, he informed Catherine that he had "spent four
hours with her [Elizabeth], talking about a variety of things, including the
great and perfect friendship that she says she has for the king, your majesty, and my Lord."[139] In other dispatches, the ambassador assured the
king that Elizabeth had "an immortal friendship that she always wants to
have for my Lord, your brother," as well as "a lot of love and affection"
for him.[140] On the same day (May 18, 1580), he told Catherine that
Elizabeth "prays always to be assured of a perpetual and satisfying
friendship"[141] and the following month he informed Henry of "the
[queen's] friendship that she wants you to have all her life."[142] As these
reports indicate, the preservation of the Anglo-French alliance remained a
priority for both royal courts.

The French royal family also employed overt displays of affection in a
bid to retain Elizabeth's goodwill, even as the marriage negotiations slid
inexorably toward ultimate collapse. As we have seen, she was downgraded
from "germayne sister" to "good sister" and even "good friend" in the
diplomatic correspondence, but in December 1580 Henry ordered the
French ambassador to express his ongoing "goodwill and perfect affection" toward Elizabeth.[143] The following May, he wrote directly to the
queen herself with an assurance that she was still "the princess of this

---

[138] Mauvissière to Henry III of France, 265th Report, September 18, 1579, BNF MS. Fr.
15973, fol. 185r°, "vostre reciproque et bonne et parfaite amytié."

[139] Mauvissière to Catherine de Medici, October 16, 1579, BNF MS. Fr. 15973, fol.
194v°, "passé quatre heures avec elle me parlant de differentes choses mesmement de cette
grande et parfait amityé qu'elle dit portée au roy, a vostre majeste, et a Monseigneur."

[140] Mauvissière to Henry III of France, 287th Report, May 18, 1580, BNF MS. Fr. 15973,
fol. 276r°, "lamitié immortelle quelle vouloit a jamais portee à Monseigneur vostre frere"
and Mauvissière to Henry III of France, 288th Report, May 27, 1580, BNF MS. Fr. 15973,
fol. 278r°, "de beaucoup d'amour et d'affection quelle porte a Monseigneur."

[141] Mauvissière to Catherine de Medici, May 18, 1580, BNF MS. Fr. 15973, fol. 277v°,
"quelle prie estre tousjours assuree d'une perpetuelle et contente amityé."

[142] Mauvissière to Henry III of France, 291st Report, June 26, 1580, BNF MS. Fr. 15973,
fol. 295v°, "lamityé quelle vous voulez porter toute sa vye."

[143] Henry III of France to Mauvissière, December 8, 1580, BNF MS. Fr. 3307, fol. 23v°,
"asseurer que de ma part la même correspondence a sa même bonne volonté et parfaicte
affection."

world whom we see as the dearest."[144] Similarly, Catherine left Elizabeth in no doubt about "the great affection we have toward your friendship."[145]

Perhaps unsurprisingly, while the French royal family and their ambassador often informed Elizabeth of the warmth of their feelings toward her, their letters to one another contain little evidence of genuine affection for the English queen. However, they do include countless references to Elizabeth's affection for them. For instance, Mauvissière repeatedly alluded to Elizabeth's displays of "friendship and fraternal love" toward the Valois rulers,[146] assured Catherine that "the words that the queen told me show the great affection she has toward you," and informed Henry that Elizabeth was "the most affectionate good sister you could have."[147] It is impossible to know whether the French royal family accepted all of these dispatches at face value or rather suspected that Elizabeth was just as disingenuous toward them as they were toward her, but the fact that both sides were willing to preserve the veneer of affection reveals the importance of the alliance for all concerned.

As with the correspondence relating to the marriage negotiations, it is Catherine's letters that shed the most light on the relationship between the two courts. For instance, although she echoed her son's references to eternal, unbreakable Anglo-French amity, she also hinted that both sides could and should do more to strengthen the alliance. At the end of 1579, she assured Elizabeth that "you will always find reciprocity on our part, with firm words and a desire to fortify and embrace our mutual friendship with an indissoluble bond and make it perpetual between our common realms, countries, and subjects."[148] Similarly, the previous month, she had expressed her commitment to "the continuation and fortification of the

---

[144] Henry III of France to Elizabeth I of England, May 5, 1581, TNA SP 78/5, fol. 66, "la princesse de ce monde que nous tenons pour la plus chère."

[145] Catherine to Elizabeth, November 18, 1579, in *LCM*, Tome VII, 196, "grande affection que nous avons à vostre amytié."

[146] Mauvissière to Henry III of France, 236th Report, February 22, 1579, BNF MS. Fr. 15973, fol. 105v°, "la grande affection quelle avoit pour vous."

[147] Mauvissière to Catherine de Medici, April 29, 1579, BNF MS. Fr. 15973, fol. 132v°°, "les mots que m'a dit la royne monstre fort la grande affection d'elle envers vous" and Mauvissière to Henry III of France, 252nd Report, June 16, 1579, BNF MS. Fr. 3307, fol. 152r°, "plus affectionnee bonne seur que vous pourriez avoir."

[148] Catherine de Medici to Elizabeth, December 27, 1579, in *LCM*, Tome VII, 213, "vous trouverez tousjours le réciproque de nostre costé, avec ferme propos et volunté de fortiffier et estraindre nostre mutuelle amityé d'un lien indissoluble et de la rendre perpétuelle entre noz commungs royaulmes, pays et subjectz."

friendship between these two crowns."[149] Even more significantly, in September 1581, after the collapse of the marriage negotiations, she articulated "the singular desire and affection that we have not only to conserve and maintain our good friendship, alliance, and confederation but also to increase, fortify, and expand it."[150] Therefore, whereas Henry merely expected Elizabeth to honor the alliance as it stood, Catherine hoped to forge a rather stronger union between the two nations, even though her dream of cementing it through marriage had now all but died.

## Conclusion

As this chapter has demonstrated, Anglo-French relations became increasingly fraught during the last few years of marriage negotiations between Elizabeth and the Duke of Anjou. In part, this may be attributed to the tense and complicated European political context, but the French court's changing perception of the English queen certainly played a role, too. The diplomatic correspondence between the French royal family and their ambassador provides ample evidence of their increasing irritation and frustration with Elizabeth, particularly in response to her procrastination and indecision over the marriage.

Furthermore, this chapter has shown that there was a marked difference in perceptions of Elizabeth in England and France. Whereas the image of the Virgin Queen rose to prominence within her own realm at the start of the 1580s—especially among those who were opposed to the French match—in the French royal correspondence she was often portrayed as an indecisive, deceitful, and immoral monarch who promoted piracy against French vessels.[151] Although this image of a pirate queen dated back to the early years of Elizabeth's reign, it became far more prevalent between 1579 and 1581, reflecting the lack of trust between the two crowns, especially on the French side. However, there was a parallel—and

---

[149] Catherine de Medici to Elizabeth, November 18, 1579, in *LCM*, Tome VII, 195, "la continuation et fortification de l'amitié d'netre ces deux couronnes."

[150] Catherine de Medici to Elizabeth, September 13, 1581, in *LCM*, Tome VII, 397, "le singulier désir et affection que nous avons, non seulement de conserver et entretenir nostre bonne amytié, alliance et confédération, mais aussy l'acroistre, fortiffier et augmenter."

[151] Helen Hackett has argued that "the Anjou courtship is important because it marks some important changes: the realisation by Elizabeth's subjects that a Virgin Queen might be preferable to a married Queen [...] From now on she wold be unequivocally celebrated as ever-virgin." in Hackett, *Virgin Mother, Maiden Queen*, 95.

contrasting—development in perceptions of Elizabeth around the same time: she was increasingly seen as a weak woman who could not reach a decision without the advice of strong men. This was certainly the view of her own Privy Council and the French court, but it was also evident in the work of the pamphleteers, poets, and authors who criticized her rule and advised her to abandon the marriage negotiations.[152]

The French king and especially his mother continued to represent Elizabeth as an essential ally and indeed a member of their own family, but she was no longer the "germayne sister" she had been for Charles IX. Rather, she became a mere "good sister and cousin." Similarly, Mauvissière's relationship with the English queen was far cooler than his predecessor's had been. Even Catherine, who still occasionally advanced the notion of a mother–daughter relationship with Elizabeth, increasingly reverted to the formal diplomatic idiom of the time. Nevertheless, preservation of the alliance with England remained paramount for the French royal family because of the urgent need to counteract Spain's rapidly expanding power on the continent. Hence, their expressions of warmth and affection toward Elizabeth continued, regardless of their annoyance about English pirates' activities in the Channel and frustration over the queen's indecision in the marriage negotiations.

Although many studies have addressed the political fallout following the failure of those negotiations, scholars have tended to overlook the consequences for monarchical representation. How the French royal family reacted to the collapse of the Anjou match and how they subsequently perceived Elizabeth and depicted her in their correspondence challenged all of the accepted diplomatic conventions of the time. From ambivalence to inconsistency, French representations of the English queen came to mirror increasingly tense relations between the two nations in a decade that witnessed the outbreak of the eighth French religious civil war in 1585, Mary Stuart's execution in February 1587, and the English victory over the Spanish Armada in 1588.

---

[152] Hackett, "The rhetoric of (in)fertility, Shifting responses to Elizabeth I's childlessness," 149–71. On the reaction of the English on the Anjou Match, see Sir Philip Sidney, "From a Discourse of Sir Philip Sidney to the Queen's Majesty Touching Her Marriage with Monsieur (1579)," in *The Complete Works of Sir Philip Sidney*, ed. Albert Feuillerat, vol. 3 (Cambridge: Cambridge University Press, 1923), 51–60; William Elderton, *A newe ballade, declaring the dangerons shootynge of the gunne at the courte* (London: Edward White, 1579; STC 7557.4); Sir Philip Sidney, "From Arcadia (ca. 1578–80)," in *The Covntess of Pembrokes Arcadia* (London: William Ponsonbie, 1593; STC 22540).

# "declared herself as our enemy": Crisis, Confrontation, and Secret Correspondence, 1584–1588

On June 10, 1584, Francis, Duke of Anjou, heir to the French throne, died, triggering a major succession crisis. The Huguenot leader Henry III, King of Navarre, had the strongest claim to the throne, but the Catholic League, founded in 1576 and led by Henry I, Duke of Guise, and Charles II of Bourbon, could not accept a Protestant as the King of France.[1] As a result, the nation's nobility divided into two rival, mutually hostile camps.

In March 1585, the members of the League issued a declaration in which they voiced their opposition to

> the complete subversion of the Catholic Apostolic and Roman religion in this very Christian realm, inside which we will never suffer the reign of a heretic [...] or suffer the domination of a non-Christian Catholic Prince, given that this is the first oath that our Kings take when they are crowned— to maintain the Catholic Apostolic and Roman religion.[2]

---

[1] Holt, *The French Wars of Religion*, 122 and Knecht, *Hero or Tyrant?*, 228. Charles II, Cardinal of Bourbon was the uncle of Henry of Navarre. Despite his name, he fought alongside the Guises and the Catholic League against his nephew and the House of Bourbon in the 1580s.

[2] Déclaration des causes qui ont mu monseigneur le cardinal de bourbon et les pairs, princes, seigneurs, villes et communautés catholiques de ce royaume de France, de s'opposer à ceux qui par tous moyens s'efforcent de subvertir la religion catholique et l'Etat, March 31, 1585, *Mémoires de la Ligue*, Tome I (Amsterdam: Arkstee & Merkus, 1758), 56.

© The Author(s) 2019      171
E. Paranque, *Elizabeth I of England through Valois Eyes*, Queenship and Power, https://doi.org/10.1007/978-3-030-01529-9_6

The meaning was clear: the Catholic faith had precedence over any dynastic claim to the throne. Just four months later, Henry III addressed the League's concerns in the Treaty of Nemours, which revoked all previous religious treaties and explicitly forbade Protestantism in the realm.[3] Outraged, the Huguenots initiated the eighth religious civil war, which sucked Henry and the whole of France into four years of incessant conflict and violence.[4]

The political situation was febrile in England, too. During the Throckmorton Plot of 1583 a group of powerful Catholics attempted to assassinate Elizabeth and replace her with Mary Stuart. The following year, the Privy Council, under the leadership of Burghley and Walsingham, drafted the Bond of Association,[5] which specified that the signatories would assassinate any claimant to the throne who profited from Elizabeth's assassination. Nevertheless, suspicions continued to mount against Mary and her Catholic supporters, especially after the discovery of Anthony Babington's plot to install her as queen in 1586. It was this plot that led directly to Mary's trial and execution.

Therefore, between 1584 and 1588, both Henry III of France and Elizabeth of England faced unprecedented challenges to their rule. Moreover, distrust between the two nations continued to grow, not least because Walsingham's network of spies strongly suspected that the French

---

[3] Edit de Nemours, July 7, 1585, in Eugène et Emile Haag, *La France Protestante*, vol. 10 (Paris, 1858), 184, "il ne se fera dorénavant aucun exercice de la nouvelle religion prétendue réformée, mais seulement celui de notre religion catholique, apostolique et romaine. Ce que nous inhibons et défendons très-expressément à tous nos sujets de quelque qualité et condition qu'ils soient, sur peine de confiscation de corps et de biens, nonobstant la permission qui était donnée de ce faire par nos édits de pacification précédens, laquelle nous avons révoquée et révoquons par ces presents, par lesquelles voulons et ordonnons, sur les mêmes peines que dessus est dit, que tous ministres de ladite nouvelle religion, aident à vuider et sortir de celui notredit royaume."

[4] Denis Crouzet, *Les Guerriers de Dieu: la Violence au Temps des Troubles de Religion, 1525–1610*, Tome 2 (Seyssel: Champ Vallon, 1990), 467; Denis Crouzet, *Dieu en ses royaumes* (Seyssel: Camp Vallon, 2008), 313–4; see also the works of Elie Barnavi and Robert Decimon, *La Sainte Ligue, le Juge et la Potence* (Paris: Hachette, 1985); Hugues Daussy, *Les Huguenots et le roi: le combat politique de Philippe Duplessy-Mornay, 1572–1600* (Genève: Droz, 2002) and Agrippa d'Aubigné, *Histoire universelle*, ed. A. Thierry, Tome VI (Genève: Droz, 1992).

[5] BL MS Cottonian Library Caligula C.IX, art. 41, fol. 122. And see, Carole Levin, *The Reign of Elizabeth I* (New York: Palgrave, 2002), 95.

were conspiring with Mary.[6] This complicated and frequently dangerous political context had a significant impact not only on the Anglo-French alliance but also on representations of Elizabeth within the French royal family's diplomatic correspondence. The virtual family ties that had bound the two courts together for decades started to dissolve after Francis's death, changing the dynamics of the alliance and increasing the likelihood that it would collapse altogether. Largely due to the chaos of the final four years of his reign, Henry III found himself isolated on the international stage and started to gain a reputation for tyranny both at home and abroad.[7] Meanwhile, Philip II's Spain asserted ever more authority on the continent and became a serious threat to both England and France.[8]

This chapter explores the French royal family's mounting distrust of Elizabeth in this period of domestic crisis. As we shall see, some old grievances resurfaced—such as suspicions that the English queen was sending aid to the Huguenots and doing little to stop English pirates' attacks on French vessels—but the French diplomatic correspondence also reveals a court that was riven by indecision over how to react to the various conspiracies that threatened Elizabeth's life and faced the dilemma of imperiling the Anglo-French alliance or abandoning Mary Stuart to her fate. All of these issues contributed to the French court's increasingly complex perceptions and representations of the English queen throughout the latter half of the 1580s. By contrast, the Catholic League's entirely negative depictions of Elizabeth were much more simplistic. Finally, we shall examine Henry III's desperate efforts to preserve the Anglo-French alliance amid the domestic turmoil that would eventually claim his life and confirm the end of the Valois dynasty.

---

[6] Bossy, *Giordano Bruno*, 33–35.

[7] See the works of Annie Duprat, *Les rois de papier, la caricature de Henry III à Louis XVI* (Paris: Belin, 2002) which examines the bad reputation of Henry III by his contemporaries, and Katherine Crawford, "Love, Sodomy, and Scandal: Controlling the Sexual Reputation of Henry III," *Journal of the History of Sexuality*, vol. 12 (2003): 513–42, which argues that those critics were created to reproach the king's effeminate appearance as well as his failure to produce an heir.

[8] Richardson, "'Your most assured sister': Elizabeth I and the Kings of France", 194.

## The Anglo-French Alliance in the Balance: Threats, Piracy, and War

The period 1584 to 1588 was one of ongoing distrust and defiance, as well as rising tension, between the crowns of England and France.[9] To some extent, the mutual suspicion was understandable, given the incessant Catholic conspiracies against Elizabeth's rule. Take the case of Thomas Morgan, who fled to France following accusations of involvement in the Parry Plot of 1585—one of countless conspiracies (both real and imagined) that aimed to depose Elizabeth and install Mary Stuart in her stead on the English throne.[10] Both Morgan himself and the leader of the plot, William Parry, were said to have strong links with the French Embassy,[11] although Leo Hicks suggests that Morgan was actually working for Francis Walsingham, Elizabeth's loyal "spymaster."[12] Either way, the important point is that London was rife with suspicion in the 1580s, and much of it inevitably fell on England's closest—but Catholic—ally.

On February 12, 1585, Elizabeth wrote directly to her French counterpart to ask for his help in locating Morgan:

> It having been discovered a few days ago that one of our subjects intended to make an attempt upon our life, he has confessed that another of our subjects, now a fugitive in your realm, expressly incited him thereto; an act so detestable and of such dangerous consequence for all princes, that with one accord they ought to exert themselves that severe and exemplary punishment may be given to all the supporters of so unhappy an enterprise.

As we saw in her correspondence with Charles IX, Elizabeth firmly believed that the maintenance of royal authority was paramount, and there are obvious echoes of that attitude in this appeal to Charles's successor. Later in the same letter, she invoked another familiar theme, the principle of justice:

---

[9] Bossy, *Under The Molehill*, 94.

[10] Bossy, *Giordano Bruno*, 54 and Elizabeth Jenkins, *Elizabeth and Leicester* (London: The Phoenix Press, 2002), 290.

[11] Bossy, *Under The Molehill*, 97.

[12] Leo Hicks, *An Elizabethan Problem: Some Aspects of the Careers of Two Exile-Adventurers* (New York: Fordham University Press, 1964), 172–85. John Bossy also made a case against Edward Stafford and how he was actually paid by the French rulers, see Bossy, *Giordano Bruno*, 96–97.

We hope for this above all from you, as from a prince who loves right and justice, ever holds honor dear, and has vowed to us true affection, friendship and mutual good correspondence, of which we have already made proof on many occasions, and that you will make no difficulty—according to the right of the ancient treaties between the two crowns—in putting into our hands the author of so unhappy an enterprise [...] our request being so just and reasonable and the matter of such great consequence from the imminent danger to our person, which your own honor and the duty of friendship will not permit you to deny.[13]

Clearly, Elizabeth felt that the Parry Plot was sufficiently grave to warrant maximum diplomatic pressure, hence her explicit reference to the Anglo-French alliance and the "ancient treaties between the two crowns." Having received such a strong appeal for assistance, Henry must have understood that any refusal to cooperate would jeopardize the alliance, yet he was also under concerted pressure from the Catholic League, who did not want to see Morgan sent back to England. In a bid to appease both sides, although the king refused to hand over the fugitive,[14] he did imprison him in the Bastille. Infuriated, the English queen dispatched another personal letter to Henry:

But this pleasure [*liesse*] is like a fire made of straw, which flames up more than it endures, for now I have a packet which has made me very angry hearing that not only was he not delivered into my hands, but that my ambassadors have not been permitted to see his ciphers and writings.[15]

Morgan remained in the Bastille for the next two and a half years, during which time he continued to communicate freely with his accomplices in France and England.[16] Inevitably, his case remained a bone of contention and a source of considerable tension between the two crowns. But it was just one of many disputes that ultimately caused the French royal family to perceive and portray Elizabeth as a potential enemy, which obviously had serious repercussions for the Anglo-French alliance.

[13] Elizabeth I of England to Henry III of France, 12 March 1585, TNA SP 78/13 fol. 24.

[14] In a letter to Mauvissière, Henry III explained the reasons he could not send back Morgan to England, Henry III of France to Mauvissière, March 17, 1585, BNF Cinq Cent Colbert n° 470, fol. 113–5.

[15] Elizabeth I of England to Henry III of France, March 10, 1585, TNA SP, 78/13 fol. 55.

[16] ODNB, Thomas Morgan (1543–in or after 1611), Alison Plowden. Accessed on April 28, 2018.

Two years after Morgan's flight from England, Walsingham heard of yet another plot. William Stafford, the younger brother of Edward Stafford, English ambassador at the French court, had allegedly joined a conspiracy to poison Elizabeth organized by the new French ambassador, Guillaume de l'Aubespine, Baron de Chasteauneuf, and his secretary, Leonard des Trappes.[17] No charges were ever brought against Chasteauneuf, although suspicions remained about his knowledge of the plot, whereas Trappes was arrested in Dover while attempting to flee to France.[18] Henry expressed both surprise and dismay on hearing the news of his diplomatic mission's alleged involvement in a plot to assassinate the queen, but then insisted that he—and he alone—had the right to judge any member of his embassy's staff.[19] However, Elizabeth refused his request to send Trappes back to France; instead, she reiterated her demand for Morgan's return to England.[20] The English ambassador reported Henry's indignant response to Walsingham:

> he told me that she did so evil to refuse the sending of Trappes hither with his depositions to have him here examined, and worse to ask for Morgan in exchange for Trappes [...] the King took it marvelous evil that her Majesty would neither receive letters from his ambassador nor hear him.[21]

It is not known what became of Trappes, but given the circumstances, it seems safe to assume that he never made it home.

The rising tension between the two crowns was also linked to Spain's growing power throughout mainland Europe and even within France itself. Indeed, as the eighth religious civil war continued to ravage French cities, the Catholic League formed an alliance with Spain to obtain financial support and weapons.[22] Moreover, the continued displays of distrust and

---

[17] ODNB, William Stafford (1554–1612), Peter Holmes. Accessed on April 28, 2018 and William Stafford's report [before the Lords], SP 15/30 fol. 10.

[18] Note that in 1583 [1587], or the year preceding, a design to attempt the life of the Queen was discovered, SP 15/30 fol. 12.

[19] Henry III of France to Elizabeth I of England, February 14, 1587, TNA SP/78/17 fol. 49.

[20] Henry III of France to Elizabeth I of England, February 5, 1587, TNA SP 78/17 fol. 24.

[21] Stafford to Walsingham, March 24, 1587, TNA SP 78/17 fol. 101.

[22] Cauvin, *Henry de Guise Le Balafré*, 233; Nicolas Le Roux, *Un régicide au nom de Dieu* (Paris: Gallimard, 2006), 116–9; Robert Knecht, *Hero or Tyrant?*, 230 and Geoffrey Parker, *The Grand Strategy of Philip II* (New Haven: Yale University Press, 1989), 172.

defiance by—or on behalf of—Elizabeth led to increased fears of an Anglo-Spanish alliance. In 1584, Henry ordered Mauvissière, who was still his ambassador in London at the time, to ensure that "the queen of England is not making an alliance with the king of Spain against my realm."[23] Three years later, Catherine expressed the same concern, writing to one of her closest advisers, Monsieur de Bellièvre: "she [Elizabeth] will agree if she can with the said king of Spain; and they will both agree on instigating trouble for this realm."[24] Furthermore, in a letter to Chasteauneuf, she insisted that Elizabeth "evidently contravenes the treaties of alliance that are between monsieur the king, my son, and her, which you should continue to complain about and explain in a good way that [...] we clearly see the wrong she is doing to us."[25] This is just one of several references to Elizabeth breaching the terms of treaties in Catherine's correspondence of the late 1580s, which demonstrate not only that the queen mother remained an influential political adviser until the very end of her life but also that she ultimately came to view the English queen as deceitful and untrustworthy.[26]

---

[23] Henry III of France to Mauvissière, November 30, 1584, BNF MS. Fr. 3305, fol. 57r°, "Asseurez vous que la royne d'Angletere ne fasse pas d'alliance avecques le roy d'Espagnes constre mon royaume."

[24] Catherine de Medici to Bellièvre, February 14, 1587, in *LCM*, Tome IX, 166, "elle s'accordera, si elle peut, avec ledict roy d'Espaigne; et eulx deulx s'accorderont aussi à fommenter les troubles en ce roiaulme."

[25] Catherine de Medici to Chasteauneuf, February 2, 1588, in *LCM*, Tome IX, 326, "elle contrevient manifestement aux traictez d'alliance qui sont entre le Roy monsieur mon filz et elle, dont vous debvez continuer à vous plaindre et faire instance de si bonne façon qu'elle veoye que [...] nous n'appercevions clairement le tort qu'elle nous faict."

[26] For other letters mentioning Elizabeth's attitude regarding the treaties, see Catherine de Medici to Chasteauneuf, January 5, 1588, in *LCM*, Tome IX, 323 and Catherine de Medici to Henry III of France, May 29, 1587, in *LCM*, Tome IX, 213. As for Catherine a powerful adviser and politician, see the works of: Nicola M. Sutherland, *Catherine de Medici and the Ancien Regime* (London: Historical Association, 1966); Mark Strage, *Women of Power: The Life and Times of Catherine de Medici* (New York and London: Harcourt, Brace Jovanovich, 1976); Katherine Crawford, "Catherine de Medicis and the Performance of Political Motherhood," *The Sixteenth Century Journal*, vol. 31, No. 3 (Autumn, 2000): 643–73 and Sheila ffolliott, "Catherine de' Medici as Artemisia: Figuring the Powerful Widow," in *Rewriting the Renaissance: The Discourses of Sexual Difference in Early Modern Europe*, eds. Margaret W Ferguson, Maureen Vickers, and Nancy J. Vickers (Chicago: University of Chicago Press, 1986), 227–41.

In early 1588, Edward Stafford informed Elizabeth, "there were evil-disposed people to break the amity between France and England,"[27] but there can be little doubt that Catherine reached her own conclusions about the English queen. Her chief fear was the formation of an Anglo-Spanish alliance against France, and Elizabeth's scheming behavior and defiance did little to assuage her suspicions. Such perceptions were soon reflected in pervasive images of the English queen as a pirate and a warrior. Indeed, as the Spanish threat became increasingly serious—for England as well as France—Elizabeth turned to the nation's pirates to lead the counterattack,[28] and her "rhetoric also became more powerful."[29] While this image of a strong pirate queen was welcomed and celebrated by most of Elizabeth's subjects, the attitude on the other side of the Channel was rather different, as the French royal family developed an almost identical—but wholly pejorative—representation of Elizabeth in their correspondence.

As we saw in Chap. 5, Henry admired England's most notorious pirate—Francis Drake—and he was well aware of the scale of Drake's activities on behalf of the English queen. In 1585, he told Mauvissière that Elizabeth had "ordered Drake to get ready for a voyage to the West and East Indies with 18 great vessels and 3,000 Englishmen."[30] By the following May, it was clear that the French king had followed this expedition closely. In a letter to Mauvissière's successor at the English court, Chasteauneuf, he discussed "the exploits of Drake in Peru, Saint Domingo and Cuba."[31] Catherine was similarly smitten, telling Chasteauneuf: "I believe that Drake has made good progress up to now [as] he is better supported [...] When you see him, will you give him my affectionate greetings and assure him of the affection I have toward him."[32] Yet, while

[27] Stafford to Elizabeth I of England, February 25, 1588, TNA SP 78/18 fol. 52.

[28] Ronald, *The Pirate Queen*, 277–305.

[29] Levin, *The Heart and Stomach of a King*, 140.

[30] Henry III of France to Mauvissière, July 2, 1585, BNF Cinf Cents Colbert, n° 470, fol. 133, "elle as aussy donne ordre à Drac de se presparer pour un voyage vers les Indes orientales et occidentales avec 18 grands vaisseaux et 3000 Anglois."

[31] Henry III of France to Chasteauneuf, May 8, 1586, BNF MS. Fr. 3305, fol. 24v°, "les exploits de Drak au Perou, Sain Domingue et Cuba."

[32] Catherine de Medici to Chasteauneuf, June 30, 1586, in *LCM*, Tome IX, 18, "Je croy qu'à present que Drach faict si bon progrez, il est mieulz assisté [...]. Quand vous le verrez vous luy ferez mes affectionnées recommandations, et l'asseurez tousjours de l'affection que je luy porte."

the French royal family could not contain their excitement over Drake's exploits, his activities and those of other English pirates placed ever more strain on Anglo-French diplomatic relations.

Henry raised the issue of English attacks on French vessels in numerous letters to his ambassadors and often Elizabeth herself. For instance, on December 21, 1585, he complained to the English queen:

> Drake, general of the English navy, met at sea near Cape Finister a vessel named "La Magdeleine" which was new and sailing her first voyage with a cargo of salt from Portugal belonging to Jacques Procheau, a marine trader from Sables Dollones. He seized the said vessel with its crew and goods.[33]

On the very same day, the king instructed Chasteauneuf to "press the queen, my good sister and cousin, for justice."[34] Three months later, when another of his subjects, Estienne Dasmeguettes, was attacked near the Isle of Wight, Henry was rather more insistent, as he told Chasteauneuf that "she [Elizabeth] must order that the sea is purged of so many pirates, her subjects are ruining commerce" and promised to "send her retaliation" if the queen failed to act.[35] By May 1587, according to Henry, the situation had deteriorated to such an extent that "our friendship is in danger because of English pirates, who seize French commercial vessels and take them to England. The queen of England does not act against such practices and does not order restitution for the king's subjects."[36]

---

[33] Henry III of France to Elizabeth I of England, December 21, 1585, BNF MS. Fr. 3309, fol. 95v°, "Drac general de l'armée navalle angloise ayant rencorstre en mer pres du cap Finistere un navire nomme "La Magdeleine" neuf et qui faisait son premier voyage retoursnant charge de sel de Portugal, appurtenant a Jacques Procheau, marchans marinier des Sables Dollone. Il auroit retenu ledict navire ainsi que lequipaige et marchandises."

[34] Henry III of France to Chasteauneuf, December 21, 1585, BNF MS. Fr. 3309, fol. 96r°, "Drak general de larmee navalle de la royne d'Angleterre madame ma bonne seur et cousine a pris un navire appurtenan a Jacques Procheau [...] insiste au pres de la royne ma bonne seur et cousine pour que justice soit fait."

[35] Henry III of France to Chasteauneuf, March 13, 1586, BNF MS. Fr 3305, fol. 20v°, "depredations du vaisseau et des marchandises faicte par les gens du sr de Quevry, gouverneur de lisle de Wicht (Wight) sur Estienne Dasmesguettes, marchan de sain jean de luz [...] la royne d'Angleterre doist lui rensdre justice, si ce nest pas le cas, je lui enverrai des lettres de represailles [...] elle doist ordonner que la mer soist purgee de tant de pirates, ses subjectz ruinnent le commerce."

[36] Henry III of France to Chasteauneuf, May 11, 1587, BNF MS. Fr. 3305, fol. 28v°, "nostre amytie est en danger a cause de la piratterie angloise qui arreste les navires marchan

Henry made countless direct appeals to Elizabeth on behalf of merchants from Paris, Toulouse, Troyes, Rouen, Calais, and elsewhere throughout the mid-1580s, but it seems that most—if not all—of these petitions were ignored.[37] As a result, his image of her as a corrupt pirate queen gradually overwhelmed all previous representations of the English monarch. Moreover, some of Catherine's letters suggest that she started to share the king's view toward the end of her life, such as when she confided to Chasteauneuf that "my son is continually solicited by his subjects, victims of depravity done against them by the English."[38] Six months later, in May 1588, Catherine told Henry that the Spanish ambassador had asked for an audience with the French king in order to inform him that

the king of Spain, his master, seeing so many English pirates at sea who are so prejudicial to him and his subjects, has been forced to muster a navy, which is going to sail at the beginning of the month to purge the sea of these said pirates [...] He does not know for what it will be used next, but it will not be at our expense; on the contrary, it will serve you, if you need it.[39]

francois et les conduit en Angleterre. La royne d'Angleterre n'agit pas contre ces pratiques et ne fait pas restituer aux subjectz du roy."

[37] See Henry III of France to Elizabeth I of England, April 1586, TNA SP 78/15 fol. 89, "On behalf of Francois de Troyes—Narrates the seizing of his ship, the St. Jehan "au port d'Artemue" the sale of the cargo of salt by the late Vice-Admiral Champernon and the vain attempts of des Troyes to obtain redress and prays her to give him the value of the salt—taken against the treaties between their crowns and the liberty of commerce between their subjects;" Henry III of France to Elizabeth I of England, May 1586, TNA SP 78/15 fol. 91, "On behalf of Jehan Menaut, merchant of Paris, whose ship, laden with wine at Rouen for Calais was taken by pirates;" Henry III of France to Elizabeth I of England, July 19, 1586, TNA SP 78/16 fol. 58, "Complaining that in spite of remonstrances on my part and promises on yours, your ships at sea have lately taken four or five vessels laden with corn belonging to my subject" and Henry III of France to Elizabeth I of England, October 15, 1586, TNA SP 78/16 fol. 122, "Philip Destailleur, a burgess and sheriff of Calais, had laden in two English ships at Hambourg for Calais 36 lasts of wheat and 30 of rye for that place, the same in the way was taken by one Captain [...] and conveyed to Zeeland [...] it was declared good price and sold, without restitution of money or goods made."

[38] Catherine de Medici to Chasteaneuf, November 23, 1587, in *LCM*, Tome IX, 301, "mon filz estant continuellement sollicité par ses subjectz, interessés des déprédations faictes sur eux par les Anglois."

[39] Catherine de Medici to Henry III of France, May 23, 1588, in *LCM*, Tome IX, 301, "Monsieur mon filz, l'ambassadeur d'Espaigne m'est ceste après-diner veneu trouver et m'a dict que l'occazion pour laquelle il vous avoit demandé audiance ces jours icy estoit pour vous faire entendre que le roy d'Espagne son maistre, veoyant tant de pirates anglois à la mer,

This is certainly an oversimplification, as there were many other reasons why Philip II decided to launch the Spanish Armada against England. However, English piracy was undoubtedly a significant contributory factor. Furthermore, it should be noted that there is no evidence of sympathy for Elizabeth herself or England in Catherine's letter. By 1588, the image of the warrior, pirate queen was so ingrained in the French royal family's discourse that they knew precisely who to blame when war eventually, inevitably, broke out.

Elizabeth's warlike rhetoric is exemplified in a rousing speech that she gave to the troops at Tilbury as they prepared to face the anticipated Spanish invasion: "I know I have the body but of a weak and feeble woman but I have the heart and stomach of a king and of a king of England too— and take foul scorn that Parma or any prince of Europe should dare to invade the borders of my realm."[40] Although some scholars have questioned the authenticity of this oration, Janet M. Green has assembled a substantial body of evidence—including comparisons between Elizabeth's "internal rhetoric" at Tilbury and her use of similar phrases in other verifiable speeches—that seems to prove that it did indeed take place as reported at the time.[41]

Once the remnants of the Armada had limped back to Spain, the image of Elizabeth as a powerful—maybe even invincible—warrior queen became embedded in the English national psyche. By contrast, the reaction on the other side of the Channel was rather more muted. Indeed, in a letter to Chasteauneuf of August 27, 1588, Henry merely mentioned "the victory of the queen of England over the Spanish" before moving on to other topics.[42] In part, his apparent lack of interest in her triumph may be

---

qui lui faisoient et à ses subjectz tant de prejudice, il avoit esté contrainct de mettre une armée navalle, qui debvoit faire voille dez le commencement de ce mois, pour repurger la mer desdictz pirates; qu'il ne sçavoit après cela ce qu'elle feroit, mais que ce ne seroit rien à vostre prejudice, au contraire qu'elle vous serviroit, sy vous en aviez besoing."

[40] Queen Elizabeth's Armada Speech to the troops at Tilbury, 9 August 1588, in *Elizabeth I: Collected Works*, 326.

[41] Janet M. Green, "'I My Self': Queen Elizabeth's Oration at Tilbury Camp," *The Sixteenth Century Journal*, 28/2 (Summer, 1997): 421–45. See, *Elizabeth I: Collected Works*, 326 and Levin, *The Heart and Stomach of a King*, 143–5. Also see brief discussion in Chap. 2.

[42] Henry III of France to Chasteauneuf, August 27, 1588, BNF MS. Fr. 3305, fol. 44v°, "la victoire de la royne d'Angleterre sur lEspagne."

explained by the fact that his own realm had been in a state of brutal civil war for the previous three years, and there was still no end in sight.[43]

Many of Henry's subjects were even less enthusiastic about the defeat of the Armada. For instance, Pierre de L'Estoile reported that

> this so great and fearsome Spanish navy that threatened England [...] was miraculously ruined, defeated, and reduced to wind and nothingness not so much by the English (though they are given the honor of such a victory that belongs only to God) but by a headwind.[44]

This was typical of contemporary French accounts, which tended to give no credit whatsoever to the English navy, the English government, or Elizabeth herself. Instead, they attributed the victory entirely to dumb luck. The English propaganda that elevated Elizabeth to almost mythical warrior queen status seemingly never made it across the Channel.[45] Understandably, most of the studies of Elizabeth's representation and self-representation as a warrior have focused on these laudatory English pamphlets and poems,[46] but the Gloriana persona never gained a foothold

---

[43] Pierre de L'Estoile, *Première Partie du Tome Premier, Registre-Journal de Henry III 1574–1589*, 261–4 and see Arlette Jouanna, "Le Temps des Guerres de Religion en France (1559–1598)," in *Histoire et Dictionnaire des Guerres de Religion*, eds. Arlette Jouanna, Jacqueline Boucher, Dominique Biloghi and Guy Le Thiec (Robert Laffont: Turin, 1998), 329–40.

[44] L'Estoile, 262, "ceste grande et effroiable armée navalle d'Hespagne menassant l'Angleterre [...] fut miraculeusement ruinée, desfaite et réduitte au vent et à néant, non pas tant par les Anglois (encore qu'on lui en donne l'honneur de ceste victoire, qui appartient à Dieu seul), que par un vent contraire."

[45] Thomas Deloney, *The Queenes visiting of the campe at Tilsburie* (London: Edward White, 1588), STC 6565; Thomas Sorocold, "Queen Elizabeth: The Queen in Victory (1588), Prayer of Thanksgiving for the Overthrow of the Spanish Navy" in *Supplications of saints A booke of prayers* (London: Nicholars Bourne, 1612), STC 22932, N7r–N8v and James Aske, *Elizabetha triumphans Conteyning the damnes practizes, that the diuelish popes of Rome have vsed euer sihence her Highnesse first coming to the Crowne* (London: Thomas Gubbin and Thomas Newman, 1588), STC 847.

[46] The analysis of Elizabeth's warrior representations have been analysed in various works. See for examples: Anna Whitelock, "'Woman, Warrior, Queen?': Rethinking Mary and Elizabeth," in *Tudor Queenship: the Reigns of Mary and Elizabeth*, eds. Alice Hunt and Anna Whitelock (New York: Palgrave Macmillan, 2010), 173–89; Ben Spiller, "Warlike Mates? Queen Elizabeth and Joan La Pucelle in 1 Henry VI," in *Goddesses and Queens: the Iconography of Elizabeth I*, eds. Annaliese Connolly and Lisa Hopkins (Manchester and New York: Manchester University Press, 2007), 34–44; Susan Doran, *Elizabeth I and Foreign*

in France or indeed anywhere else in the late sixteenth century.[47] As we have seen, the warrior queen image became prevalent in the French royal correspondence long before the defeat of the Armada, but it was never a flattering portrait. Rather, while Catherine and especially Henry might have envied Elizabeth's capacity to avert civil war in her realm, they viewed her as a deceitful, unjust monarch who promoted piracy with impunity.

Indeed, Henry lost, at times, all confidence in Elizabeth as an ally and feared she would launch a direct attack against France, should the opportunity arise. With that prospect in mind, in March 1587 he wrote to one of his closest advisers, Anne de Batarnay, Duke of Joyeuse, and urged him

> to reinforce the fight against the maritime piracy by increasing the number of vessels that are engaged in surveillance of the English Channel [...] and ensure that we have more armaments in case the said queen of England should arm against me.[48]

The previous summer, the king had ordered Chasteauneuf to "let the said lady queen, my sister and cousin, know that because of the piracy at sea, I am arming vessels in Normandy and Brittany to counterattack English vessels' piracy."[49] Of course, any monarch had a right—and indeed a duty—to protect his subjects from attack at sea, but this letter gives a clear

---

*Policy, 1558–1603* (New York, 2000); Paul E. J. Hammer, "The Catholic Threat and the Military Response," in *The Elizabethan World*, eds. Susan Doran and Norman Jones (London: Routledge, 2000), 629–45; Nicola M. Sutherland, "The Origins of Queen Elizabeth's Relations with the Huguenots, 1558–1562," in *Princes, Politics and Religion, 1547–1589* (London: Bloomsbury, 1984), 73–96 and Paranque, "The representations and ambiguities of the warlike female kingship of Elizabeth I of England," 163–76.

[47] See the works of Roy Strong, *The Cult of Elizabeth* and Roy Strong, *Gloriana: The Portraits of Queen Elizabeth I* (London: Random House, 2003). Furthermore, in his book Louis Montrose analyses how the English participated in the creation of the cult of Elizabeth, Montrose, *The Subject of Elizabeth*, 89–93.

[48] Henry III of France to Duke of Joyeuse, March 31, 1587, BNF MS. Fr. 3394, fol. 2, "Il fault renforcer la luttre contre la pirattterie maritime en augmentant le nombre de navires charges de la surveillance de la Manche [...] et sasseurer un plus gran armement au cas ou ladite dame royne d'Angleterre sarmerait davantage contre moi." On Henry's relations to Duke of Joyeuse or his mignons, see Knecht, *Hero or Tyrant?*, 205–24.

[49] Henry III of France to Chasteauneuf, June 29, 1586, BNF MS. Fr. 3305, fol. 25r°, "vous ferez savoir a la dicte dame royne ma soeur et cousine que a cause des pillages en mer, je fais armer des vaisseaux en Normandie et Bretagne pour sopposer a la piraterie des vaisseaux anglois."

indication that Henry did not consider the English pirates as rogue, independent criminals; rather, by letting the queen know of his intentions, he signaled his belief that they were under her jurisdiction, if not quite her control. And once this image of a *pirate* queen had been established, it was almost inevitable that the image of a warlord queen who might threaten a neighboring country would follow.

Elizabeth herself must take some of the responsibility for the development of both of these representations within the French court. For instance, in January 1587, she issued the following robust response to Henry's plans to arm French vessels:

> I was not born in so lowly a place, nor have I been ruling such little realms that in right and honor I will yield to a living prince who insults me [...] I beg you to fortify our friendship rather than diminish it: living states do not allow too many enemies, and do not put bridles on startled horses for fear that they will shake your saddle.[50]

This letter, written in Elizabeth's own hand, surely did nothing to reassure Henry of the queen's goodwill and peaceful intent. The phrase "your saddle" was an obvious reference to the king's increasingly tenuous grip on the French throne, which might be shaken loose at any moment, especially if he made "too many enemies." The clear implication was that Elizabeth might become one of those enemies herself, especially if Henry continued to "insult" her. In light of this combative rhetoric, it is little wonder that the French king formed the impression that he was corresponding with a belligerent potential adversary, rather than an ally.

Moreover, Elizabeth had latterly provided ample evidence that she was prepared to back up her bellicose words with deeds. In July 1585, Henry informed Mauvissière that "the said queen of England wishes to start actions against the king of Spain in Flanders,"[51] and just six months later

[50] Elizabeth I of England to Henry III of France, January 1587, TNA SP 78/17 fol. 7, "je ne suis nay de si bas lieu, ni gouverne si petites royaumes que en droict et honneur je cederay a prince vivant qui minjure [...] je vous prie plustot a fortifier nostre amitie que la minuer: vis estats ne permettent trop d'enemis, et ne donnes la bride a chevaux effarouches, de peur qu'ils nesbranlent vostre selle."

[51] Henry III of France to Mauvissière, July 15, 1585, BNF Cinq Cents Colbert, n° 470, fol. 127, "jay compris par vos despeches que la royne d'Angleterre souhaisté renstrer en actions contre le roy d'Espagne en Flandres."

he told the ambassador's successor that "the queen of England, my good sister and cousin, has rescued the Netherlands to prevent them from a new conquest and tyranny from Spain."[52] The fact that Henry presented Elizabeth as the savior of the Dutch people as well as a warrior reveals that his perception of the English queen was not entirely negative at this time, regardless of his misgivings about her intentions and suspicions about her support for piracy.

Less than two weeks earlier, Henry had instructed Chasteauneuf to explain France's domestic situation to the English queen in the following terms: "religion is not the reason for this new war of religion [...] she must understand that it is a dispute between two houses, the Bourbons and the Guises."[53] However, if he hoped to secure her neutrality through this clarification, he failed. Elizabeth and Henry of Navarre, leader of the Huguenots, shared a mutual hatred of the Guises and formed an alliance against them.[54]

As early as May 1585, Catherine had warned her son that his royal authority was being undermined because the King of Navarre "is being helped by the queen of England."[55] Thereafter, Elizabeth's support for the Huguenot leader remained a prominent theme in Catherine's letters to her son. For instance, almost two years later, she received an intelligence report relating to an intercepted letter in which Elizabeth had allegedly promised further assistance to the Huguenots' cause, as per the terms of a treaty she had signed with Henry of Navarre. According to Catherine, this proved "the ill-will the said king [Henry of Navarre] and this queen [Elizabeth] have toward you [Henry III] and your realm."[56] Perhaps she

---

[52] Henry III of France to Chasteauneuf, February 27, 1586, BNF MS. Fr. 3305, fol. 19r°, "la royne d'Angleterre ma bonne seur et cousine a secourru les Pays-Bas pour leur evister une nouvelle conqueste et tyranny de la part de lEspagne."

[53] Henry III of France to Chasteauneuf, February 16, 1586, BNF MS. Fr. 3305, fol. 18v°, "la religion nest pas en cause dans ceste nouvelle guerre de religion, elle doist comprendre que cest un differend entre les maysons de Bourbon et de Guisez."

[54] Richardson has explored details of Elizabeth's support of the Huguenot leader after Henry III's death in 1589, in Richardson, "Your most assured sister": Elizabeth I and the Kings of France," 195–6.

[55] Catherine de Medici to Henry III of France, May 5, 1585, in LCM, Tome VIII, 275, "lors le roy de Naverre eties huguenots, ayent donné hordre à leur fayst, faset entrer des reystres, aystant aydé de la royne d'Angleterre."

[56] Catherine de Medici to Henry III of France, February 7, 1587, in LCM, Tome IX, 156, "Et à ce propos je vous diray que j'ay sceu certainement que ce Portuguais, qui a esté quelque

deemed Henry's response to this information rather too casual, because the following week she dispatched a follow-up letter: "I have always thought that she was providing clandestine help [...] but now that she has declared herself it is imperative that you reinforce the garrisons of your maritime cities."[57] The message was clear: Elizabeth was a Protestant troublemaker and an enemy of the French royal family.

Little had changed by the following January, when Catherine informed Chasteauneuf that Elizabeth was still "favoring and assisting, openly and with animosity, with money and goods, the king of Navarre and those of the new opinion [Protestants] of this realm, which prevents them from conforming and submitting to the king's will."[58] In light of this, she instructed the ambassador to try to "slow down and delay the aid and relief she is giving in support of those of the new opinion."[59] The following month, Catherine's representation of Elizabeth as the savior of the Huguenots was even more explicit: "the said queen of England will never abandon the king of Navarre and his cause [...] when he is distressed, she will aim to help him up and rescue him by all possible means."[60]

As we have seen, Henry III was not entirely averse to depicting Elizabeth as a savior of the Protestant cause himself, such as when he acknowledged that she had "rescued the Netherlands" from Spanish "tyr-

---

temps prisonnier en Angleterre [...] Touttesfois il fut pris par eulz, et a esté trouvé saisy de plusieurs papiers, lettres, instructions et mémoires des intelligences, menées et praticques, que a ledict roy d'Espagne en vostre roiaulme [...] au doz d'icelle, y avait escript de la royne d'Angleterre, une promesse et asseurance que par leur traicté ledict roy de Navarre y seroit compris et soustenu d'eulz, en continuant de faire ce qu'il faict, dont je vous ay bien voullu donner advis, affin que vous entendiez la mauvaise voulunté que ledict roy et icelle royne ont envers vous et vostre roiaulme."

[57] Catherine de Medici to Henry III of France, February 15, 1587, in *LCM*, Tome IX, 170, "J'avois tousjours bien pensé qu'elle aideroit soubz main, comme on voyoit bien qu'elle faisoit, vos subjectz de la nouvelle opinion, mais se declairant, comme elle fait, il est aussy très nécessaire que vous renforciez les garnisons de voz villes maritimes."

[58] Catherine de Medici to Chasteauneuf, January 5, 1588, in *LCM*, Tome IX, 323, "la royne d'Angleterre, favorisant et assistant si manifestement et animeusement d'apgent et de moyens le roy de Navarre et ceulz de la nouvelle oppinion de ce royaume, pour les empescher de se conformer et rànger à la voluntè du Roy."

[59] Catherine de Medici to Chasteauneuf, January 5, 1588, "vous rallentissiez et retardiez l'ayde et secours qu'elle faict en la cause desdicts de la nouvelle oppinion."

[60] Catherine de Medici to Chasteauneuf, February 2, 1588 in *LCM*, Tome IX, 326, "la royne d'Angleterre n'abandonnera aulcunement le roy de Navarre en ceste cause, mais que, lorsqu'il se verra le plus abbatu, elle tachera par tous moiens de le rellever et secourir."

anny." However, overall, Catherine's opinion of the English queen's behavior was much more definitive, as can be seen from her repeated use of forceful terms such as "favoring and assisting," "all possible means," and "openly and with animosity" in her correspondence. Henry's language was rather more ambiguous, although he did exhibit considerable annoyance over Elizabeth's ongoing support for the Huguenots, especially in his letters to Chasteauneuf. For example, in February 1586, he complained that "I am very offended by the aid that the queen of England, madam my good sister and cousin, is sending to my disobedient subjects."[61] Then, a few months later, he first instructed the ambassador to tell Elizabeth that "I cannot abide the aid that she sends to the king of Navarre and my rebellious subjects,"[62] before informing him that he expected the queen "to renounce the assistance she is giving to my reformed subjects."[63] Unfortunately, Henry did not offer Chasteauneuf any advice regarding how he might go about securing such a renouncement.

In all of these letters, it is evident that Henry was fully aware of Elizabeth's activities, but he never wholly subscribed to the Protestant protector queen portrait that his mother was painting at the time. Instead, he continued to view and represent his English counterpart as a deceitful, unnecessarily belligerent, and, above all, unjust ruler. Elizabeth's treatment of Mary Stuart merely cemented that image in his mind.

## The French Court's Reaction to Mary Stuart's Imprisonment and Execution

Mary Stuart's position became much more precarious on discovery of the Throckmorton Plot, which had attempted to elevate her to the throne of England in 1583. Catherine de Medici understood the possible consequences of that conspiracy's failure, and the following year she urged the French ambassador to do all he could to ensure that Mary was "favorably

---

[61] Henry III of France to Chasteauneuf, February 16, 1586, BNF MS. Fr. 3305, fol. 17v°, "je suys tres offense de layde que la royne d'Angleterre madame ma bonne seur et cousine a apportee a mes subjetz desobeissantz."

[62] Henry III of France to Chasteauneuf, April 7, 1586, BNF MS. Fr. 3305, fol. 26v°, "faites lui savoir que je ne peulx supporter layde quelle apporte au roy de Navarre et mes subjects rebelles."

[63] Henry III of France to Chasteauneuf, May 11, 1586, BNF MS. Fr. 3305, fol. 28v°, "quelle renonce a lassistance quelle donne a mes subjectz reformes."

treated, which I know is also the wish of the King, my son."[64] Unfortunately for Mary, though, in 1586 Walsingham's spies uncovered another plot, headed by Anthony Babington, and this time they found evidence of Mary's personal involvement in and support for the conspiracy.[65] She was accused of high treason against the queen, found guilty, and executed on February 8, 1587.[66]

While historians such as Alexander Wilkinson, Charles Labitte, John Guy, and Jenny Wormald have analyzed the impact of Mary Stuart's death on English public opinion, very little attention has been paid to the French royal family's reaction to what was a pivotal event in Anglo-French relations as well as British history.[67] Their correspondence on this subject is characterized by the emergence of even more negative representations of the English queen, who is portrayed first as a jailor and then as a cold-blooded murderer.

At the end of 1586, Henry and Catherine sent Pomponne de Bellièvre to the English court in an effort to "assist by all means the queen of Scotland."[68] Concern over Mary's fate was a strong theme in both Catherine's and Henry's letters to their adviser. The former told Bellièvre that saving the Scottish queen was "important for the service of the king [...] [as well as] the king's and the realm's honor."[69] Meanwhile, the Guise family and the Catholic League increased the pressure on Henry to rescue their niece by spreading rumors that he was happy to see Mary executed,

---

[64] Catherine de Medici to Mauvissière, December 1, 1584, in *Lettres de Catherine de Médicis*, publiées par M. Le Cte Baguenault de Puchesse, Tome VIII, 1582–85 (Paris: Imprimerie Nationale, 1901), 27, "elle puisse estre favorablement traictée, comme je sais que c'est aussy l'intention du Roy mon fils."

[65] Guy, "*My Heart is my Own*," 484–5 and Antonia Fraser, *Mary Queen of Scots* (London: Weidenfeld and Nicolson, 1994), 493.

[66] Guy, "*My Heart is my Own*," 498.

[67] See Wilkinson, *Mary Queen of Scots and French Public Opinion*, 111–21; Charles Labitte, *De la Démocratie chez les Prédicateurs de la Ligue* (first edition Paris Joubet 1841, Geneva: Slatkine Reprints, 1971), 108; Guy, "*My Heart is my Own*," 505–6 and Jenny Wolmald, *Mary, Queen of Scots* (London: George Philip, 1988), 13–14.

[68] Catherine de Medici to the Scottish Ambassador, December 20, 1586, in *Lettres de Catherine de Médicis*, publiées par M. Le Cte Baguenault de Puchesse, Tome IX, 1586–88 (Paris: Imprimerie Nationale, 1905), 125, "d'envoier le sieur de Bellievre en Angleterre, pour assister de tous ses moiens la royne d'Escosse."

[69] Catherine de Medici to Bellièvre, January 1587, in *LCM*, Tome IX, 135, "Angletere pour une si bonne aucasion et qui ayst ynportente pour le servyse du Roy, il ne la vous fault pas recomender, mes touchent à l'onneur du Roy et du royaume."

because he despised "the whole race from Lorraine."[70] In reality, of course, the king did as much as he could to save the Scottish queen. For instance, in a letter to Chasteauneuf at the start of November 1586, he expressed the hope

> that she [Elizabeth] will not refuse this request, which I desire you to reiterate on my behalf, and once again beg you to embrace the protection of my said sister-in-law as this is something that is close to my heart and concerns the preservation of my reputation.[71]

Catherine also understood the importance of preserving her son's reputation. In a letter to Bellièvre, she explained that Mary's execution would "touch the king's authority and diminish the greatness of the name of this realm."[72] In other words, both Henry and Catherine realized that France's fate was inextricably linked to Mary's. Unfortunately for the Valois family, though, their efforts to lobby on Mary's behalf were severely curtailed, because Elizabeth repeatedly postponed or canceled audiences with Chasteauneuf, the official French ambassador at the English court. On November 2, 1586, he complained to Lord Burghley, "I pray you therefore to lay this my request before her Majesty, since I cannot have audience before Tuesday, a thing which I infinitely desire, to fulfil my Master's order, who will esteem judgement given against the Queen of Scotland to greatly touch his reputation."[73]

Although maintenance of Henry's status at home and abroad was a recurring theme in the French diplomatic correspondence, this was mirrored by genuine, deep-seated anxiety over Mary's wellbeing in the vast majority of the royal family's letters. Catherine and Henry both referred

---

[70] Pierre de L'Estoile, *Première Partie du Tome Premier, Registre-Journal de Henry III 1574–1589*, eds. MM. Champollion-Figeac and Aimé Champollion fils (Paris: Edouard Proux et Compagnie, 1837), 208–9, "Sa Majesté arresta de dépescher M. De Bellièvre par devers la roine d'Angleterre pour empescher sil estoit possible l'exécution de l'arrest contre ladite roine d'Escosse, sa bonne et proche parente. Toutefois ceux de la Ligue eurent opinion que ledit voiage s'entreprenoit plus pour en haster l'exécution que pour l'empescher, à cause de la mauvaise volonté qu'ils disoient que le Roy portoit à toute la race des Lorrains." Also see, Cauvin, *Henry de Guise Le Balafré*, 265–70.

[71] Henry III of France to Chasteauneuf, November 1, 1586, TNA SP 78/16, fol. 136.

[72] Catherine de Medici to Bellièvre, January 1587, in *LCM*, Tome IX, 135, "toucher qu'i n'y [aille] de l'aultoryté du Roy et dymynutyon de la grendeur du nom de cet royaume."

[73] Chasteauneuf to Lord Burghley, November 2, 1586, TNA SP 78/16 fol. 140.

to her as "the poor queen of Scotland,"[74] and the king told Chasteauneuf that he was "glad to see that you are continuing, in accordance with my orders, to give all the assistance you can to the Queen of Scotland, my sister-in-law."[75] Two years earlier, in letters to Mauvissière, he had signaled his determination "to promote with all my power the affairs of the said lady and sister, the queen of Scotland [...] I find it very distressing to see her languishing for so long in the condition she is in,"[76] so "rescuing the poor queen Mary Stuart"[77] was imperative. However, all of the French royal family's efforts proved futile, and on February 14, 1587, before news of Mary's execution had reached Paris, Catherine lamented that it was a "great pity to see her so weakened."[78]

These representations of Mary Stuart as a "poor" victim who was "languishing" and "weakened" in prison and therefore needed "rescuing" had a direct and significant impact on how the French royal family perceived Elizabeth. Henry portrayed the English queen as Mary's all-powerful jailer, writing to Bellièvre and Chasteauneuf that "we have to safeguard Mary Stuart's life [...] although this is something that is entirely within her [Elizabeth's] hands and power, having taken her as a prisoner as she did."[79] To some extent, the French king hoped to act as mediator between the two cousins, and initially, at least, he felt that "affectionate petitions to her [Elizabeth] to display kindness and clemency in regard to the Queen, her near kinsman, ought to move her."[80] However, the following month,

---

[74] Catherine de Medici to Bellièvre, February 2, 1587, in *LCM*, Tome IX, 153, "le byen de la pouvre royne d'Ecosse;" Catherine de Medici to Henry III of France, February 7, 1587, in *LCM*, Tome IX, 155, "pauvre royne d'Escosse" and Catherine de Medici to Bellièvre, February 14, 1587, in *LCM*, Tome IX, 166, "myeux fayre pour ceste pouvre royne d'Ecosse."

[75] Henry III of France to Chasteaneuf, November 1, 1586, TNA SP 78/16 fol. 136.

[76] Henry III of France to Mauvissière, April 6, 1584, BNF MS. Fr. 15972, fol. 5v°, "je desire veirtablement favriser de tout mon pouvoir les affaire de ladite dame & seur la royne descosse et que je voys tres desplaisant de la veoir si longuement languir en l'estat auquel elle est."

[77] Henry III of France to Mauvissière, November 30, 1584, BNF MS. Fr. 3305, fol. 57r°, "délivrer la pouvre royne Marie Stuart."

[78] Catherine de Medici to Bellièvre, 14 February 1587, in *LCM*, Tome IX, 166, "J'enn é grent pytyé et regret de la voyr ynsill reduyte."

[79] Henry III of France to Bellièvre and Chasteauneuf, December 4, 1586, BNF MS. Fr. 15907, fol. 345v°, "il faut garantir la vie de Marie Stuart en choses que ladite royne d'Angleterre pourroit desirer, encores que ce soit chose qui soit entierement entre ses mains et sa puissance, la tenant prisonniere comme elle faict."

[80] Henry III of France to Chasteaneuf, November 1, 1586, TNA SP 78/16 fol. 136.

December 1586, he took a rather different tack and explained to Chasteauneuf and Bellièvre that "we need to guarantee the queen of England's life [in order] to save that of the queen of Scots" and this might be achieved by persuading "the queen of Scotland to renounce her rights to the English crown [...] [W]e have to advise her [Mary] of this."[81] In the first letter, Henry clearly still entertained the hope that simple appeals for mercy might be sufficient to secure Mary's release, whereas in the second he finally acknowledged—possibly decades too late—that the Scottish queen's claim to the English throne was a serious threat that Elizabeth could not ignore. Therefore, to Henry's mind, if Mary were to "renounce" that claim, harmony would be restored between the two cousins. Unfortunately, it is not known if Mary ever received the king's counsel or what her response was if she did.

While he positioned himself as a mediator, Henry did not wish to appear weak, so he also instructed Bellièvre and Chasteauneuf to inform Elizabeth that "if she continues to want to execute her [Mary], which is in her power, I will be very offended, as will other Christian kings and potentates."[82] Although couched in the polite, diplomatic language of the day, this amounted to a stark warning: Elizabeth was running the risk of shattering the Anglo-French alliance and turning Henry into an implacable enemy if she insisted on executing Mary.

Therefore, Henry adopted three distinct tactics in his efforts to secure Mary's release and finally resolve a diplomatic nightmare that had been rumbling on since the 1560s: simple appeals to Elizabeth's clemency; convince Mary to abandon her claim to the throne; and direct threats to the English queen. Although the French king acknowledged that Mary may have "in some sort participated in the [Babington] conspiracy," he still believed that she deserved to be pardoned because she had colluded with the plotters only to regain "her liberty and deliver herself from the captivity in which she had been held for many years."[83] In other words, Henry

---

[81] Henry III of France to Bellièvre and Chasteauneuf, December 24, 1586, BNF MS. Fr. 15908, fol. 345, "il fault garantir la vie de la royne d'Angleterre pour saulver celle de la royne d'Escosse. [...] je suys davis d'une proposition pourroit estre de faire renoncer a la royne d'Escosse ses droits sur la couronne d'Angleterre, il fault la lui conseiller."

[82] Henry III of France to Bellièvre and Chasteauneuf, December 24, 1586, "insistez que si elle continue de voulloir la faire executer, qui est son pouvoir, jen serois tres offensé ainsi que tous les aultres roys et potentas chrétiens."

[83] Henry III of France to Chasteauneuf, November 1, 1586, TNA SP 78/16 fol. 136.

excused Mary's involvement in English Catholics' efforts to dethrone Elizabeth by presenting her as a victim who had been unjustly imprisoned. Once again, he depicted the English queen as Mary's jailer and therefore ultimately responsible not only for the Queen of Scots' suffering but also for her participation in the plots against Elizabeth.

Understandably, Elizabeth had little time for Henry's version of events. In January 1587, one month before Mary's execution, she wrote a furious letter to the French king. First, she insisted that his instructions to Bellièvre and Chasteauneuf had "forced [her] to change [her] style and, instead of grace, to add complaints." Next, she criticized Henry's repeated interventions in the Mary affair, and asked, "how can you be so mad as to believe that it is honorable or friendly to lecture the one who is oppressed and to seek the death of an innocent by making [her] a murderer?" Finally, she issued a pointed reminder that she was still the French king's equal and had "almost lost my reputation among all the princes of my persuasion [Protestants]" by remaining loyal to him, despite facing "greater danger than any prince has ever endured."[84]

This letter demonstrates that Elizabeth was well aware of the French royal family's perception of her as the heartless jailer of an innocent victim, and that she was not afraid to defend herself, even to the point of calling the French king "mad." She also had the audacity to suggest that she—rather than Mary—was the innocent victim because Henry had unjustly accused her of being a murderer.[85] Moreover, his attitude was especially hurtful because she had risked losing her good reputation among her fellow Protestant rulers by remaining his staunch ally in the most trying circumstances.

---

[84] Elizabeth I of England to Henry III of France, January 1587, TNA SP 78/17 fol. 7, "Monsieur mon frère, le viel argument sur qui jay basty souvent mes lettres me semble si extrement esbranlé que suis constrainct de changer de stile, et au lieu de graces, adjouster plainctes. Comment estes vous forcené a croire que ce soit honneur ou bonne amitié a resprendre l'opprimé et rechercher la mort d'une innocent pour la faire proye d'une meutriere. Mon Dieu, postposant ma qualité, non moindre digne que la vostre, ne vous souvenant de mon affection la plus sincere en vostre endroict, ayant quasi perdu la reputation entre tous princes de ma profession, leur ayant tous, tous negligé pour ne pas contrarier le royaulme, aussy souffrant jusque present le plus grand danger que jamais prince endure."

[85] See the English propaganda that defended Elizabeth's decision not to pardon Mary in Sharpe, *Selling the Tudor Monarchy*, 448.

All of this illustrates the importance of personal representations in diplomatic correspondence and reveals that Elizabeth's own words had a significant impact on how Henry perceived his English counterpart. When Elizabeth learned that Henry was blaming her for the treasonous plots against her rule as well as Mary's plight, she counterattacked, tried to reaffirm her authority as the French king's equal, and attempted to reestablish her reputation as a just ruler by insisting on her innocence.[86] This marked the start of a new dynamic in the king and queen's diplomatic relationship. Elizabeth now felt obliged to justify her actions and decisions because she had lost the upper hand over the French royal family that she had enjoyed in the aftermath of the St. Bartholomew's Day Massacre and during the marriage negotiations.

This shift in the balance of power is also evident in Henry's letters to his ambassador at the English court. While he was prepared to accept that Elizabeth was his equal, he certainly did not view her as any more than that, as the following message to Chasteauneuf illustrates:

> there is no law in England that would render my sister-in-law guilty and subject to any jurisdiction, whether for this accusation or any other that might be brought forward against her, as she was born a sovereign princess, who, by the privilege common to all other Kings, is exempt from human jurisdiction and subject only to the judgment of God.[87]

Around the same time, Bellièvre also reminded the English queen that only God could judge another monarch.[88] Pierre de L'Estoile recorded Elizabeth's tetchy response: "One must understand the preciousness of my royal dignity and rank [...] [Mary is] my inferior, since she is in my realm, [and] I have shown her many tokens of friendship, which have not

---

[86] This theme of innocence was also used by Elizabeth in her speeches. See Estelle Paranque, "The representations and ambiguities of the warlike female kingship of Elizabeth I of England," in *Medieval and Early Modern Representations of Authority in Scotland and Great Britain*, eds. Katherine Buchanan, Lucinda Dean, and Michael Pennman (London: Routledge, 2016), 168 and 172.

[87] Henry III of France to Chasteauneuf, November 1, 1586, TNA SP 78/16 fol. 136, "il n'existe pas de loi en Angletrre qui forceroist ma belle soeur coupable et subjet de quelque juridiction, que ce soit pour ceste accusation ou quelle autre qui pourroit estre avance contre elle, estant une princesse souveraigne qui avec le prisvilege commun de chaque austres rois est exempte de juridiction humayne et subget seullement au jugement de Dieu."

[88] Extrait & Aphorisme de la harangue de Monsieur de Bellièvre à la Reine d'Angleterre, 1586, in *Mémoires de la Ligue*, Tome I, 411–5.

prevented her from [displaying] ill-will toward me."[89] By insisting on Mary's inferiority, on the grounds that she was no longer a queen in her own right, as well as her unjustified hostility, Elizabeth hoped to demonstrate her right to judge her cousin. Her words did not convince the French royal family, however, and Catherine told Bellièvre that "it is something that never happens that a queen has justice over another."[90] Nevertheless, she and Henry both recognized that the English queen enjoyed almost unprecedented power in her own realm, with a level of authority that was close to "the judgment of God." Hence, in their letters, there is an implicit acknowledgment of their powerlessness to influence the course of events. Despite all of their petitions and threats, they knew that Elizabeth herself had to grasp the potentially dire consequences of ordering the death of a fellow monarch (and, indeed, her closest kinswoman). Otherwise, Mary would surely die.

As we saw in the previous chapter, Henry instructed his ambassador Mauvissière to "keep an eye on" Elizabeth as early as 1579, but there were no such indications of suspicion in Catherine's correspondence until early 1587. Thereafter, however, Elizabeth's untrustworthiness became a dominant theme in the queen mother's letters to her closest advisers and her envoys in England. For instance, on February 7, 1587 (the day before Mary's execution), she instructed the French secretary of state, Pierre Brulard, "more than ever to have an eye on the said queen's actions,"[91] while the next day she warned Bellièvre that "we have to be cautious and have an eye on the said queen's actions."[92] Similarly, the following week, she drew Henry's attention to "the ill-will that I see in the queen of England."[93] According to Catherine, Elizabeth "openly declared herself as

---

[89] L'Estoile, *Première Partie du Tome Premier, Registre-Journal de Henry III 1574–1589*, 211, "On doit peser combien est précieuse la dignité royale et le rang que je tiens, estant mon inférieur, puisqu'elle est en mon roiaume, je luy ay démonstré beaucoup d'offices d'amitié; ce qui ne l'a divertie de sa mauvaise volonté en mon endroit."

[90] Catherine de Medici to Bellièvre, February 14, 1587, in *LCM*, Tome IX, 166, "C'est chause qui ne feust james que une royne aye justice sur une aultre."

[91] Catherine de Medici to Brulard, February 7, 1587, in *LCM*, Tome IX, 158, "Et fault avoir l'oeil aux deportemens de ladicte royne plus que jamais."

[92] Catherine de Medici to Bellièvre, February 8, 1587, in *LCM*, Tome IX, 160, "qu'il fault se prendre garde et avoir l'oeil aux deportemens de ladicte royne."

[93] Catherine de Medici to Henry III of France, February 15, 1587, in *LCM*, Tome IX, 170, "la mauvaise volonté que je vois en la royne d'Angleterre."

our enemy" by choosing to execute Mary.[94] Such comments not only reflected but escalated the tension between the two crowns. Perhaps surprisingly, Henry was rather more circumspect about expressing his distrust in his letters, although he did order his ambassador to "inform me of everything the queen tells you,"[95] and he treated Elizabeth's "displays of friendship" with caution: "let her know that in order to believe her, I will need to see results."[96]

This lack of trust was mutual, and Chasteauneuf was forced to operate in an atmosphere of considerable antipathy within the English court. In one letter to Henry, sent shortly after Mary's execution, he even reported that his belongings had been confiscated and complained that he had "asked for the truth [...] a thing that I was never able to obtain."[97] The ambassador's frustration over such treatment and Elizabeth's increasing unavailability was also evident in a message he sent to Lord Burghley in November 1586: "it having pleased her Majesty to postpone my audience to another day, I am forced, to my great regret, to make the present request to her in writing."[98] Two months earlier, he had informed Burghley that

On Sunday I complained to her Majesty of an Englishman named Turner who had insulted one of my men by saying publicly that this conspiracy [the Babington Plot] had been contrived in France, and that I had some with me who deserved to be killed, even in my lodging. I also complained that many others, English and French, had said loudly on the Exchange that the King my master was the author of this plot, a thing which I could not suffer. Her Majesty promised me to have justice done, and desired me to name to you the said Frenchman and also the said Turner.[99]

[94] Catherine de Medici to Bellièvre, February 14, 1587, in *LCM*, Tome IX, 166, "puysque n'a voleu gratyfier le Roy mon fils de sa requete, qu'ele set declere ouvertement nostre ennomye."
[95] Henry III of France to Chasteauneuf, March 31, 1586, BNF MS. Fr. 3305, fol. 23r°, "informez moi de toult ce que la royne pourra vous dire."
[96] Henry III of France to Chasteauneuf, March 31, 1586, 24v°, "concernant ses demonstrations d'amytié, faites lui savoir que pour la croire, il fauldroit que jen vois les effets."
[97] Chasteauneuf to Henry III of France, February 12, 1587, BNF MS. Fr. 3377, fols. 1r–v, "la royne d'Angleterre a fait arester dastraper qui est a moy [...] j'y ai demandé la verite [...] chose que je n'ay jamais pu obtenir."
[98] Chasteauneuf to Lord Burghley, November 2, 1586, TNA SP 78/16 fol. 140.
[99] Chasteauneuf to Lord Burghley, September 3, 1586, TNA SP 78/16 fol. 92.

The next day, Chasteauneuf raised the same issue with Walsingham, and the following month Robert Turner was duly arrested under a warrant signed by Elizabeth's spymaster.[100] Yet, this was a rare example of the English court acceding to one of the French ambassador's requests. Overall, Chasteauneuf was treated with suspicion and more than a little disdain, and he responded in kind.

In October 1586, the ambassador informed Brulard that "we have little hope for the salvation of this Princess who was condemned; she has been told her sentence."[101] His prediction was proved correct as Mary Stuart was executed on February 8, 1587. There was an outpouring of grief when news of her death reached the French court several days later, and

> on the 13th of the same month, in the great Church of Paris, a solemn memorial service was given in her honor [...] her death was infinitely regretted and denounced by Catholics, mostly Leaguers, who cried and said out loud that she died as a martyr for the Catholic faith.[102]

Some of the mourners went further and decried the execution in pamphlet form. Pierre de L'Estoile

> collected the ones that [...] were posted on the door of the Church of Notre-Dame of Paris on the day of the solemn memorial service [...] they are entitled: I. *De Jezabelis Angliae parricidiis ad pios Mariae Scoticae reginae Manes, Carmen*, II. *Regale monumentum*, III. *A la Jezebel Angloise*, IV. *Aux Anglois ses subjetcs*, V. *Vers funèbres faits par Du Perron qui ne ressentent en rien sa vieille profession hérétique*, VI. *Du Bartas, en sa 2e semaine et 2e jour, intitulé: Babilone parle de la roine d'Angleterre et de ses rares vertus et perfections. Un ligueur en a fait une antithèse respondant vers pour vers aux susdits de Du Bartas.*[103]

---

[100] Chasteauneuf to Walsingham, September 4, 1586, SP 78/16 fol. 96 and Robert Turner to Sec. Davison, October 8, 1586, SP 12/194 fol. 46.

[101] Chasteauneuf to Brulard, October 15, 1586, BNF Cinq Cents de Colbert, n°337, fol. 850, "nous voyons peu desperence au salut de ceste Princesse laquelle estant condamnee, on luy a prononcé sa sentence."

[102] L'Estoile, *Première Partie du Tome Premier, Registre-Journal de Henry III 1574–1589*, 217–8, "A la nouvelle de ceste mort, on fist en la cour de France grande démonstration de deuil [...] Et le 13 du dit mois, en la grande église de Paris, lui fust fait un solennel service [...] Sa mort fut infiniment regrettée et plainte par les catholiques, principalement par les Ligueurs, qui crioient et disoient tout haut, qu'elle estoit morte martyre pour la foi catholique." Carroll also examines how Mary's death had an impact on the French, see Carroll, *Martyrs and Murderers*, 265.

[103] L'Estoile, 218, "j'ai recueilli ceux qui suivent, desquels le premier fust affiché aux portes de l'église de Nostre-Dame de Paris, le jour de la solemnité du service; et ils sont ainsi tiltrés...".

All of these pamphleteers blamed Elizabeth for Mary's death and por-trayed the English queen as "Jezebel."[104]

The French royal family never resorted to comparing Elizabeth to the wife of Ahab, King of Israel, who persuaded her husband to become a tyrant, even though they must have been aware of the analogy's preva-lence among their subjects.[105] Instead, their correspondence was charac-terized by an air of impending defeat and despondency, which was an accurate reflection of their predicament following Mary's death. Henry well understood that her execution had dealt a hammer blow to his care-fully cultivated image as a warrior Catholic king. In April 1587, he told Nicolas de Neufville, Sr de Villeroy, his principal adviser, that he would soon have to say "farewell to everything that might remain as a sign of royalty."[106] Indeed, he alluded to Mary's death and his sadness about it in only one letter, which he sent to the Scottish ambassador, Sr de Courcelles, the day after the memorial service.[107] The king's mind was already else-where as he attempted to quell a new uprising in the south of France.[108] Furthermore, the Guises were in the process of extracting maximum polit-ical capital out of their niece's death by stressing that Henry had been too weak to prevent her execution. They even accused him of collaborating with Elizabeth.[109] In the face of all these troubles, Henry had neither the time nor the inclination to express his grief over Mary's death.

---

[104] For further information on how the news was received in France, see Anne Dillon, *The Construction of Martyrdom in the English Catholic Community, 1535–1603* (London: Routledge, 2003), 163–9 and 273–5; Stuart Carroll, "The Revolt of Paris, 1588: Aristocratic Insurgency and the Mobilization of Popular Support," *French Historical Studies*, 23 (2000): 301–37; Richard Williams, "'Libels and Paintings': Elizabethan Catholics and the International Campaign of Visual Propaganda," in *John Foxe and his World*, eds. Christopher Highley and John N. King (London: Routledge, 2002) and Mark Greengrass, "Mary, Dowager Queen of France," in *Mary Stewart: Queen in Three Kingdoms*, ed. Michael Lynch (Oxford: Wiley Blackwell 1988), 186–8.

[105] Elizabeth Knowles, "Jezebel," in *The Oxford Dictionary of Phrases and Fable* (2006, *encyclopedia.com*).

[106] Henry III of France to Nicolas de Neufville, Sr de Villeroy, April 1587, BNF MS. Fr. 3398, fol. 17, "adiey tout se qu'il me pouroyt rester de marque de royauté."

[107] Henry III of France to Sr de Courcelles, March 14, 1587, BL Cottonian Library, Caligula D.I., fol. 220.

[108] See, for example: Henry III of France to the Duke of Epernon, February 26, 1587, BNF MS. Fr. 24168, fol. 145v°; Henry III of France to the Duke of Epernon, February 28, 1587, BNF MS. Fr. 24168 fol. 146v°.

[109] Keith Cameron, "La polémique, la mort de Marie Stuart et l'assassinat de Henry III," in *Henry III et son temps*, ed. Robert Sauzet (Paris: Librairie Philosophique J. Vrin, 1992), 188.

By contrast, in a letter to Bellièvre, Catherine wrote, "among so many issues I have been plunged into during this miserable time, the cruelty that has been used against the queen of Scotland, madam my daughter-in-law, has made me so upset."[110] Similarly, she informed Villeroy of the "extreme discontent that I have due to the cruel death of this poor queen [...] and those who are of the same religion as the queen of England should still feel repulsed by such inhumanity."[111] This marked a significant change in Catherine's representations of Elizabeth in her correspondence, with a new emphasis on the English queen's "cruelty" and "inhumanity."

The two ambassadors—Chasteauneuf at the English court and Stafford at the French court—endeavored to minimize the impact of Mary's execution on Anglo-French relations. In a report of one of his audiences with Henry, Stafford told Elizabeth:

> Then of the Queen of Scots and her death, which I was glad he fell into, because I know there hath been great cunning used to keep that still in his mind against your Majesty (as he himself confessed and that particularly) for I think I left him satisfaction of it better than he hath had, and especially for your quiet ignorance thereof, and mere unwillingness to it, which at the first he smiled at, as not believing it, asking if it were possible.[112]

Stafford's references to "satisfaction" and Henry's reaction—"the first he smiled at"—indicate that he was doing his best to preserve Anglo-French amity in difficult circumstances. Meanwhile, from the other side of the Channel, Chasteauneuf tried to reassure Henry that Elizabeth was deeply upset over Mary's death, confiding that "she took me by the hand and took me to one of the corners of her room [...] and told me the greatest grief that she had ever suffered was the death of her germayne cousin."[113] This information seemed to confirm the rumor that Elizabeth had been

---

[110] Catherine de Medici to Bellièvre, March 8, 1587, in *LCM*, Tome IX, 191, "parmy tant d'ennuiz où je suis plongée en ce miserable temps, la cruaullé dont l'on a usé envers la royne d'Escoase, madame ma belle-fille, m'a acreu tellement l'afliction."

[111] Catherine de Medici to Villeroy, March 14, 1587, in *LCM*, Tome IX, 194, "l'extreme desplesir que j'ay de la cruele mort de cete pauvre royne [...] ceux mesmes qui sont de la religion de la royne d'Angleterre, encor doyvent-ils avoyr horreur d'une tele inhumanité."

[112] Stafford to Elizabeth I of England, February 25, 1588, TNA SP 78/18 fol. 52.

[113] Chasteausneuf to Henry III of France, May 13, 1587, BNF MS. Fr. 3377, fol. 17v°, "elle me prit par la main et me retira en ung coing de sa chambre [...] et me dit le plus grand malheur venu que jamais elle eust souffert estoit la mort de sa cousine germaine."

reluctant to sign the death warrant.[114] In a later letter to Catherine, the French ambassador reported that "the said Queen ordered that the funeral of the deceased queen of Scotland should take place on the first day of the next month that is the first with all the required ceremonials for a Queen."[115] By highlighting Elizabeth's grief and desire to commemorate Mary as a legitimate monarch, Chasteauneuf counterbalanced, to some extent at least, Catherine's characterization of the English queen as "cruel." Incidentally, scholars who have analyzed Elizabeth's declarations of sadness over her cousin's death have found no reason to believe they were anything other than genuine.

The final few years of petitions and discussions regarding Mary Stuart's fate had a significant impact on Anglo-French relations. Although Henry was rather more concerned about his own reputation than Mary's wellbeing, he did send several senior advisers to England to plead her case. Meanwhile, on a personal level, he acknowledged her guilt but appealed for her life and begged Elizabeth for mercy.

Some interesting representations developed as a result of this prolonged diplomatic campaign. From Elizabeth's assertion that she was Henry's equal and the very public demonstration of her autocratic power to Catherine's characterization of the execution, and therefore Elizabeth, as cruel and inhuman, the Anglo-French relationship seemed to shift and deteriorate, which generated further negative images of the English queen. Yet, given Henry's own struggles with the Catholic League, he could not afford to alienate his English counterpart—and one of his few remaining allies—completely. Consequently, he bit his tongue over Mary's execution and tried to persuade Elizabeth either to turn her back on Henry of Navarre or at least play the role of a mediator between himself and the leader of the Huguenots.

[114] See Levin, *The Reign of. Elizabeth I*, 99 and Alison Plowden, *Two Queens in One Isle* (Stroud: Sutton Publishing Limited, 1984), 211–2.

[115] Chasteauneuf to Catherine de Medici, July 28, 1587, BNF MS. Fr. 3377, fol. 41°, "la dite dame Royne a ordonné les obseque de la defunte royne descosse estre faicte au premier jour du mois prochain qui nous est le unzieme avec toutes les ceremonies requises a une Royne."

## Renewed Optimism About Preserving the Anglo-French Alliance

Tensions between the Huguenots and the Catholic League continued to intensify in the years 1585 to 1587. Open warfare erupted in several French provinces, and Henry's royal authority was challenged on all sides.[116] Meanwhile, although Catherine and the king suspected that Elizabeth was supporting the Huguenots, they remained hopeful that she would eventually rally to their cause and convince the King of Navarre to surrender. This complicated, perilous situation generated a number of surprising representations of the English queen in the French royal correspondence, not least Henry's attempt to cast Elizabeth as a personal adviser and potential mediator between himself and the King of Navarre.

By 1587, the French king was finding it increasingly difficult to maintain any royal authority over his subjects. That February, Catherine suggested that her son should do everything in his power to persuade Elizabeth to "advise and beg the king of Navarre and those of the new opinion [Protestants] to respect their duties toward you and make peace."[117] Three months later, she again urged him to lobby the English queen so "that she and her subjects do not give any assistance to the king of Navarre and those of the new opinion, but advises them to respect their duties toward you."[118]

Given the incessant Catholic plots in England and the ever-present fear of a Spanish invasion, Henry himself had long been surprised "that the queen does not advise obedience to the king of Navarre and those who follow him, because if peace were restored in France, it would be easier to oppose the might of Spain, which she fears greatly."[119] A week later, he

---

[116] Knecht, *Hero or Tyrant?*, 240.

[117] Catherine de Medici to Henry III of France, February 7, 1587, in *LCM*, Tome IX, 155–6, "proffiter envers ladicte royne d'Angleterre pour l'induire à inciter, conseiller et prier le roy de Navarre et ceulz de la nouvelle oppinion à se ranger à leur devoir envers vous, et faire la paiz."

[118] Catherine de Medici to Henry III of France, May 23, 1587, in *LCM*, Tome IX, 213, "en leur disant aussi que vous desirez bien qu'elle et ses subjectz ne donnent aulcune assistance au roy de Navarre et ceulx de la nouvelle oppinion, mais qu'elle les conseille de se ranger à leur debvoir envers vous."

[119] Henry III of France to Chasteauneuf, March 23, 1586, BNF MS. Fr. 3305, fol. 21r°, "Je suys etonnee que la royne ne conseille pas la soumission au roi de Navarre et a ceulx qui

admitted that he needed "the queen of England to convince the king of Navarre to agree to peace."[120]

While it was reasonable enough for Henry to hope that Elizabeth might persuade the leader of the Huguenots to call a ceasefire—after all, both sides had suffered terribly in the civil war—another of his aspirations was far more ambitious: he suggested that the (Protestant) English queen should try to convince the (Protestant) Henry of Navarre to convert to Catholicism in order to solve France's succession crisis. Elizabeth's ambassador at the French court, Edward Stafford, issued the following—admirably restrained—response on behalf of his monarch:

> Whereupon, I replied to him the impossibility that it was for the Queen's Majesty to deal with the King of Navarre in religion, for the reasons that I had both told him the other day [...] That her Majesty, I durst answer, would do what she could any way, but to persuade the King of Navarre any more to change than she had persuaded him to take it, that it was a thing she would not meddle in.[121]

Clearly, then, the English queen was not prepared to intervene in a matter of personal faith, particularly when that faith was Protestantism. Furthermore, Elizabeth was much more likely to do everything in her power to retain one of her few Protestant allies, rather than urge him to convert to Catholicism simply to assist a neighboring king. Her angry reaction when Henry of Navarre did convert to Catholicism in 1593 seems to confirm this conclusion.[122] Stafford's report continued:

> I answered him [...] that for persuading the King of Navarre to obey the King ever in all he could, you [Elizabeth] had never given other counsel; but particularly to persuade him to change his religion you neither would nor could do it.[123]

---

le suilvent car si la paix revenoit en France, il seroit plus facile d'opposer la grandeur de lespagne dont elle monstre avoir grande crainte."

[120] Henry III of France to Chasteauneuf, March 31, 1586, BNF MS. Fr. 3305, fol. 22v°, "Il fault que la royne d'Angleterre convainc le roy de Navarre de se resoudre a la paix."

[121] Stafford to Elizabeth I of England, February 25, 1588, TNA SP 78/18 fol. 52.

[122] Richardson, "'Your most assured sister': Elizabeth I and the Kings of France," 191.

[123] Stafford to Elizabeth I of England, April 5, 1588, TNA SP 78/18 fol. 119.

The use of the phrase "neither would nor could" at the end of this report reveals Elizabeth's uncompromised authority: even if she had been able to fulfill Henry's, she was not willing to do so.

Interestingly, notwithstanding his doubts about her trustworthiness, Henry's representation of Elizabeth as an experienced counsellor and mediator was a prominent feature of his letters at this time. For instance, in March 1586, he told Chasteauneuf that "she therefore advises me to let them live in the exercise of their religion."[124] Then, a month later, he assured the ambassador:

> I have very well understood all the words that you have reported from the said queen of England. She denies any aid given to the king of Navarre but has replied to you that if she did help him, it was more in my interest than his. She therefore advises me to pacify my realm and to grant the exercise of the reformed religion.[125]

In this context, Elizabeth was portrayed as a sage adviser—someone who knew what was best for Henry's realm and the restoration of peace. However, given her problems with religious dissent in her own realm, her advice to Henry was somewhat sanctimonious. The French king confessed to Chasteauneuf: "I no longer want to suffer from the exercise of two religions as I have experienced the hardships of such granted freedom. There is no prince, and particularly that queen, who does not wish to suppress another's religion."[126] More vividly, the following month, he declared, "to live at peace, it is necessary to have the exercise of only one religion [...] as in the example of the said lady queen, who does not want

---

[124] Henry III of France to Chasteauneuf, March 23, 1586, BNF MS. Fr. 3305, fol. 21r°, "Elle me conseille doncques de les laysser vivre en l'exercice de leur religion."

[125] Henry III of France to Chasteauneuf, April 26, 1586, BNF MS. Fr. 3305, fol. 23v°, "jay bien compris les propoz que vous m'avez reporté de la dicte royne d'Angleterre. Elle nie toute ayde au roy de Navarre mais vous as repondu que si elle laydait cetoit plus dans mon interest que le sien. Elle me conseille doncques de pacifier mon royaulme et daccorder lexercice de la religion reformee."

[126] Henry III of France to Chasteauneuf, March 31, 1586, BNF MS. Fr. 3305, fol. 22r°, "je ne veulx plus souffrir de l'exercice de deux religions pour avoir en experimente les afflictions de cette liberte donnee. Il ny a aulcun prince et particulierement ceste royne, qu ne veuille supprimer aultre religion que la sienne."

to suffer in her realm the exercise of a religion other than hers."[127] Therefore, although Henry continued to seek Elizabeth's counsel, he struggled to follow her advice, not least because she seemed to have little or no intention of following it herself.

Of course, it was the English queen herself who was most active in promoting her wise counsellor image. For instance, when the French king refused to send Thomas Morgan back to England, she explained, "My God, what necromancer has blinded your eyes, that you cannot see your own danger?"[128] For Elizabeth, the Catholic League represented a serious threat to both rulers, as its members did not recognize Henry's authority any more than hers. Five months later, in August 1585, she assured the French king that she had offered "my very genuine prayers to God, who will inspire you to open your eyes and see clearly your detractors, among whom, I will be in the last place. Your abused good sister."[129] By 1588, according to Stafford, Henry was finally willing to concede that "his enemies were hers."[130] That February, before the Catholic League besieged Paris and forced the French king to flee to Chartres, he met with the English ambassador. Stafford reported that Henry

desired you [Elizabeth] to put your helping hand to it; that though his Council, and especially Queen Mother dissuaded him to desire at your hands, as a thing unhonorable to him to desire that you should meddle between him and his subjects, yet he did secretly by me desire and beseech you, and that he should think himself beholding to you for it and most of all for doing it upon his request, and keeping secret that he hath requested you.[131]

---

[127] Henry III of France to Chasteauneuf, April 26, 1586, BNF MS. Fr. 3305, fol. 24r°, "Pour vivre dans un repos il faut lexercice dune seule religion dont me sert d'exemple ladicte dame Royne qui ne veult souffrir en son royaulme exercice daultre religion que la sienne."

[128] Elizabeth I of England to Henry III of France, March 10, 1585, TNA SP 78/13 fol. 55.

[129] Elizabeth I of England to Henry III of France, August 4, 1585, TNA SP 78/14 fol. 64, "Avec mes très cordialles prieres au seigneur Dieu qui vous inspire tout le meilleur et vous ouvrir les yeux à pouvoir voir clairement vos abuseurs, entre lesquels je ne me mettray en dernier rang. Votre abusée bonne sœur."

[130] Stafford to Elizabeth I of England, February 25, 1588, TNA SP 78/18 fol. 52.

[131] Stafford to Elizabeth I of England, February 25, 1588.

This report marked a significant shift in Elizabeth and Henry's diplomatic relations, one year after the execution of Mary Stuart. Clearly, the French king was now in urgent need of Elizabeth's help. They were still allies, despite their previous differences and his annoyance over her continuing aid to the Huguenots, and he pleaded for her advice and support at a moment when his royal authority was under serious threat.

Two months later, the English ambassador reported another audience with Henry:

> I could show him the letter first written in your Majesty's own hand [...] When he had heard me (for I read as though I had read word by word as it was in the letter), the first word he said when I had made an end, he began with a fair oath, *Vertu Dieu, voyla une femme c'est la*, and added withal that he desired of God that he had broken one of his fingers that the King and they all together were as wise as your Majesty. He desired me that I would let him take an extract in short of the argument as they were set down in order with the reasons to them, for he protested that he never saw more sufficient nor weighty argument in his life.[132]

The allusion to Elizabeth's womanhood—"*Vertu Dieu, voyla une femme c'est la*" (Holy God, what a woman she is)—was meant as a compliment: Henry acknowledged that the queen was wiser than any of the men who listened to her advice, despite her gender. Indeed, on the assumption that Stafford's report was accurate, the French king admired Elizabeth's political skill as well as the sagacity of her counsel.

Therefore, despite the numerous negative images of Elizabeth that prevailed in the French diplomatic correspondence of the 1580s—enemy, pirate queen, belligerent warrior, Protestant savior—Henry's desire for peace forced him not only to work with his English counterpart but also to represent—and, crucially, perceive—her as a close adviser. Even in the darkest years of their diplomatic relationship, Elizabeth remained an essential ally of the French king.

As Rayne Allinson has rightly noted, the correspondence between Catherine and Elizabeth became more sporadic in the latter half of the 1580s.[133] This was hardly surprising, given that Catherine's perception of the English queen became increasingly negative from 1584 onwards. As

[132] Stafford to Elizabeth I of England, April 5, 1588, TNA SP 78/18 fol. 119.
[133] Allinson, *A Monarchy in Letters*, 108.

we have seen, in earlier years, she did more than anyone else to promote an image of Elizabeth as a member of the French royal family, but she adopted rather different language after the final collapse of the marriage negotiations at the start of the decade. There were no more allusions to an intimate mother–daughter relationship. Instead, Catherine increasingly referred to Elizabeth simply by her title ("queen of England") or used the traditional diplomatic term of address ("my good sister and cousin").

Nevertheless, their personal correspondence continued to contain a trace of the old affection, for a time at least. For instance, Elizabeth wrote to Catherine to express her sincere condolences after Francis's death in 1584. It seems that the duke's mother was genuinely touched, as she replied:

> I beg you to believe that nothing has moved me more than the friendship I have for you and the desire I have, not that it needs to be stated, for every-one to know how much the King my son loves and esteems you.[134]

Interestingly, here and elsewhere, Catherine had a tendency to express her son's affection for Elizabeth, rather than her own. Two weeks later, she instructed Mauvissière to convey the message that "the King the said lord and son and myself very much esteem this lady's friendship, with true and perfect resolution to pursue it, as on her part she is well disposed to it."[135] Catherine's use of the word "lady" is significant here, as this was a much cooler term of address than "my daughter" or even "sister."

Over the next few months, she first acknowledged "the affection and good friendship she continues always to display toward the King my son and myself [...] [Please assure] her that she will always find the same in us"[136] and then reiterated that it was essential "to maintain the said lady

---

[134] Catherine de Medici to Elizabeth I of England, July 25, 1584, in *LCM*, Tome VIII, 199, "pour vous supplier croire que rien ne m'a esmeue a ce faire que l'amitié que je vous porte et l'envie que j'ay que, non pas vous que je sçais en estre aseurée, mais tout le monde cognoisse combien le Roy mon filz vous aime et estime."

[135] Catherine de Medici to Mauvissière, August 4, 1584, in *LCM*, Tome VIII, 202, "luy avoir bien faict congnoistre que le Roy mondict Sr et filz et moy estimons beaucoup l'amytié d'icelle dame, avec vraie et parfaicte résolution d'y persévérer, y estant de sa part si bien disposée."

[136] Catherine de Medici to Mauvissière, October 12, 1584, in *LCM*, Tome VIII, 223, "l'affection et bonne démonstration d'amytié qu'elle continue tousjours à l'endroit du Roy mon filz et de moy, qui l'asseure que en nous elle trouvera tousjours le semblable."

queen in our good friendship and affection, [and] assure her that she will always find the same in the King my son and myself."[137] As these messages to Mauvissière clearly indicate, Catherine remained keen to express her amity toward Elizabeth, for she knew that doing so would help to reinforce the Anglo-French alliance, but it seems highly doubtful that she still felt the powerful personal affection that was so prevalent in her letters of previous years.

Meanwhile, as we have seen, Henry's relationship with Elizabeth was extremely complex and continued to evolve in rather unexpected ways. Between 1584 and 1588, he often employed the polite but formal "good sister and cousin"[138] when discussing Elizabeth with his ambassadors, as in his instruction to Mauvissière "to reinforce the friendship I have for the queen of England my good sister and cousin."[139] Specifically, he tended to use this term when his focus was on the Anglo-French alliance, such as when he ordered Mauvissière to "maintain the peace and alliance with the queen of England my good sister and cousin,"[140] and when he informed Chasteauneuf that "the queen of England my good sister and cousin indeed desires peace in my realm [...] judging that this peace could be useful to her."[141] On one occasion, he even signed a letter to Elizabeth "your good brother and cousin."[142] Therefore, while the relationship between Elizabeth and Charles IX was built on strong familial terms of affection—such as a "germayne sister" and "second mother"—which undeniably helped the English queen to assert her dominance over her French counterpart, her relationship with Charles's successor was always

---

[137] Catherine de Medici to Mauvissière, December 1, 1584, in *LCM*, Tome VIII, 227, "mainctenir ladicte dame royne en nostre bonne amitié et affection, l'asseurant qu'elle trouvera tousjours au Roy mon fils et en moy le semblable."

[138] Henry III of France to Elizabeth I of England, June 11, 1584, BNF MS. Fr. 3308, fol. 84v°, "nostre bonne seur et cousine."

[139] Henry III of France to Mauvissière, July 20, 1584, BNF MS. Fr. 3305, fol. 54v°, "renouvelesz lamytié que jay pour la royne d'Angleterre ma bonne seur et cousine."

[140] Henry III of France to Mauvissière, July 2, 1585, BNF Cinq Cents Colbert n° 470, fol. 133, "maintenir la paix et l'alliance avec la royne d'Angleterre ma bonne seur et cousine."

[141] Henry III of France to Chasteauneuf, March 31, 1586, BNF MS. Fr. 3305, fol. 21v°, "je pense que la royne d'Angleterre ma bonne seur et cousine desire en effet la paix dans mon royaume [...] jugeant que cette paix lui seroit utile."

[142] Henry III of France to Elizabeth I of England, February 14, 1587, TNA SP 78/17 fol. 49, "vostre bon frere et cousin."

more formal and therefore more distant, possibly because Henry was not a young man when he acceded to the throne of France.

However, this is not to say that there is no evidence of friendship between the two monarchs. For instance, in May 1585, Henry assured Mauvissière "I am her perfect friend" and instructed the ambassador to tell Elizabeth "that, on my part, I only desire a perfect friendship and relationship between our two realms."[143] The French king went even further later that year when declaring that "she has no better friend than me in the whole of Christendom,"[144] while in November 1586 he insisted that he was "her best and most perfect friend."[145] These demonstrations of amity were a means of counterbalancing the negative images of Elizabeth in Henry's—and his ambassadors'—correspondence, and they reveal that he appreciated the importance of buttressing what had become a very shaky alliance.

Elizabeth reciprocated this rhetoric of friendship in her letters to Henry, and for precisely the same reason. Most notably, in January 1585, she wrote:

> If the Kings our predecessors, have, in all times, been accustomed to choose those amongst our own order, who by their heroic virtues and private affections towards them have obliged them to testify to them a like correspondence of good friendship and mutual intelligence: We must confess that hardly any one of them had greater cause than we have to fulfil the obligation demanded by so many proofs and testimonies as we have received of your sincere and perfect friendship and affection toward us.

Therefore, in Elizabeth's opinion, maintaining good diplomatic relations and preserving a strong alliance between the two courts was an "obligation" that both rulers should respect and safeguard. She continued:

> And therefore we have dispatched our well-beloved cousin, the Earl of Derby, knight and companion of our Order, to present to you the Garter and other ornaments thereto appertaining, and have also given express charge to our ordinary ambassador resident with you to join with him

---

[143] Henry III of France to Mauvissière, May 30 1585, BNF Cinq Cents Colbert n° 470, fol. 119, "je suys son parfaicte amy […] je veulx quelle sache que de mon coste je ne desire quune parfaicte amytie et intelligence entre nos deulx royaulmes."

[144] Henry III of France to Mauvissière, July 2, 1585, BNF Cinq Cents Colbert, n° 470, fol. 133, "elle n'as pas de meylleur amy dans toute la chretienneté que moy."

[145] Henry III of France to Chasteauneuf, November 1, 1586, TNA SP 78/16 fol. 136.

therein, so that together they may accomplish it on our behalf with all due completeness; praying you very affectionately to accept in good part this proof of the honor and sincere affection which we bear to you.[146]

Elizabeth undoubtedly stressed her "affection" for Henry in the hope of reinforcing their friendship at a moment when both rulers were facing significant challenges within their respective realms.

Henry repeatedly expressed similar sentiments not only in his letters to Elizabeth herself but also in his dispatches to his ambassadors at her court. For instance, in October 1584, he ordered Mauvissière "to assure the queen of England of my friendship as well as my mother the queen's."[147] Later, in the summer of 1585, he first instructed the ambassador "to assure the queen of England of my good intentions toward her and of the perfect friendship that I desire to maintain with her,"[148] then insisted that "my profound desire is to preserve our friendship and alliance."[149]

Interestingly, then, between 1584 and 1588, even as suspicion and defiance continued to grow between the two courts, both monarchs attempted to preserve their "perfect friendship" in order to safeguard an alliance that was constantly challenged and at times very fragile. Moreover, in the process of continually restating his commitment to their friendship, Henry ultimately defended Elizabeth herself and her honor. For instance, in a letter of June 4, 1584, he asserted that he was "against all forms of contestation, against her or against myself,"[150] and the following May he instructed Mauvissière to "tell the earl of Leicester that I have forbidden this defamatory libel against my good sister and cousin [as] proof of my

[146] Elizabeth I of England to Henry III of France, January 1585, TNA SP 78/13 fol. 21. The Most Noble Order of the Garter is the third most prestigious and the highest order of chilvary in England. To some extent, this was therefore a token of Elizabeth's appreciation and respect for Henry.

[147] Henry III to Mauvissière, 11 October 1584, BNF MS. Fr. 3305, fol. 55v°, "asseurez la royne d'Angleterre de mon amytie et celle de la royne ma mere".

[148] Henry III of France to Mauvissière, May 16, 1585, BNF Collection Moreau 721, fol. 145, "asseurez la royne d'Anglerrre de mes bonnes intentions à son encontre et de la parfaicte amytié que je desire maintenir avecques elle."

[149] Henry III of France to Mauvissière, July 15, 1585, BNF Cinq Cents Colbert, n° 470, fol. 137, "mon desir profond est de conserver nostre amytié et alliance."

[150] Henry III of France to Mauvissière, June 4, 1584, BNF MS. Fr. 3305, fol. 51r°, "je suys constre touste formes de contestation, envers elle ou envers moi."

sincerity toward her."[151] All of these demonstrations of goodwill and sincerity were designed to reinforce the Anglo-French alliance. Indeed, in another letter to Mauvissière, Henry insisted that he would not allow his "name to be mingled in things that would thwart my friendship and the good peace that exists between the said queen of England and myself."[152] Two years later, in February 1586, the king again clarified his position, this time to Mauvissière's successor, Chasteauneuf:

> I have never been involved in any of the enterprises that have been made against her and her state [...] [Indeed, I have gone beyond] my treaty obligations, because I could have overlooked the plots against her, but I stopped them and meted out justice on the captains and soldiers who had gathered against her.[153]

Here, again, the king was at pains to emphasize that he had always done his best to protect Elizabeth. Two days earlier, he had expressed similar sentiments to the queen herself when raising the delicate matter of the arrest of Leonard des Trappes, Chasteauneuf's secretary, in Dover:

> regarding Trappes, who is our subject [...] I promise you that if he is found guilty of the accusations against him, we will impose such a punishment that everyone will know how much we abhor such action [...] For our part, we desire to maintain our common and fraternal friendship.[154]

---

[151] Henry III of France to Mauvissière, May 16, 1585, BNF Collection Moreau, fol. 145, "faites savoir au conte de Leicester que jay faict interdir ce libelle diffamatoire constre ma bonne seur et cousine, preuve de ma sincerite envers elle." Unfortunately we do not have clear information on the libel the king is referring to.

[152] Henry III of France to Mauvissière, April 6 1584, BNF MS. Fr. 15972, fol. 5v°, "je n'entendz que mon nom soit meslé en chose qui contrarienne a lamitié & bonne paix qui est entre ladite royne d'Angleterre & moi."

[153] Henry III of France to Chasteauneuf, February 16, 1586, BNF MS. Fr. 3305, fol. 17v°, "je nay jamais preste la main a des entreprinses faicte contre elle et son estat et mesme plus que les traites my obliegeaient car j'aurois pu fermer les yeux sur les actions prinses contre elle mais faisant courre sus et procedder par justice allencontre des capitaines et soldats que l'on assembloit et levoit contre elle."

[154] Henry III of France to Elizabeth I of England, February 14, 1587, SP 78/17 fol. 49, "que pour le regard de Trapes, qui est nostre subject, a la suicte de nostre dict ambassadeur, et nostre justiciable, que vous le faictes remectre entre ses mains, vous promectant que s'il se trouve coulpable de l'accusation que luy est mise sus, nous en ferons faire telle pugnition que chacun cognoistra combien nous abhorrons ung tel faict, et nous affectionnons ce que peult concerner la conservacion de vostre vye, qui ne nous sera jamais moings chère que celle de la nostre propre. Desirans pour nostre part mainctenir nostre commune et fraternelle amitye."

Therefore, even in the midst of a potentially damaging diplomatic incident, Henry's concern for the alliance remained paramount, which was why he concluded the letter by highlighting his "fraternal friendship" with his English counterpart.

Of course, it is easy to argue that Henry's declarations of affection were totally insincere, nothing more than disingenuous flattery to maintain peace with a powerful potential enemy at a time when his country was already in the midst of yet another civil war and seemingly on the brink of an international conflict with Spain. Yet, it should be noted that he did not merely instruct his diplomats to convey his thoughts to the English queen, as was standard practice between heads of state at the time. Rather, he wrote a private letter to Elizabeth, in his own hand, which suggests that their alliance—and their friendship—meant a great deal to him.

It is important to remember that, by the mid-1580s, Henry and Elizabeth had been communicating directly with each other as rulers of their respective nations for almost a decade, and this level of familiarity allowed both of them to speak their minds without too much fear of inflicting permanent damage on the relationship. This was particularly true of Elizabeth, but Henry could be forthright with the English queen, too. For example, in March 1585, as we have seen, she left Henry in no doubt about her displeasure at his refusal to send the traitor Thomas Morgan back to England. However, she then concluded her letter as follows:

> My good brother, you will excuse this roundness, which is only from my love to your renown throughout all lands, which I hold so dear that I desire to have no just cause to abate the affection I have vowed to you; coming not from deceitful lips (from which may God guard you) that under cloak of piety have little care for your greatness. I sent this gentleman to show my heart to you, and pray you to give him credit and listen favorably to what he has to say to you on my behalf. Pardon me if these last dealings have made me forget to thank you for the honors you have shown to my ambassadors.[155]

The phrases "from my love to your renown," "the affection I have vowed to you," and "to show my heart to you" are all strong signals of the amity Elizabeth still felt for her French counterpart. Similarly, two years later, after lambasting Henry for his repeated interventions in the Mary Stuart

---

[155] Elizabeth I of England to Henry III of France, March 10, 1585, TNA SP 78/13 fol. 55.

case, she concluded, "I am telling you this with sincere love, your very affectionate good sister and cousin."[156] In other words, she bore him no ill-will, even though she thought he had been "mad" to criticize her.

When the Catholic League besieged Paris in early 1588, Elizabeth sent a messenger, Thomas Bodley, to the French court to deliver a message. Bodley was an eminent scholar and a fervent Protestant, but more importantly a highly skilled diplomat whom the queen trusted implicitly.[157] In the letter that he carried, Elizabeth insisted that

> you cannot truly believe that I am on any other side but yours [...] I beg you, do me the honor of reading this letter yourself, without any secretary, and give a favorable audience to this messenger as secretly as it pleases you.[158]

These caring, loving words, as well as Elizabeth's plea that Henry should read the letter in private, suggest that the two rulers' friendship was fundamentally sincere, even amid the mutual suspicion and occasional animosity. Moreover, Elizabeth was just as keen as Henry to maintain the alliance, as she also feared Spain and knew that the Catholic League despised her. In his report on his audience with the king, Bodley informed Elizabeth that Henry "found more kindness in his good sister the Queen of England than in all the Princes, his friends and allies besides, in that it pleased her to send so carefully and circumspectly to him in his troublesome state."[159]

By maintaining this amicable personal correspondence with the French king and resolutely characterizing herself as his most loyal friend and ally, even when the tension between the two courts was at its height in early 1587, Elizabeth undoubtedly had a significant impact on Henry's perception of the English queen as well as his representations of her in his own

---

[156] Elizabeth I of England to Henry III of France, January 1587, TNA SP 78/17 fol. 7, "Je le vous dis en sincere amour, vostre bien affectionne bonne seur et cousine."

[157] Thomas Bodley, *Oxford Dictionary of National Biography*, W. H. Clennell, accessed on 31 August 2016.

[158] Elizabeth I of England to Henry III of France, May 11, 1588, TNA SP 78/18 fol. 178, "Vous me pouvez hardiment croire que je ne suis d'aultre partie que la vostre. Et mesme, je vous supplie, faites moy cest honneur de lire ceste-cy vous memes, sans secretaire et donner favorable audience a ce porteur aussy secretement que bon vous semblera."

[159] Mr Bodley to Elizabeth I of England, substance of the French king's answer, May 1588, TNA SP 78/18 fol. 122.

letters. Moreover, the English ambassador at the French court, Edward Stafford, felt that the king's professed attitude toward his English counterpart and England itself was entirely sincere:

> I am not wise enough to advise your Majesty what to resolve upon it, but I think he hath dealt truly in most things, and according as he meaneth I would with your Majesty to do what you could well do to content him; for I am of that opinion that there will hardly be ever in France a King of a disposition fitter for England, for surely he hath a desire, if he can live in peace, to attempt nothing against England or any else.[160]

Henry's depiction of himself as England's premier ally once again indicated that he knew the importance of maintaining a strong alliance and a benevolent relationship with Elizabeth. Furthermore, Stafford's letter revealed that the French king was extremely receptive to Elizabeth's advice and had no desire to join her enemies.

The correspondence between these two monarchs reveals that reputations and representations cannot be separated from diplomatic relations. Furthermore, it shows that, despite their clashes over Mary's imprisonment and execution, piracy, and other issues, the English queen was repeatedly portrayed—and portrayed herself—as Henry's close friend. The French king's eagerness to pursue stronger ties with Elizabeth reinforced the image of the English queen as a staunch ally of the French royal family even at a time of considerable tension.

## CONCLUSION

The period 1584 to 1588 was fraught with danger for the monarchies of France and England. The growing power of Spain, the Catholic plots in England, and the eighth religious civil war in France, not to mention the death of Mary Stuart, forced Henry and Elizabeth to reevaluate their alliance, their diplomatic exchanges, and their personal relationship. Interestingly, this process contributed to increasing divergence between the king's and his mother's perceptions and representations of Elizabeth. As a result, the cohesion that the French royal family had maintained for decades in their dealings with England started to dissolve at the very end

---

[160] Stafford to Elizabeth I of England, February, 25 1588, TNA SP 78/18 fol. 52.

of the Valois dynasty. This was exemplified in Catherine's and Henry's contrasting responses to Mary Stuart's death, for which the queen mother never forgave Elizabeth whereas her son adopted a much more neutral stance.

On the other hand, at various times, both Catherine and Henry portrayed Elizabeth as a potential enemy, a pirate queen, a bellicose warrior, and a Protestant savior, although neither stooped to the level of the French pamphleteers by depicting her as Jezebel. While English commentators started to paint Gloriana, Virgin Queen, and even goddess portraits of their monarch—or, as Frances Yates called her, "the imperial virgin"[161]—the French royal family's representations of their counterpart came in far more shades of grey, which added nuance to her overall, enduring, historic image.[162] As we have seen, all of these contrasting perceptions and representations were inextricably intertwined with—and had a significant impact on—Anglo-French diplomatic relations throughout the 1580s.

The French royal correspondence is an invaluable source in any attempt to evaluate Elizabeth's reputation outside of the borders of her own realm. Furthermore, analysis of the queen's own correspondence with Henry has revealed that she herself might have been an important factor in his reluctance to follow his mother's lead and turn against Elizabeth in the final years of his life. Their personal relationship was an accurate reflection of the ebbs and flows of the Anglo-French alliance itself in this period, and just as unpredictable. For instance, given their disputes over so many issues, few people would have thought that Henry would ever represent Elizabeth as one of his most trusted counsellors, yet he did so repeatedly in their private correspondence.

Studying the images of Elizabeth through the eyes of the French royal family results in a deeper understanding of their diplomatic relations. It also reveals that the hagiography of Elizabeth in English poems, plays, and pamphlets never crossed the Channel and so never influenced the French rulers' perceptions of the English queen. Rather, the French royal family developed and fashioned their own perceptions and representations of the final Tudor queen, adding layer upon layer of complexity to her reputation.

---

[161] Frances A. Yates, *Astrea* (London: Taylor & Francis, 1999), 79.
[162] See Sharpe, *Selling the Tudor Monarchy*, 378–85.

Catherine de Medici died in January 1589 and her son Henry was assassinated seven months later. By contrast, Elizabeth continued to rule England until 1603, and continued to engage with countless foreign dynasties and their ambassadors. However, her interactions and diplomatic correspondence with the Valois were unique in terms of their depth, longevity, and complexity. More importantly, despite their differences, mutual suspicion, and occasional outbursts of fury, they managed to maintain the peace between their two nations for more than three decades—a feat that most of their predecessors, and many of their successors, failed to achieve.

# BIBLIOGRAPHY

## PRIMARY SOURCES

### MANUSCRIPTS

Bibliothèque Impériale, Fonds de Saint Germain, n° 223.
BNF, Cinq Cent Colbert, n° 470.
BNF, Cinq Cent Colbert, n° 337.
BNF, Collection Clairambault.
BNF, Collection Moreau, n° 720.
BNF, Collection Moreau, n° 721.
BNF, MS. Fr. 3305.
BNF, MS. Fr. 3307.
BNF, MS. Fr. 3308.
BNF, MS. Fr. 3309.
BNF, MS. Fr. 3330.
BNF, MS. Fr. 3377.
BNF, MS. Fr. 3394.
BNF, MS. Fr. 3398.
BNF, MS. Fr. 10752.
BNF, MS. Fr. 15907.
BNF, MS. Fr. 15908.
BNF, MS. Fr. 15971.
BNF, MS. Fr. 15973.
BNF, MS. Fr. 24168.
BNF, Nouvelles Acquisitions, Fr. 6003.

© The Author(s) 2019                                                               215
E. Paranque, *Elizabeth I of England through Valois Eyes*, Queenship
and Power, https://doi.org/10.1007/978-3-030-01529-9

BNF, V° Colbert, n° 337.
BNF, V° Colbert, n° 471.
BL, Add. MS. n° 19398.
BL, Cottonian Library, Caligula D.I., fol. 220.
BL, Cottonian Library, Caligula, C.1, Plut XX D, fol. 74.
BL, Cottonian Library, Caligula E, vol. VI, fol. 60.
BL, Cottonian Library, EVI, 106.
SP 12/130.
SP 70/113.
SP 78/4.
SP 78/5.
SP 78/12.
SP 78/13.
SP 78/15.
SP 78/16.
SP 78/17.
SP 78/18.

## Printed Sources

### Main Printed Sources

*Ambassades de Messieurs de Noailles en Angleterre*, rédigées par feu M. L'Abbé de Vertot. Tome 1. Leyden: Dessaint & Saillant Libraires, 1763.

*Correspondence diplomatique de Bertrand de Salignac de la Mothe Fénélon, ambassadeur de France en Angleterre, de 1568 à 1575.* Tome Premier, Années 1568 et 1569. Archives du Royaume: Paris et Londres, 1838.

*Correspondence diplomatique de Bertrand de Salignac de la Mothe Fénélon, ambassadeur de France en Angleterre, de 1568 à 1575.* Tome II, Année 1569. Archives du Royaume: Paris et Londres, 1838.

*Correspondence diplomatique de Bertrand de Salignac de la Mothe Fénélon, ambassadeur de France en Angleterre, de 1568 à 1575.* Tome III, Années 1570 et 1571. Archives du Royaume: Paris et Londres, 1840.

*Correspondence diplomatique de Bertrand de Salignac de la Mothe Fénélon, ambassadeur de France en Angleterre, de 1568 à 1575.* Tome Cinquième, Années 1572 et 1573. Archives du Royaume: Paris et Londres, 1840.

*Correspondence diplomatique de Bertrand de Salignac de la Mothe Fénélon, ambassadeur de France en Angleterre, de 1568 à 1575.* Tome Sixième, Années 1574 et 1575. Archives du Royaume: Paris et Londres, 1840.

*Correspondence diplomatique de Bertrand de Salignac de la Mothe Fénélon, ambassadeur de France en Angleterre, de 1568 à 1575.* Tome Septième, Supplément. Archives du Royaume: Paris et Londres, 1840.

*Lettres de Catherine de Médicis* publiées par M. Le Cte Hector de la Ferrière. Tome III, 1567–70. Paris: Imprimerie Nationale, 1887.

*Lettres de Catherine de Médicis* publiées par M. Le Cte Hector de la Ferrière. Tome IV, 1570–75. Paris: Imprimerie Nationale, 1889.

*Lettres de Catherine de Médicis* publiées par M. Le Cte Baguenault de Puchesse. Tome VII, 1579–81. Paris: Imprimerie Nationale, 1899.

*Lettres de Catherine de Médicis,* publiées par M. Le Cte Baguenault de Puchesse. Tome VIII, 1582–85. Paris: Imprimerie Nationale, 1901.

*Lettres de Catherine de Médicis,* publiées par M. Le Cte Baguenault de Puchesse. Tome IX, 1586–88. Paris: Imprimerie Nationale, 1905.

*Mémoires de Messire Michel de Castelnau, Seigneur de Mauvissière et de Concressaut, Baron de Jonville,* par M. Petitot. Paris: Foucault Librairie, 1823.

Potter, David, ed. *A Knight of Malta at the Court of Elizabeth I: The Correspondence of Michel de Seure, French Ambassador, 1560–1561.* Cambridge: Cambridge University Press, Camden Series, 2014.

OTHER PRINTED SOURCES

*Annales Ecclésiastiques du Diocèse de Toulouse,* par un prêtre du diocese. Toulouse: Imprimerie de Bellegarrigue, 1825.

Aylmer, John. *An Harborowe for faithful and trewe subjects.* N4v. London, 1559.

de Belleforest, Francis. *LInnocence de la trèsillustre, très-chaste, et débonnaire Princesse Madame Marie Royne d'Escosse. Où sont amplement refutes les calmonies faulces, & impositions iniques, publiées par un livre secrettement divulgué en France, l'an 1572.* Reims, Jean de Foigny, 1572 & Lyon: Jean de Tournes, 1572.

*Calendar of the Letters and State Papers to English Affairs Preserved in, originally Belonging to, the Archives of Simancas,* edited by Martin Hume, Vol. 1. London: HMSO, 1892.

Camden, William. *Annales: The True and Royal History of the Famous Empress Elizabeth.* London: B. Fisher, 1625.

———. *The History of the Most Renowned and Victorious Princess Elizabeth, Late Queen of England,* (first published in 1625), edited and with an introduction by Wallace T. MacCaffrey. Chicago and London: The University of Chicago Press, 1970.

*Christian Prayers and Meditations in English, French, Italian, Spanish, Greeke, and Latine.* STC 6428. London: John Day, 1569.

*Continuation des choses plus celebres et memorables advenues en Angleterre, Ecosse et Irlande.* BNF, Résac. 8 NC 155. Michel Jove, Lyon, 1570.

De L'Estoile, Pierre. *Première Partie du Tome Premier, Registre-Journal de Henry III 1574–1589,* edited by MM. Champollion-Figeac and Aimé Champollion fils. Paris: Edouard Proux et Compagnie, 1837.

Déclaration des causes qui ont mu monseigneur le cardinal de bourbon et les pairs, princes, seigneurs, villes et communautés catholiques de ce royaume de France, de s'opposer à ceux qui par tous moyens s'efforcent de subvertir la religion catholique et l'Etat, 31 Mars 1585. *Mémoires de la Ligue*, Tome I. Amsterdam: Arkstee & Merkus, 1758.

Digges, Dudley. *The Compleat Ambassador: Or Two Treaties of the intended marriage of Qu. Elizabeth of Glorious Memory: Comprised in Letters of Negotiation of Sir Francis Walsingham, her Resident in France Together with the Answers of the Lord Burleigh, the Earl of Leicester, Sir Tho: smith, and others Wherein, as in a dear Mirror, may be seen the Faces of the two Courts of England and France, as they then stood; with many remarkable passed of State, not at all mentioned in any History.* London: Thomas Newcomb, 1655.

*Discours des troubles nouvellement advenuz au royaume d'Angleterre.* BNF, Resac. 8 NC 154 A. Chez Nicolas Chesneau, Paris, 4 October 1570.

Edit de Nemours, 7 July 1585. Eugène et Emile Haag, eds. *La France Protestante*, Vol. 10. Paris: 1858.

*Elizabeth I: Collected Works.* Leah Marcus, Janel Mueller and Mary Beth Rose, eds. Chicago and London: University of Chicago Press, 2000.

Extrait & Aphorisme de la harangue de Monsieur de Belièvre à la Reine d'Angleterre, 1586. *Mémoires de la Ligue*, Tome I. Amsterdam, 1758.

*Histoire des Chancelliers et des Gardes des Sceaux de France dinstingués par les règnes de nos Monarques depuis Clovis Premer Roy Chrétien jusques à Louis Le Grand XIVe du nom, heureusement régnant,* by Francis du Chesne. Paris: Chez l'auteur avec privilège du roy, 1680.

*Hymne sur la naissance de Madame de France, fille du roy très-chrétien Charles IX,* dédié à Jacques Fouyn, prieur et seigneur d'Argenteuil, signé J. S. P. Lyon: Benoist Rigaud, 1572 et Paris: Mathurin Martin, 1572.

Knox, John. *The first blast of the trumpet against the monstruous regiment of women.* STC 15070. Geneva: J. Poullain and A. Rebul, 1558.

*Le Réveille-Matin des Francis et de leurs voisins,* composé par Eusebe Philadelphe Cosmopolite, en forme de Dialogues. Edinburgh: Jacques James, 1574.

*Lettre de Pierre Charpentier addressée à Francis Portes, Candiois, par laquelle il monstre que les persécutions des Églises de France sont advenues non par la faulte de ceux qui faisoient profession de la religion, mais de ceux qui nourrissoient les factions et conspirations qu'on appelle la Cause.* 1572.

Queen of Scots to the Queen of Spain, Elisabeth, wife of Philip, 24 September 1568, in *Letters of Mary, Queen of Scots, and documents connected with her personal history.* Agnes Strickland ed., Volume 1. London: Henry Colburn Publisher, 1842.

Stubbs, John. *The discoverie of a galping gulf whereinto England is like to be swallowed by another French marriage, if the Lord forbid not the banes, by letting her maiestie see the sin and punishment thereof.* London: H. Singleton for W. Page.

SECONDARY SOURCES

Adams, Simon. *Leicester and The Court: Essays on Elizabethan Politics.* Manchester: Manchester University Press, 2002.

Alford, Stephen. *The Early Elizabethan Polity: William Cecil and the British Succession Crisis, 1558–1569.* Cambridge: Cambridge University Press, 1998.

Allinson, Rayne. *A Monarchy in Letters: Royal Correspondence and English Diplomacy in the Reign of Elizabeth I.* New York: Palgrave Macmillan, 2012.

———. "Conversations on kingship: the letters of Queen Elizabeth I and King James VI," in eds. Liz Oakley-Brown and Louise J. Wilkinson. *Rituals and Rhetoric of Queenship: Medieval to Early Modern.* Portland: Four Court Press, 2009.

Angenot, Marc. "Les traités de l'éloquence du corps." *Semiotica* Vol. 8 (1) (1973).

Axton, Marie. *The Queen's two bodies: Drama and the Elizabethan Succession.* London: Royal Historical Society, 1977.

Barnavi, Elie, and Decimon, Robert. *La Sainte Ligue, le Juge et la Potence.* Paris: Hachette, 1985.

Barnavi, Elie. *Le Parti de Dieu: Etude sociale et politique des chefs de la Ligue parisienne, 1585–1594.* Louvain: Nauwelaerts, 1980.

Barraclough Pullman, Michael. *The Elizabethan privy council in the fifteen-seventies.* Berkeley and Los Angeles: CA, 1971.

Barrett-Graves, Debra. "'Highly touched in honour': Elizabeth I and the Alençon Controversy," in Carole Levin, Jo Eldridge Carney and Debra Barrett-Graves eds. *Elizabeth I: Always her own free woman.* Aldershot: Ashgate, 2003.

Beem, Charles, ed. *The Foreign Relations of Elizabeth I.* New York: Palgrave Macmillan, 2011.

Bell, Ilona. *Elizabeth I: The Voice of a Monarch.* New York: Palgrave Macmillan, 2010.

———. "'Soueraigne Lord of lordly Lady of this land': Elizabeth, Stubbs, and the Gaping Gvlf," in Julia M. Walker ed. *Dissing Elizabeth: Negative Representations of Gloriana.* Durham and London: Duke University Press, 1998.

Benedict, Philip. "Un roi, une loi, deux foix: Parameters for the History of Catholic-Reformed Co-existence in France, 1555–1685," in Ole Peter Grell and Bob Scribner eds. *Tolerance and Intolerance in the European Reformation.* Cambridge: Cambridge University Press, 1996.

Bernard, G. W. *Power and Politics in Tudor England.* Aldershot: Asghate, 2000.

Blessing, Carol. "Elizabeth I as Deborah the Judge: exceptional women of power," in Annaliese Connolly and Lisa Hopkins eds. *Goddesses and Queens: the Iconography of Elizabeth I.* Manchester and New York: Manchester University Press, 2007.

Bossy, John. *Giordano Bruno and the Embassy Affair.* New Haven and London: Yale Nota Bene and Yale University Press, 2002, first published 1991.

———. *Under The Molehill: An Elizabethan Spy Story.* New Haven and London: Yale University Press, 2001.

Boucher, Jacqueline. "Autour de Francis, duc d'Alençon et d'Anjou, un parti d'opposition à Charles IX et Henry III." *Henry III et son temps: actes du Colloque international du Centre de la Renaissance de Tours, octobre 1989.* Paris: Librairie philosophique J. Vrin, 1992.

———. *La cour de Henry III.* Rennes: Ouest France, 1986.

———. *Société et mentalités autour de Henry III.* Lille: Honoré Champion, 2007.

Bourgeon, Jean-Louis. *Charles IX devant la Saint Barthélémy.* Geneva: Droz, 1995.

Braddick, Michael J. *State Formation in Early Modern England, c. 1550–1700.* Cambridge: Cambridge University Press, 2000.

Brigg, Robin. *Early Modern France 1560–1715.* Oxford, London, New York: Oxford University Press, 1977.

Cameron, Keith. "La polémique, la mort de Marie Stuart et l'assassinat de Henry III," in Robert Sauzet ed. *Henry III et son temps.* Paris: Librairie Philosophique J. Vrin, 1992.

Campbell, Kenneth L. *Window's Into Men's Soul: Religious nonconformity in Tudor and Early Stuart England.* Plymouth: Lexington Books, 2012.

Carroll, Stuart. *Martyrs & Murderers: The Guise Family and the Making of Europe.* Oxford: Oxford University Press, 2009.

———. "The Revolt of Paris, 1588: Aristocratic Insurgency and the Mobilization of Popular Support." *French Historical Studies,* 23 (2000).

Cauvin, Charles. *Henry de Guise, Le Balafré: Histoire de France de 1563 à 1589.* Tours: Alfred Mame et Fils, 1881.

Chang, Leah L., and Kong, Katherine. *Catherine de Médicis and Others, Portraits of the Queen Mother: Polemics, Panegyrics, Letters.* Toronto: Centre for Reformation and Renaissance Studies, 2014.

Coatalen, Guillaume. "'Ma plume vous pourra exprimer', Elizabeth's French Correspondence," in Alessandra Petrina and Laura Tosi eds. *Representations of Elizabeth I in Early Modern Culture,* 83–104. New York: Palgrave Macmillan, 2011.

Coatalen, Guillaume, and Gibson, Jonathan. "Six Holographs Letters in French from Queen Elizabeth I to the Duke of Anjou: Texts and Analysis," in Carlo M. Bajetta, Guillaume Coatalen and Jonathan Gibson eds. *Elizabeth I's Foreign Correspondence: Letters, Rhetoric, and Politics,* 27–62. New York: Palgrave Macmillan, 2014.

Coch, Christine. "'Mother of my Contreye': Elizabeth I and Tudor Constructions of Motherhood." *English Literary Renaissance,* 26. 3 (1996): 423–450.

Cocula, Anne Marie. *Brantôme, Amour et gloire au temps des Valois.* Paris: Michel, 1986.

Collinson, Patrick. *Elizabethan Essays.* London: The Hambledon Press, 1994.

Cooper, John. *The Queen's Agent: Francis Walsingham at the Court of Elizabeth I.* London: Faber & Faber, 2011.

Cosandey, Fanny. *La Reine de France. Symbole et Pouvoir, XVe et XVIIIe siècle.* Paris: Gallimard, 2000.

Crawford, Katherine. "Catherine de Medicis and the Performance of Political Motherhood." *The Sixteenth Century Journal*, Vol. 31, No. 3 (Autumn, 2000): 643–673.

———. "Love, Sodomy, and Scandal: Controlling the Sexual Reputation of Henry III." *Journal of the History of Sexuality*, vol. 12 (2003): 513–542.

Crouzet, Denis. *Dieu en ses royaumes.* Seyssel: Camp Vallon, 2008.

———. *Les Guerriers de Dieu: la Violence au Temps des Troubles de Religion, 1525–1610,* Tome 2. Seyssel: Champ Vallon, 1990.

Daussy, Hugues. *Les Huguenots et le roi: le combat politique de Philippe Duplessy-Mornay, 1572–1600.* Genève: Droz, 2002.

Daybell, James. *The Material Letter in Early Modern England: Manuscript Letters and the Culture and Practices of Letter-Writing, 1512–1635.* New York: Palgrave Macmillan, 2012.

Delumeau, Jean, ed. *Une Histoire du Monde aux Temps Modernes.* Lavis: Bibliothèque Historique Larousse, 2013.

Diefendorf, Barbara B. *Beneath the Cross: Catholics and Huguenots in Sixteenth Century Paris,.* Oxford and New York: Oxford University Press, 1991.

———. "The Religious Wars in France," in R. Po-Chia Hsia ed. *A Companion to the Reformation World,* 150–167. Malden: Blackwell Publishing, 2004.

Dillon, Anne. *The Construction of Martyrdom in the English Catholic Community, 1535–1603.* London: Routledge, 2003.

Doran, Susan. "An Old Testament King," in Alice Hunt and Anna Whitelock eds. *Tudor Queenship, the reigns of Mary and Elizabeth.* New York: Palgrave Macmillan, 2010.

———. *Elizabeth I and religion, 1558–1603.* London and New York: Routledge, 1994.

———. "Elizabeth I and Catherine de Medici," in Glenn Richardson ed. *The contending kingdoms: France and England 1420–1700.* Aldershot: Ashgate, 2008.

———. *Monarchy and Matrimony, the Courtships of Elizabeth I.* London New York: Routledge, 1996.

———. "Why Did Elizabeth Not Marry?" in Julia M. Walker ed. *Dissing Elizabeth: Negative Representations of Gloriana,* 30–59. Durham and London: Duke University Press, 1998.

Doran, Susan, and Richardson, Glenn, eds. *Tudor England and Its Neighbours.* New York: Palgrave Macmillan, 2005.

Duprat, Annie. *Les rois de papier, la caricature de Henry III à Louis XVI.* Paris: Belin, 2002.

Elton, G. R. *The Parliament of England, 1159–1581.* Cambridge: Cambridge University Press, 1986.

Erickson, Carolly. *The First Elizabeth.* New York: Macmillan, 1983.

Evenden, Elizabeth. "The Michael Wood Mystery: William Cecil and the Lincolnshire Printing of John Day." *Sixteenth Century Journal* 35 (2004): 383–394.

Evenden, Elizabeth, and Freeman, Thomas S. "Print, Profit and Propaganda: the Elizabethan Privy Council and the 1570 Edition of Foxe's 'Book of Martyrs'." *English Historical Review*, 119 (2004): 1288–1307.

Ferraro Parmelee, Lisa. *Good Newes from France: French Anti-League Propaganda in Late Elizabethan England*. New York: University of Rochester Press, 1996.

Ffolliott, Sheila. "Catherine de' Medici as Artemisia: Figuring the Powerful Widow," in Margaret W Ferguson, Maureen Vickers, and Nancy J. Vickers, eds. *Rewriting the Renaissance: The Discourses of Sexual Difference in Early Modern Europe*, 227–241. Chicago: University of Chicago Press, 1986.

Fraser, Antonia. *Mary Queen of Scots*. London: Weidenfeld and Nicolson, 1994.

Frye, Susan. *Elizabeth I: The Competition for Representation*. Oxford: Oxford: University Press, 1996.

Gellard, Matthieu. "Séduire par ambassadeur interposé. La négociation du mariage entre Élisabeth d'Angleterre et Henry d'Anjou en 1570–1571," in Pierre-Yves Beaurepaire ed. *La Communication en Europe de l'âge classique au siècle des Lumières*. Paris: Belin, 2014.

————. *Une Reine Epistolaire: Lettres et pouvoir au temps de Catherine de Médicis*. Paris: Classsiques Garnier, 2014.

Gibson, Jonathan. "'Dedans la plié de mon fidelle affection': Familiarity and Materiality in Elizabeth's Letters to Anjou," in Carlo M. Bajetta, Guillaume Coatalen and Jonathan Gibson, eds. *Elizabeth I's Foreign Correspondence: Letters, Rhetoric, and Politics*, 63–89. New York: Palgrave Macmillan, 2014.

Graves, Michael. *Burgley, William Cecil Lord Burghley*. London, 1998.

Green, Janet M. "'I My Self': Queen Elizabeth's Oration at Tilbury Camp." *The Sixteenth Century Journal*, 28/2 (Summer, 1997): 421–445.

Greengrass, Mark. "Mary, Dowager Queen of France," in Michael Lynch, ed. *Mary Stewart: Queen in Three Kingdoms*. Oxford: Wiley Blackwell, 1988.

Guy, John. *"My Heart is my Own": The Life of Mary Queen of Scots*. London: Fourth Estate, 2004.

————. *Politics, Law and Counsel in Tudor and Early Stuart England*. Aldershot: Ashgate, 2000.

————, ed. *The Reign of Elizabeth I: Court and Culture in the Last Decade*. Cambridge: Cambridge University Press, 2003.

————. "The Rhetoric of Counsel in early modern England," in Dale Hoak ed. *Tudor political culture*, 292–310. Cambridge: Cambridge University Press, 1995.

Haan, Bertrand. *L'Amitié entre princes. Une alliance franco-espagnole au temps des guerres de Religion (1560–1570)*. Paris: PUF, 2011.

Hackett, Helen. "The rhetoric of (in)fertility, Shifting responses to Elizabeth I's childlessness," in Jennifer Richards and Alison Thorne eds. *Rhetoric, Women and Politics in Early Modern England*, 149–171. London and New York: Routledge, 2007.

———. *Virgin Mother, Maiden Queen: Elizabeth I and the Cult of the Virgin Mary*. GB: Palgrave Macmillan, 1994.

Haigh, Christopher. *Elizabeth I*. London: Longman, 1988.

Hall, Bert S. *Weapons and Warfaire in Renaissance Europe: Gunpowder, Technology, and Tactics*. Baltimore: Johns Hopkins University Press, 1997.

Hammer, Paul E. J. "The Catholic Threat and the Military Response," in Susan Doran and Norman Jones eds. *The Elizabethan World*, 629–645. London: Routledge, 2000.

Heisch, Alison. "Queen Elizabeth I and the Persistence of Patriarchy." *Feminist Review*, 4 (1980): 45–56.

Hicks, Leo. *An Elizabethan Problem: Some Aspects of the Careers of Two Exile-Adventurers*. New York: Fordham University Press, 1964.

Holt, Mack P. *The Duke of Anjou and the Politique Struggle during the Wars of Religion*. Cambridge: Cambridge University Press, 1986.

———. *The French wars of religion*. New York: Cambridge University Press, 1995.

Hulse, Clark. *Elizabeth I: Ruler and Legend*. Urbana: University of Illinois Press, 2003.

Huneycutt, Lois L. "Public Lives, Private Ties: Royal Mothers in England and Scotland, 1070–1204," in John Carmi Parson and Bonnie Wheeler eds. *Medieval Mothering*, 295–312. New York and London: Garland Publishing Inc., 1996.

Hunt, Alice, and Whitelock, Anna, (eds.), *Tudor Queenship: The Reigns of Mary and Elizabeth*. New York: Palgrave Macmillan, 2010.

Hunter, Dard. *Papermaking: The History and Technique of an Ancient Craft*. New York: Courier Dover Publications, 1978.

Hurstfield, Joel. *Elizabeth I and the Unity of England*. London: The English University Press, 1960.

———. *Freedom, Corruption and Government in Elizabethan England*. London: Jonathan Cape, 1973.

Hutchinson, Robert. *Elizabeth's Spy Master: Francis Walsingham and the Secret War that Saved England*. London: Weidenfeld & Nicolson, 2002.

Jansen, Sharon L. *The Monstrous Regiment of Women: Female Rulers in Early Modern Europe*. New York: Palgrave Macmillan, 2002.

Jenkins, Elizabeth. *Elizabeth and Leicester*. London: The Phoenix Press, 2002.

Jones, Norman. "Governing Elizabethan England," in Susan Doran and Norman Jones eds. *The Elizabethan World*, 19–34. Oxon and New York: Routledge, 2011.

Jouanna, Arlette. *La France du XVIe siècle, 1483–1598*. Paris: Presses Universitaires de France, 1996.

———. "Le Temps des Guerres de Religion en France (1559–1598)," in Arlette Jouanna, Jacqueline Boucher, Dominique Biloghi and Guy Le Thiec eds. *Histoire et Dictionnaire des Guerres de Religion*, 329–340. Robert Laffont: Turin, 1998.

Kelsey, Harry. *Sir John Hawkins, Queen Elizabeth's Slave Trader*. New York: Yale University Press, 2003.

Knecht, Robert. *Hero or Tyrant? Henry III, King of France, 1574–89*. Farnham: Ashgate, 2014.

Kruse, Elaine. "The Virgin and the Widow: The political finesse of Elizabeth I and Catherine de Médici," in Carole Levin and Robert Bulcholz eds. *Queens and Power in Medieval and Early Modern England*, 126–140. Lincoln and London: University of Nebraska, 2009.

Labitte, Charles. *De la Démocratie chez les Prédicateurs de la Ligue*. First edition Paris Joubert, 1841, second edition, Geneva: Slatkine Reprints, 1971.

Lake, Peter. *Bad Queen Bess? Libels, Secret Histories, and the Politics of Publicity in the Reign of Queen Elizabeth I*. Oxford: Oxford University Press, 2016.

Le Person, Xavier. *"Practiques et Practiqueurs", La vie politique à la fin du règne de Henry III (1584–1589)*. Genève: Droz, 2002.

Levin, Carole. *Dreaming the English Renaissance: Politics and Desire in Court and Culture*, (New York: Palgrave Macmillan, 2008.

———. *'The heart and stomach of a King': Elizabeth I and the politics of sex and power*. Philadelphia: University of Pennsylvania Press, 2013, first published in 1994.

———. *The Reign of Elizabeth I*. New York: Palgrave, 2002.

———. "'We shall never have a merry world while the Queen lyveth' Gender, Monarchy, and the Power of Seditious Words," in Julia M. Walker ed. *Dissing Elizabeth: Negative Representations of Gloriana*. Durham and London: Duke University Press, 1998.

Levin, Carole, and Jo Eldridge Carney. "Young Elizabeth in Peril: From Seventeenth-century Drama to Modern Movie," in Carole Levin, Jo Eldridge Carney and Debra Barrett-Graves eds. *Elizabeth I Always Her Own Free Woman*, 215–238. Aldershot: Ashgate, 2003.

Levine, Mortimer. *The Early Elizabethan Succession Question 1558–1568*. Stanford: Stanford University Press, 1966.

Limm, Peter. *The Dutch Revolt, 1559–1648*. London: Longman, 1989.

Loades, David. *The Tudor Court*. London: Headstart History Publishing, 1986.

Lockyer, Roger. *James VI and I*. London: Longman, 1998.

Loomis, Catherine. "'Bear your Body More Seeming': Open-Kneed Portraits of Elizabeth I," in Debra Barrett-Graves ed. *The Emblematic Queen: Extra-Literary Representations of Early Modern Queenship*, 53–68. New York: Palgrave Macmillan, 2013.

MacCaffrey, Wallace T. *Queen Elizabeth and the Making of Policy 1572–1588*. Princeton: Princeton University Press, 1981.

———. *The Shaping of the Elizabethan Regime*. Princeton: NJ, 1968.

Martin, Lynn A. "Papal Policy and the European Conflict, 1559–1572." *Sixteenth Century Journal*, volume 11, No. 2 Catholic Reformation (Summer, 1980): 35–48.

Matar, Nabil, "Elizabeth through Moroccan Eyes," in Charles Beem ed. *The Foreign Relations of Elizabeth I*, 145–158. New York: Palgrave Macmillan, 2011.

May, Steven. "Queen Elizabeth Prays for the Living and the Dead," in Peter Beal and Grace Ioppolo eds. *Elizabeth I and the Culture of Writing*, 201–211. London: British Library, 2007.

———. *Queen Elizabeth: Selected Works*. New York: Washington Square Press, 2004.

McLaren, Anne, "Elizabeth I as Deborah: Biblical typology, prophecy and political power," in Jessica Munns and Penny Richards eds. *Gender, Power and Privilege in Early Modern Europe*, 90–107. London: Longman, 2003.

———. *Political Culture in the Reign of Elizabeth: Queen and Commonwealth, 1558–1585*. Cambridge: Cambridge University Press, 1999.

Mears, Natalie. "Counsel, Public Debate and Queenship: John Stubbs's The discoverie of a gaping gulf." *The Historical Journal*, 44 (2001): 629–650.

———. *Queenship and Political Discourse in the Elizabethan* Realms. Cambridge: Cambridge University Press, 2005.

Montrose, Louis. *The Subject of Elizabeth: Authority, Gender, and Representation*. Chicago: University of Chicago Press, 2006.

Nagy, Piroska. *Le don des larmes au Moyen-Âge*. Paris: Albin Michel, 2000.

Neale, John E. *Elizabeth I and her Parliaments*, 2 vols. London: 1953–1957.

O'Callaghan, Joseph F. "The Many Roles of the Medieval Queen: Some Examples from Castile," in Theresa Earenfeight ed. *Queenship and Political Power in Medieval and Early Modern Spain*. Aldershot: Ashgate, 2005.

Orlin, Lena. "The Fictional Families of Elizabeth I," in Carole Levin and Patricia A. Sullivan eds. *Political Rhetoric, Power and Renaissance Women*, 85–110. Albany: Suny Press, 1995.

Page-Bayne, Sheila. "Tears and Weeping: An Aspect of Emotional Climate reflected in Seventeenth Century French Literature." *Etudes Littéraires Françaises* (vol. 16, 1981).

Paranque, Estelle, "Catherine of Medici: Henry III's Inspiration to be a Father to his People," in Elena Woodacre and Carey Fleiner eds. *Royal Mothers and their Ruling Children: Wielding Political Authority from Antiquity to the Early Modern Era*, 225–240. New York: Palgrave Macmillan, 2015.

———. "Elisabeth of Austria and Marie-Elisabeth of France: Represented and remembered," in Valerie Schutte and Estelle Paranque eds. *Forgotten Queens in Medieval and Early Modern Europe: Political Agency, Myth-Making, and Patronage*, 114–128. London: Routledge, 2018.

————. "Queen Elizabeth I and the Elizabethan Court in the French Ambassador's Eyes," in Anna Riehl-Bertolet ed. *Queens Matter in Early Modern Studies*, 257–284. New York: Palgrave Macmillan, 2017.

————. "Royal Representations Through the Warrior and Father Figures in Early Modern Europe," in Elena Woodacre ed. *History of Monarchy*. London: Routledge, forthcoming 2019.

————. "The representations and ambiguities of the warlike female kingship of Elizabeth I of England," in Katherine Buchanan, Lucinda Dean, and Michael Pennman eds. *Medieval and Early Modern Representations of Authority in Scotland and Great Britain*, 163–176. Routledge: London, 2016.

Pender, Patricia. *Early Modern Women's Writing and The Rhetoric of Modesty*. New York, NY: Palgrave Macmillan, 2012.

Perry, Maria. *The word of a prince*. Woodbridge: The Boydell Press, 1990.

Phillips, James Emerson. *Images of a Queen: Mary Stuart in Sixteenth Century Literature*. Berkeley and Los Angeles: University of California Press, 1964.

Probasco, Nate. "Queen Elizabeth's reaction to the St. Bartholomew's Day Massacre," in Charles Beem ed. *The Foreign Relation of Elizabeth I*, 77–110. New York: Palgrave Macmillan, 2012.

Questier, Michael C. *Catholicism and Community in Early Modern England: Politics, Aristocratic Patroage and Religion, c. 1550–1640*. Cambridge: Cambridge University Press, 2006.

————. "Elizabeth and the Catholics," in Ethan Shagan ed. *Catholics and the 'Protestant Nation': Religious Politics and Identity in Early Modern England*. Manchester: Manchester University Press, 2005.

Read, Conyers. *Lord Burghley and Queen Elizabeth*. London and New York, 1960.

————. *Mr. Secretary Cecil and Queen Elizabeth*. London, 1955.

————. *Mr. Secretary Walsingham and the Policy of Queen Elizabeth*. 3 Vols. Oxford, 1925.

————. "Walsingham and Burghley in Queen Elizabeth's privy council." *English Historical Review*, 28 (1913): 34–58.

Richardson, Glenn. ""Your most assured sister": Elizabeth I and the Kings of France," in Alice Hunt and Anna Whitelock eds. *Tudor Queenship: the reigns of Mary and Elizabeth*. New York: Palgrave Macmillan, 2010.

Ronald, Susan. *The Pirate Queen: Queen Elizabeth I, Her Pirate Adventurers, and the Dawn of Empire*. New York: HarperCollins Publishers, 2007.

Riehl Bertolet, Anna. *The Face of Queenship, Early modern Representations of Elizabeth I*. New York: Palgrave Macmillan, 2010.

Rhorchi, Fatima, "Consorts of Moroccan Sultans: Lalla Khnata Bint Bakkar 'A Woman With Three Kings'," in Elena Woodacre ed. *Queenship in the Mediterranean: Negotiating the Role of the Queen in the Medieval and Early Modern Eras*. New York: Palgrave Macmillan, 2013.

Schneider, Gary. *The Culture of Espitolarity: Vernacular Letters and Letter Writing in Early Modern England, 1500–1700.* Newark, Delaware: University of Delaware Press, 2005.

Sharpe, Kevin. *Selling the Tudor Monarchy: Authority and Image in Sixteenth Century England.* New Haven: Yale University Press, 2009.

Shenk, Linda. *Learned Queen: The Image of Elizabeth I in Politics and Poetry.* New York: Palgrave Macmillan, 2010.

———. "Queen Solomon," in Carole Levin and Robert Bucholz eds. Queens and Power in Medieval and Early Modern England. Aldershot: Ashgate Publications, 2009.

Smith, Alan G. R. *The Government of Elizabethan England.* London: Hodder and Stougthton, 1967.

Spiller, Ben. "Warlike Mates? Queen Elizabeth and Joan La Pucelle in 1 Henry VI," in Annaliese Connolly and Lisa Hopkins eds. *Goddesses and Queens: the Iconography of Elizabeth I.* Manchester and New York: Manchester University Press, 2007.

Stewart, Alan. *The Cradle King: A Life of James VI & I.* London: Chatto and Windus, 2003.

Stewart, Alan, and Heather Wolfe. *Letterwriting in Renaissance England.* Washington: Folger Shakespeare Library, 2004.

Strage, Mark. *Women of Power: The Life and Times of Catherine de Medici.* New York and London: Harcourt, Brace Jovanovich, 1976.

Strauss, Paul. "The Virgin Queen as Nurse of the Church: Manipulating an Image of Elizabeth I in Court Sermons," in Carole Levin and Christine Stewart-Nunez eds. *Scholars and Poets Talk about Queens*, 185–202. New York: Palgrave Macmillan, 2015.

Strong, Roy. *Gloriana: The Portraits of Queen Elizabeth I.* London: Thames and Hudson, 1987.

———. *The Cult of Elizabeth: Elizabethan Portraiture and Pageantry.* London: Pimlico, 1999.

Sutherland, Nicola-Mary. *Catherine de Medici and the Ancien Regime.* London: Historical Association, 1966.

———. *The Massacre of St Bartholomew and the European Conflict, 1559–1572.* London: Macmillan, 1973.

———. "The Origins of Queen Elizabeth's Relations with the Huguenots, 1558–1562," in *Princes, Politics and Religion, 1547–1589.* London: Bloomsbury, 1984.

Tallon, Alain. "Les puissances catholiques face à la tolérance religieuse en France au XVIe siècle; droit d'ingérence ou non intervention," in Lucien Bély ed. *L'Europe des traités des Westphalie. Esprit de la diplomatie et diplomatie de l'esprit.* Paris: PUF, 2000.

Teagues, Frances, "Queen Elizabeth in her speeches," in S.P. Cerasano and Marion Wynne-Davies eds. *Gloriana's Face: Women, Public and Private, in the English Renaissance*. Detroit: Wayne State University Press, 1992.

Villeponteaux, Mary. *The Queen's Mercy: Gender and Judgment in Representations of Elizabeth I*. New York: Palgrave Macmillan, 2014.

Vincent-Buffaut, Anne. *Histoire des larmes, XVIIIe-XIXe siècles*. Marseille: Rivages, 1986.

Wanegffelen, Thierry. *Ni Rome Ni Genève: Des fidèles entre deux chaires en France au XVIe siècle*. Paris: Honoré Champion, 1997.

Walker, Julia M. *The Elizabethan Icon, 1603–2003*. Basingstoke: Palgrave Macmillan, 2004.

Walsham, Alexandra. "'A Very Deborah?' The Myth of Elizabeth I as a Providential Monarch," in Susan Doran and Thomas S. Freeman eds. *The Myth of Elizabeth*. New York: Palgrave Macmillan, 2003.

Watkins, John. "Elizabeth Through Venetian Eyes." *Explorations in Renaissance Culture*, vol. 30, 1 (Summer 2004).

Wernham, Robert Bruce. *Before the Armada: The Emergence of the English Nation, 1485–1588*. Norton, 1966.

Wernham, Robert. *The Making of Elizabethan Foreign Policy 1558–1603*. Berkeley & Los Angeles: University of California Press, 1980.

Wilkinson, Alexander. *Mary Queen of Scots and French Public Opinion, 1542–1600*. New York: Palgrave Macmillan, 2004.

Williams, Richard. "'Libels and Paintings': Elizabethan Catholics and the International Campaign of Visual Propaganda," in Christopher Highley and John N. Kin eds. *John Foxe and his World*. London: Routledge, 2002.

Whitelock, Anna. "'Woman, Warrior, Queen?': Rethinking Mary and Elizabeth," in Alice Hunt and Anna Whitelock eds. *Tudor Queenship: the Reigns of Mary and Elizabeth*. New York: Palgrave Macmillan, 2010.

Wolmald, Jenny. *Mary, Queen of Scots*. London: George Philip, 1988.

Yates, Frances A. *Astraea*. London and New York: Routledge, 1999, first published in 1975.

# Index[1]

[1] Note: Page numbers followed by 'n' refer to notes.

© The Author(s) 2019
E. Paranque, *Elizabeth I of England through Valois Eyes*, Queenship
and Power, https://doi.org/10.1007/978-3-030-01529-9

Printed by Printforce, the Netherlands